CRIMINOLOGY

About the Author

Isidore Silver is a professor of constitutional law and history at John Jay College of Criminal Justice, City University of New York. He is also a practicing attorney who has been deeply involved in criminal and constitutional cases. Among his publications are *The Crime Control Establishment* (Prentice-Hall) and *A National Strategy to Reduce Crime* (Avon).

CRIMINOLOGY

An Introduction

Isidore Silver

John Jay College of Criminal Justice

BARNES & NOBLE BOOKS
A DIVISION OF HARPER & ROW, PUBLISHERS
New York, Cambridge, Hagerstown, Philadelphia,
San Francisco, London, Mexico City, São Paulo, Sydney

CRIMINOLOGY: *An Introduction.* Copyright © 1981 by Isidore Silver. All rights reserved. Printed in the United States of America. No part of this book may be used or reproduced in any manner whatsoever without written permission except in the case of brief quotations embodied in critical articles and reviews. For information address Harper & Row, Publishers, Inc., 10 East 53rd Street, New York, N.Y. 10022. Published simultaneously in Canada by Fitzhenry & Whiteside Limited, Toronto.

FIRST EDITION

Designer: C. Linda Dingler

Library of Congress Cataloging in Publication Data

Silver, Isidore.
  Criminology : an introduction.
  (Barnes & Noble outline series ; CO 197)
  Includes index.
  1. Crime and criminals. I. Title.
HV6025.S52 1981   364   80–8417
ISBN 0–06–460197–8 (pbk.)

81 82 83 84 85 10 9 8 7 6 5 4 3 2 1

To my parents,
and Carole and Gabriel

CONTENTS

PART V: IMPRISONMENT AND POSTIMPRISONMENT

PART VI: CONCLUSIONS

CRIMINOLOGY

Introduction

Criminology is the study of crime and criminals in society. It attempts to analyze scientifically the "causes" of crime and juvenile delinquency. Criminology today in the United States is mainly oriented toward sociological explanations of those causes. Such explanations are based on the belief that crime is caused by the interrelationships among people, groups, and the society in which they live and function.

At one time, crime was attributed to physical or mental defects and was deemed to be the product of certain "inborn" or inherited traits. However, such physiological explanations have now been largely rejected. In contrast, sociological explanations—and there are many—focus upon the society itself, on the fact that crime is learned, not inherited, behavior.

Criminology deals with two separate, though related, areas: first, the nature and patterns of crime within society; second, the general processes of individual criminality. The first approach attempts to describe and explain general patterns and rates. Crime rates among societies are also compared to ascertain what factors may account for differences. The second approach studies individual criminals from a psychological or social-psychological point of view. It seeks to answer questions such as: What are the characteristics of those who participate in crime? How are they distinguished from others who live in and are affected by the same particular society? As will be seen, both types of theories are primarily descriptive rather than analytical. While general sociological theory may predict overall crime rates and changes in crime rates, the predictive value of criminality theories is low when applied to individuals.

Criminology is not true science for several reasons. Most important, scholars on the whole study behavior not from a clinical perspective (Why did an individual do what he did? Was it "functional"—that is, meaningful—to him?) but from a legalistic perspective. Law defines what is criminal and what is not, and on that basis social scientists have attempted to theorize on reasons why certain people violate the law. The subject itself, for most researchers, is bounded by the idea of "illegality." "Legality" and "illegality" are defined by particular societies in accordance with their needs and beliefs. Though criminal law may embody consistent notions of "right" and "wrong," it should be noted that not all "wrongs" (in a moral sense) are criminal. Conversely, some acts not usually considered "wrongs" may be criminalized.

Since law may well change over time and, in any case, is not always the product of a consistent, widely held belief, the study of "crime" may often be little more than a study of "fashion" or, according to many critics, something more sinister, such as economic power. Some criminologists have attempted to formulate theories of "true" wrongs that may or may not be called "criminal" by a given society at a given time. But attempts to employ moral categories instead of the perhaps too narrow legal ones have been largely fruitless. Criminologists who do this tend to become moral philosophers or even preachers and thus not truly scientific.

The law condemns acts and certain types of behavior. In general, it is not interested in the reasons ("motives") for such acts. Many different kinds of acts likely to be engaged in by many different types of people for many different reasons are lumped together under the law as criminal. People may well reasonably and rationally believe that their conduct is correct, but that conduct may nevertheless be condemned by the criminal law.

Equally, other "crimes" may be viewed, even by those committing them, as "sick" or degenerate or just wrong. If people simply believe on the one hand that particular behavior is not wrong, or on the other, that it is the result of some mental disease, attempts by criminologists to discover root causes for crime are not likely to succeed.

It thus becomes apparent that there are many different behaviors, many different types of behavior, and many different "causes" of crime. Criminologists should not assume that they can "discover" one or a few causes. This is especially true when we consider the meaning of the term "criminal." Is a criminal a person who merely commits an outlawed act once? Must there be a pattern of such acts before the label is applied? Since surveys have consistently shown that most Americans have committed at least one serious criminal act in their lives, must we assume that they are criminals and that the United States is a "criminal society"?

The sociological answer to these questions is simple and deceptive. "Society" (whatever that is) sets certain rules for behavior. While some of these rules may be minor (etiquette and fashion, for example) many are important. The most important, presumably, become embodied in the criminal law. Sociologists assume that most people, by virtue of membership in society, obey the rules, especially the serious ones. Most people are conformists who, for one reason or another, voluntarily obey rules (or follow "norms"). In turn, those rules or norms are the products of a shared belief ("consensus") among the members of society. Individual behavior that deviates from those rules must be "caused" by something, since the "natural" state of things dictates compliance. Many of these assumptions are questionable and even dubious. General norms such as the sanctity of life and of personal property embodied in the criminal law are often qualified by exceptions (justifiable homicide, for instance). Also, many criminal laws clearly reflect only what might be called "weaker norms" than those just mentioned. Property owned by institutions, for instance, is often treated by both employees and customers as available for taking. The existence of "subcultures" whose views and norms may differ from those of the dominant culture is a controversial and much-studied aspect of criminology (see Chapter 9).

Indeed, in recognition of these and other factors, criminology has expanded its horizons to include not only the study of crime and criminals but also several specific social phenomena independent of crime. Sociology of law undertakes to demonstrate how law is made, by whom, and for what purposes. Also, problems of social perception and law enforcement—which laws get enforced in which kinds of communities and against whom—have received increasing attention.

Another concern of sociologists involves the question of operation of the criminal-justice agencies themselves. How do police, prosecutors, courts, and correctional agencies *really* operate—and why? Indeed, in the last decade, most of the research in the broad field of criminology has attempted to deal with official *reactions* to crime more than with crime itself. The role of the official "system" in "labeling" those it deals with and its effect upon the lives of persons arrested have been analyzed with a view toward ascertaining just how the "criminal" comes to define himself. The structure and performance of criminal-justice personnel not only as "crime fighters" but also as members of bureaucratic institutions are now major concerns for study. What roles these personnel *really* play, rather than what roles they are thought to play, are analyzed in chapters 14 to 22. Those roles may well differ in accordance with (1) the agency itself, (2) the personalities of law enforcers themselves, and (3) the political, economic, and social environment.

There are too many variables to support the notion of criminology as a "value-free," quasi-"natural" science. Criminologists are not able to formulate laws of behavior or predict future behavior from study of past behavior. Rather, criminology is several pieces of science, different sciences, either behavioral or social, often loosely strung together. In part, it is pure sociology cataloguing consistent behavior patterns and attempting to explain that persistence. In part it is political science, attempting to demonstrate that questions of power, legitimacy, and authority are fundamental to an understanding of just how law is created and enforced. In part it is psychology, in its concern for human behavior and human personality per se. In part it is social psychology, in its raising of questions of just how specific personalities and personality traits interact to create criminal behavior, often in gang or other organized activity.

Thus we cannot formulate easy answers to questions about crime. We can more successfully deal with "correlates" than with "causes." Poverty, broken homes, lack of family discipline, and transient neighborhoods all "correlate" with crime, though they do not necessarily "cause" it. Indeed, the strong correlations are not among these factors and crime but among sex (male) and age (youthfulness) and criminal conduct. Such correlates indicate more about the nature of society than about law.

Crime, then, becomes subordinate to deeper questions of the nature of society and its values, structure, and politics. To truly understand crime, we must truly understand society—and criminology itself furnishes some tools for such understanding. The study of crime should, ideally, become the study of society, but then criminology would become irrelevant.

In this context, profound problems of social reaction to crime arise. What should "public policy"—the programs undertaken by legislators and executive officials of government—be when crime cannot be easily isolated as a social phenomenon? Public policy cannot dramatically overturn or even modify the social relationships that keep the system functioning. Laws and policies can operate only within a general framework of social activity, and that framework is relatively fixed. Yet that framework itself may be "criminogenic" (crime-causing) at the same time that it produces good effects and results. It is clear that crime cannot be singled out as something totally isolated from other ongoing processes of society. Certainly, crime control, an activity of official governmental agencies, cannot.

Criminology cannot be isolated from society for another reason. As a system of ideas about crime and crime control, criminology belongs as much to the field of the history of ideas as to any science. The study of crime has occurred in an intellectual framework, which reflect the state of society at any given moment. The history of all the ideas about crime reflects the dominant ideas of changing eras.

Of course, the idea that crime is "evil" and the unwillingness to believe that society causes it transcend any era. All societies have believed that their values and norms and processes are essentially good and that those who do not fit in are at least deviants if not outright criminals. Yet specific perceptions about crime have been shaped by particular norms of societies, by their "national characters," and by their historical experiences.

In sum, criminology's credentials as a science are limited to the tools it uses to (1) describe crime, (2) understand crime, (3) describe criminals, and

(4) understand criminals. Criminology per se cannot explain the deeper movements within all societies that produce crime—often, to be sure, different kinds of crime. Insofar as criminology attempts to understand when and perhaps why some persons apparently choose to violate the fundamental norms of society, it is exceedingly valuable. Insofar as criminology attempts more profound social analysis, especially analysis of the relationship of crime to weaker norms and values not commonly agreed upon within society, it must call for such understanding upon other insights, from the social-behavioral sciences to philosophy. It is with these reservations and qualifications that this study is undertaken.

THE NATURE, BACKGROUND, AND EXTENT OF CRIME

Part I

1. Criminal Law and Society (Sociology of Law)

Crime is a legal construction. Society has singled out and classified certain behaviors as seriously antisocial and provided for certain punishments for those found committing such acts. But history has shown that definitions of crime change and that different jurisdictions, often in the same society, have different criminal codes. Also, many definitions of crime are highly technical ("legalistic").

CRIME AND MORAL WRONG

Criminologists have differed about whether everything labeled "crime" should be within the domain of criminology and, conversely, whether moral "wrongs" or violation of "conduct norms" should also be scientifically studied. Most criminologists have concluded that to study anything but legally defined crime would make the field both unwieldy and subjective. It would be unwieldy because, even if it were possible to arrive at meaningful definitions of "conduct norms," it is impossible to ascertain the frequency of "wrongful" acts, since no social agency even attempts to chart such statistics. It is subjective because all known attempts to extract "norms" from the criminal law and to so classify them as to include conduct not now criminal have led to the creation of very broad categories; such categories also change too rapidly for possible scientific study.

Another sociological field of study is "deviance." This relates to violations of noncriminal norms and, indeed, criminally labeled violations where there are no norms or only weak norms. Although criminology and deviance may overlap (especially where laws are the result of group pressures against other groups), they should be separately studied, and the areas of overlap clearly marked out to prevent confusion.

The question of white-collar crime raises important problems for the criminologist. White-collar crimes (see pp. 30–31) often exist only on "the books" and may not be regarded as "true" crimes by society (though this view is changing) or by white-collar offenders themselves. These crimes are often complex, not easily detected, frequently unprosecuted. When they are detected, they are often dealt with not by the criminal courts but by noncriminal (or semicriminal) agencies such as administrative boards and civil courts. For instance, the United States Government often chooses to bring civil cases against companies that violate antitrust laws, although the alleged conduct is clearly criminal. Proceedings in these courts and agencies should be regarded as criminal matters if the conduct dealt with also violates criminal laws. Thus criminology can appropriately study such cases. One major difference involves the burden of proof in government action. Lesser standards of proof apply in civil and administrative proceedings than in criminal ones (which, of course, require "guilt beyond a reasonable doubt"). Since many corporations and their executives do not seriously contest civil charges, this question does not arise. Most criminologists who have studied the problem of white-collar crime simply overlook or refuse to acknowledge this situation.

CHARACTERISTICS OF LAW

Criminal law shares certain characteristics with other law. Criminal law is promulgated by a political body acting on behalf of a politically organized population and is enforceable by agents of that political body. In modern times, the political body is called the state or the nation-state. In the United States, criminal law is created by legislative bodies of either the federal government or state government rather than by other agencies, such as the courts. In contrast, much civil law is still created by the courts, although it can be superseded by legislative action. The United States Government enacts criminal laws within the area of its general powers. But most criminal laws are enacted by individual states, which have broader social powers than does the federal government. Local-government units, such as cities and towns, can also enact criminal laws, generally to supplement state criminal laws. Since only governments can enact criminal laws, rules of private organizations (for example, corporations, labor unions, social groups) are not criminal law, though many of these rules may deal with the same conduct and some may be enforceable in civil lawsuits.

CHARACTERISTICS OF CRIMINAL LAW

Criminal law differs both from other legal and from nonlegal forms of social disapproval in certain specific ways. Basically, it is a means of social control. "Social control" is the sum of all the means used by society to discourage and prevent antisocial conduct. These means may consist of "rewards" and "punishments" of a nonlegal kind, such as approval or ridicule. "Social control" must be distinguished from "personal control," which is the individual's ability to accept and internalize (make part of himself without conscious thought) prevalent social norms.

Differences from Civil Law.   Criminal law is only one part of a vast system of law that regulates human conduct and that designates certain agencies to enforce such regulation. Civil law is an important means of regulating conduct relating to such matters as the making and fulfilling of contracts, the sale and purchase of property, and redress for certain injuries inflicted by one person upon another. The civil law is enforced either by private lawsuits in courts or similar agencies or by administrative agencies of the state (such as the National Labor Relations Board, the Federal Communications Commission, state boards that license certain occupations, etc.).

Differences from Deviance.   Clearly, crime is not always synonymous with deviance; only conduct specifically punishable by the criminal law is included in the definition of crime, while deviance refers to a broader (or sometimes narrower) category of acts disliked by many (perhaps by most) people. Also, criminal law can only punish acts; deviance often stigmatizes status (for example, homosexuality as a lifestyle).

Criteria of Criminal Law.   To be called "criminal," a particular law must meet certain criteria: (1) The conduct prohibited must be spelled out in reasonable detail; (2) the law must be capable of uniform application against all persons equally and impartially; (3) violation of the law must be punishable by certain sanctions (including fines payable to the state, incarceration in jail or prison, or ultimately the death penalty); and (4) the court with jurisdiction to hear alleged violations of the law must proceed in certain ways (which differ from civil-court procedures).

All these criteria require clarification. The first has been interpreted by courts to mean as much specificity as the nature of the conduct, and the ability of human beings to use language, permit. Certain offenses such as "vagrancy" and "crimes against nature" (sodomy) are often loosely and vaguely defined. If so, they may be deemed unconstitutional under either the United States Constitution or a state constitution because the laws do not give fair and adequate notice of what conduct is condemned. While a term such as "delinquency" or "incorrigibility" may be vague, juvenile-delinquency proceedings are not generally considered criminal at all, so that greater definitional leeway has been permitted.

The second criterion is qualified by the fact that some criminal laws are directed not at the general population, but rather at particular groups (for example, for violation of liquor and professional licensing laws).

The third criterion does not include penalties such as loss of professional license or suspension of business dealings, which may be more economically severe to the individual than criminal penalties (often for the same conduct). "Penalties" in the form of money judgments by harmed individuals against civil offenders also are not criminal in nature. Conduct harmful to another individual or to the government or society may result in both criminal prosecution and civil lawsuits, in separate proceedings. The criminal penalty *may* be imposed in a case. (It need not always be; a suspended sentence and probation are often decreed by a judge in a criminal case.)

The fourth criterion requires that the state (which always prosecutes criminal charges) prove each and every element of the crime (each legally significant fact) beyond a reasonable doubt. Thus, to prove murder in the first degree, the government must show not only that the defendant killed another person but also that he did so with (1) premeditation, (2) deliberation, and (3) intent to kill. Certain constitutional safeguards also apply in criminal cases but not necessarily or to the same extent in civil ones.

Criminal Intent. Another characteristic of the criminal law is its requirement that the outlawed conduct be accompanied by criminal intent. The evil act must be voluntarily performed by the "evil mind" (*mens rea*). Criminal intent is the desire to commit the act or engage in the illegal conduct; it is not the reason ("motive") for engaging in that conduct. For certain limited categories of crime (crimes of "strict liability"), no proof of criminal intent is necessary. For example, "statutory rape" and "contributing to the delinquency of a minor" do not require that the offender know that his victim was a minor.

Insanity. Since criminal intent is generally a prerequisite to a finding of criminality, insanity is a controversial defense to a charge of crime. A person who is incapable of knowing what he was doing lacks the capacity to form criminal intent. Although this principle has been recognized throughout history, its meaning is in great doubt.

The M'Naghten Rule. Most American states have adopted this rule (named after the defendant in a famous English case tried in 1843). It requires that the defendant show that he either did not know "the nature and quality of the act" or that "what he was doing was wrong." The test was primarily designed to deal with delusional psychotics, and knowledge is the key element.

The "Irresistible Impulse" Test. Psychiatrists have argued that some criminals "know" what they are doing but cannot help themselves. Almost half the American states have supplemented *M'Naghten* with a test that finds insanity when the individual knew what he was doing and knew that it was wrong but could not control his conduct: This is the "irresistible impulse" test.

The Durham Rule. At the urging of psychiatrists and others, some states and federal courts adopted the *Durham* rule (first formulated in a federal case in 1954), which would find insanity where the criminal act was "the product of a mental disease or defect"; neither lack of knowledge nor irresistible impulse was required. However, the rule's vagueness and subjectivity and the deficiencies in the psychiatric theory underlying it became increasingly unpopular with judges and juries, and the rule has been largely abandoned.

The Model Penal Code Proposal. The American Law Institute, a private body that suggests legal changes, proposed a test in 1955 which, in essence, combines the three previous tests but emphasizes the inability of the accused to "appreciate" the wrongfulness of the act or to "conform" his conduct to the law. Several states have adopted this test, but it makes little difference since, in practice, only about 2 percent of the defendants in *any* jurisdiction are found to be insane.

The Future of Insanity Rules. The refusal of psychiatrists to accept legal definitions of insanity and vice versa (in the case of judges and prosecutors) will probably continue. Approximately fifteen states have sought to solve the problem by permitting "diminished responsibility" to reduce, but not exonerate, a criminal charge. Many have argued that the movement to limit insanity defenses should go farther and that the concept itself should be abolished.

SOURCES OF CRIMINAL LAW

Currently, there is a major controversy about how and why criminal law is created in various societies. Modern criminologists and other social scientists have agreed that it is necessary to study the origins of law, rather than merely its effects. There are several major theories, and, given the broad scope of the criminal law generally, supporting evidence for each of them.

Natural Law. "Natural law" theories, which are the oldest, most closely relate law to general morality. There are many natural-law theories, but they commonly argue that there is a "law of Nature" (or of God). Manmade law is just only insofar as it approximates natural law. Man-made law is null and void if it violates natural law. Natural law tends to be mystical, contradictory (since all sides on any problem can invoke it), and justifies either the status quo (what is is natural and therefore right) or revolution against the status quo (what is is unnatural and therefore should not be obeyed). Also, the theory tends to give great power to judges, and often is little more than a cloak for a particular judicial philosophy. For these and other reasons, it was challenged, especially by the rise of (1) democracy and its assumption that the people rather than the judges govern and (2) the nation-state, and (3) the political and legal theory of positivism (see below). Natural law in America survives as a philosophy of "natural rights," the belief that men have certain inalienable rights that the state cannot violate. But this belief is not explicated in the Constitution, and judicial decisions in the area are based largely on the Bill of Rights.

Law as Expression of Social Consensus.   The theory that law expresses a fundamental *social* consensus about right and wrong purports to explain all law, not just criminal law. In this view, law provides the "ground rules" by which diverse groups and interests agree to reconcile their conflicts and demands. In some cases, the law makes a choice about which groups will prevail, but, in a democracy no group is completely defeated, because the ensuing imbalance would cause social unrest. The legislature will reflect the balance of forces and interests of various groups and seek a consensus among them, so that resulting law reflects that consensus. Conduct deemed dangerous by all groups will probably be criminalized. This theory is obviously incomplete both as to law in general and criminal law in particular, since many laws and many crimes are not the results of any real consensus.

Law as Expression of Governmental Will.   This positivist theory argues that law is nothing more than a set of commands issued by a sovereign government; some of these commands involve criminal penalties. Law is thus based solely on the will (desire) of government rather than upon any idealist notions of the meaning of nature or of society. The duty of the student or the scholar is to study the process by which will is exercised. This theory is particularly appropriate in countries where the criminal law is a series of "commands" issued by the legislature. In the United States, however, the Constitution (promulgated in legal theory by the people) is the primary command ("the law of the land"), so that laws that violate the Constitution can be overturned by judges.

Law as Manifestation of Power.   There are several theories that emphasize this perspective; they differ on the question of defining the source of the power. The most prominent theory is the Marxist one, which contends that law is the tool of a society's dominant economic class used to repress other classes, and that both law-making and law-enforcement agencies are merely instruments of the ruling class. In modern America and western Europe, capitalists are the dominant class. The purpose of all law at all times is to serve and protect the interests of the ruling class and to maintain existing economic relationships.

Research has revealed that this perspective certainly accounts for some law. For instance, the history of English vagrancy laws shows that (1) they were first enacted to compel laborers to work at cheap wages during the labor shortage created by the Black Death plague of 1348; (2) after 1530, the laws were redefined to prevent criminality or potential criminality (highwaymen and other felons were threatening to interfere with new commercial interests); and (3) the laws have been used for both purposes in a developed capitalist economy.

Non-Marxists have argued that much criminal law reflects the wishes of local and nationally powerful social and political but not necessarily and not always economic groups. Of course, the law may serve the economic interests of social and political groups, but it often serves other interests, including "symbolic" ones. Thus, at times, the majority's tolerance of minority group habits and styles may change so that once acceptable conduct becomes threatening. For instance, in 1914, the United States passed the Harrison Act to restrict sale of certain drugs, in part because of the southern fear that cocaine made blacks stronger and more sexually assertive and in part because of the fear of white Californians that the drug increased sexual contacts between Chinese and whites. Later pressures to criminalize marijuana have been attributed to distaste for the habits of Mexicans, especially at times when Mexican labor threatened to become too competitive with native labor. As marijuana use spread into the middle class, pressures toward decriminalization have grown. One study found that the main reason why Nebraska, a normally conservative state, became the second jurisdiction in America to decriminalize marijuana possession was that a prosecutor's son was charged with the crime, causing powerful political interests to demand partial decriminalization. Another factor was the belief that a lower penalty would increase the number of convictions. The law has frequently distinguished between certain drugs: barbiturates, for instance, which have never been made illegal per se, and heroin, perhaps because the former tended to be taken by affluent people. Congressional reluctance to control the production of amphetamines (which are medically dangerous) has been attributed to the lobbying efforts of the American Pharmaceutical Association, a manufacturers' group. Similarly, Prohibition has been seen as a crusade by rural and Baptist groups against urban minorities.

Another "power" theory emphasizes the role of governmental agencies themselves as strong lobby groups for the criminalization of certain conduct (for example, marijuana possession in the 1930s), either because leaders of these groups become "moral entrepreneurs" who use their power to persuade others that society is threatened or because they seek to expand the criminal jurisdiction of their agencies by finding more conduct to criminalize.

THE DEVELOPMENT OF CRIMINAL LAW

Like all other law, criminal law has deep historical roots. Some roots relate to concern for protection of life and dignity; some, such as the law's concern for protection of private property, are more peculiar to Anglo-American history. Much law has persisted, despite a change in circumstances, simply because of the law's general inertia. Modern law is a combination of traditional concerns and newer demands, often based upon application of former concerns to a changing social and political environment.

As the population of a society increases, law grows to replace informal enforcement of social norms. Moreover, as the centralized modern nation-state developed, injuries to individuals became harmful to the state and its interest in preserving social peace. Thus, Anglo-Saxon criminal law developed from (1) a system of Saxon tribal law (prior to A.D. 1066) that was feudal and stressed blood feud between families to redress wrongs, to (2) later compensation to the injured family to (3) the Norman centralization of tribal law and its administration. After the reign of Henry II, (1154–89), the King's law prevailed throughout England until the rise of Parliament in the seventeenth century.

In America, the early colonies adopted English law, though in varying degrees. The Massachusetts Bay Colony was governed by Puritan religious principles transformed into legal codes. In 1641, a Body of Liberties was enacted; and in 1648, the Code of Laws and Liberties became the first comprehensive body of law enacted in the English-speaking world. Crimes punishable by death included idolatry, witchcraft, blasphemy, sodomy, adultery, rape and malicious homicide. Generally, criminal law shifted from protection of the moral order to protection of property and social order; but despite the vast expansion of criminal law in modern society, it has never completely shed its moral origins.

LAW AND SOCIAL PROCESS

Crimes may be fostered by evolutionary social processes. As societies become more complex, new institutions took over some tasks of older ones. Family and kinship group functions are replaced by governmental and religious institutions. Money replaces barter as the economic measurement of value. And a legal system to embody these developments grows. Technological change is accompanied by population concentration and new forms of transportation. All these processes lead to crimes unknown at earlier stages of society. Economic power gets into the hands of different groups, and older classes seeking to retain power and prestige attempt to throttle or contain the new ones. Often, the older classes use devices such as monopolies and cartels to retain their power, while newer classes seek to use government to attack them (once having gained power, the newer classes may also turn to these older devices). Often laws are enacted because of pressure from coalitions of interest groups, sometimes including those most regulated by the new laws. For instance, large business firms may try to use safety, inspection, and health regulations to increase business costs and thereby eliminate smaller competitors.

Equality before the law is in part an ideology of capitalism, which functioned to undermine class privileges of the clergy and aristocracy under feudalism. Social scientists are just now beginning to analyze such class and other influences behind modern law.

Another social process that affects criminal—and all other—law is the growing propensity of various groups to seek governmental benefits. The rise of political democracy and the ability of many people to influence government, the coming of the welfare state, and the graduated income tax have created new interest groups that seek government aid. Newer demands and newer powers breed new laws, including health and safety, pollution, antidiscrimination, and commercial fraud statutes. Thus the social processes of *differentiation* (the division of labor and function in society) and *inclusion* (more groups seeking governmental aid) reinforce each other as various new groups (1) become separate and often antagonistic and (2) rely upon government to achieve their ends. While many criminal laws are passed only after some conflict, often a consensus for their continuance builds up over time. Conflict is most acute and tends to persist when the law undertakes to punish acts that many think are not socially dangerous (see Chapter 6 regarding drugs and alcohol).

There is some evidence that the process of *differentiation* has led to less absolutist moral principles and to an emphasis upon calculation of the social costs and benefits of penalizing allegedly immoral conduct. This trend may be attributable to increasing rationality in technological processes and the spread of education to enable workers to function in a complex society. The "scientific method" may thus have become extended into social matters. Since differentiation also leads to more interchange between strangers and specialists, tolerance of differing social norms and mores may well increase. The mass media make much that has been unfamiliar quite familiar and foster increased tolerance for varying lifestyles. Perhaps increasing interdependence will lead to greater diversity and greater willingness to adapt to diversity. Unfortunately, there is also some contradictory evidence that affluent societies experience a resurgence of what they consider "moral crimes."

CLASSIFICATIONS AND TYPES OF CRIMES

Within the criminal law certain classifications and distinctions are made. For instance, the seriousness of the offense will dictate whether the crime is a felony or a misdemeanor. Felonies are usually punishable by imprisonment in a state prison or by execution; misdemeanors generally are subject to punishment by less than one year in a county jail or only a fine. Legislatures, in designating new offenses to apply to changing social conditions, have specified even lower offense designations, such as violations. Some of these categories may be expressly designated as noncriminal (for example, "civil fines" for private possession of small amounts of marijuana in some states). Of course, *actual* penalties imposed under all of these classifications may be reduced from the maximum stipulated in the laws.

Legal distinctions may involve the nature of the offense. Thus some crimes may be against the person (homicide, rape, assault, and, usually, robbery), some against property (larceny, burglary, automobile theft), some against public order (loitering, breach of the peace, alcoholism, disorderly conduct, and even riot and treason), some against public decency (sex crimes, prostitution, and sale of obscene materials). Finally, crimes against public justice include bribery and extortion; they are committed by public officials and others acting with them to disregard or corruptly administer existing laws.

Distinctions may be made according to the status of the offender. "Lower-class crime" includes much street or predatory crime, and most known offenders are relatively poor. "White-collar crime" encompasses many varieties of nonviolent crime committed by "respectable" people, often in the course of their occupations. While lower-class crime traditionally commands the headlines (and, until recently, the resources of the criminal-justice system and the interest of scholars), white-collar crime is infinitely more costly to society. One recent study concluded that in a given year there are three billion dollars' worth of bribery, ten billion dollars' worth of insurance fraud, one hundred million to possibly ten billion dollars in false credit-card payments, and about twenty billion dollars in consumer-fraud offenses (encompassing five hundred different schemes). Except for sensational cases, this form of crime is almost totally hidden from public and law-enforcement view; it is probably as frequent as street crime and is much more lucrative.

CRIMINAL LAW IN PRACTICE

Law on the books only provides a general and often misleading guide to actual enforcement practices; indeed, some of the theories of law referred to previously (such as Marxism) primarily relate to law enforcement. Enforcement in modern society is handled not by private persons or families but by government agencies. These agencies do not enforce all of the criminal law all of the time—nor are they expected to. The reasons are complex.

Role of Public Opinion.   Since the public indirectly provides funds for the criminal-justice system and its activities, the public's opinion is important. Enforcement of unpopular laws may create tensions between the police and the community. This may occur either when (1) the law itself (alcohol distribution and sales laws, for instance) may be widely disliked in a particular community or (2) the law is generally accepted but is offensive when applied (for example, traffic and speeding laws). At given moments, public opinion may demand either *underenforcement* or *complete enforcement* of particular laws. Public opinion operates on all agencies of the criminal-justice system (for example, attacks on lenient plea-bargaining practices of prosecutors and judges), not only the police. Of course, the term "public opinion" itself is vague and may only reflect the feelings of particular groups in the public or the mass media.

Criminal-Justice Agency Discretion.   Criminal-justice agencies have a substantial amount of discretion in dealing with crime, in part because of (1) the vast amount of criminal law in every jurisdiction; (2) the vagueness and ambiguity of much criminal law (despite the theoretical requirement of specificity), especially in the realm of "public order" crimes; and (3) the broadness and vagueness of juvenile misconduct laws (although much misconduct is not designated as "criminal," enforcement is within the jurisdiction of the police).

Discretion may be exercised by a particular police officer acting on his own, since he must determine whether (1) certain conduct is or probably is criminal and (2) to arrest for a particular crime. This is especially true when he does not see a crime but obtains a citizen report about it (in probably 85 percent of all arrests this is the case) and must "judge" the meaning and reliability of what he is told. Discretion may also reflect policy rather than personal decisions; for instance, a particular department may decide to consciously enforce particular laws against all known offenders (for example, arresting all prostitutes or panhandlers to "clean up" a given area, or ticketing all illegally parked cars to facilitate traffic movement) while consciously not enforcing other laws, even against known offenders. Or, in contrast, there may be a decision to consciously but selectively enforce certain laws against selected offenders (arresting one of every five gamblers).

Discretion is characteristic of the entire criminal-justice system since (1) many known or presumed violators are not arrested; (2) many of those arrested are not charged; (3) many of those charged are released by the courts prior to trial; (4) many of those charged are selected by prosecutors for plea bargains (which may result in release); (5) many of those convicted do not go to prison.

Discretion may be caused by or may merely accompany, the traditionally low budgets allocated by legislatures to criminal-justice agencies. While crime is a passionate subject of public discourse and debate, crime control is usually given a low priority when the public purse is divided.

2. The Extent of Crime: Criminal Statistics

Statistics about crime and delinquency are notoriously unreliable, especially in the United States. Much violation of law is undetected by anyone. Many crimes are detected but not reported. Some reported crimes are not recorded (or are misrecorded) by official agencies. There is no reliable way to ascertain just what the ratio between unknown and unreported crime to true crime may be at any given moment. The true crime rate, which cannot be known by present measuring devices, has been called by criminologists the "dark figure" of crime. Since recording methods may drastically change from one year to another, even in one reporting locality, even annual figures may be suspect.

THE MEANING OF STATISTICS

The "crime rate" is based upon the number of crimes per unit of population (in the United States, the unit is one hundred thousand people, and is called the "statistical base"). However, this concept is misleading. To know whether crime is rising or not, it is necessary to establish a population base; it is not enough simply to know that the number of crimes has increased unless we know whether and, if so, how much the population in a given area has simultaneously increased. The number of people living in a given area is known (approximately, since census surveys are also faulty, especially in poor and transient-inhabited areas of cities) through the census, which is taken at the beginning of each decade. That number becomes the "base" for the remainder of the decade, but, of course, population shifts occur during that decade (some shifts may be measured by a half-decade census survey, which is not complete). The crime statistics in a given area are compiled each year (or even more frequently) and, of course, have nothing necessarily to do with general population shifts. Thus, in a given year, crime may apparently increase, but population may increase even more rapidly, so that the crime rate has actually declined. Conversely, crime may remain steady or even decrease, but the crime rate may have risen because the true "base" population has been reduced. The accuracy of the assessed *national* crime rate may be unaffected by such fluctuations, since the rate of population increase nationally is fairly well known at a given time, but local population shifts are little known. It is only after the decade has passed, and the new numbers are known, that better assessments of the crime rate can be made.

Census deficiencies are also critical in that such important factors as age and sex variations in the population, urban-rural differences, and racial composition—all important factors in the "crime picture"—may be accurately known at the beginning of the decade but not during its remainder.

The notion of the "crime rate" as the relationship between crime and population (even assuming that both can be known) has been questioned. Some have suggested that the proper relationship should be between "crime" and the "opportunity" to commit that kind of crime. For instance, if auto theft goes up in proportion to population but not in proportion to the increase in the number of cars in a given area, is it proper to say that auto theft is increasing? If there are few families in a given location but a high percentage of them are victimized by rape and then the number of female residents suddenly grows while there is some increase in the number of rapes, it may turn out that the rape rate for the area (measured by total population) may be high but the risk for a particular female in that area may actually be lower. In one sense, an "environmental" approach to crime (What are the risks of what particular crimes in what general geographic area?) would be consistent with the ordinary question of how likely it is that "I" will be the victim of a crime.

While census deficiencies may mask either a rise or a decline in the crime rate, inflation of some property-crime rates may be caused by general economic inflation. In 1973, the FBI recognized the problem and so changed its "larceny-theft" category (for the Uniform Crime Reports, see p. 25) from theft amounting to "over fifty dollars" to all larceny-theft. This broadening of the category, of course, would suggest a substantial increase in it. Another factor that would increase the reported rate in all categories is more reporting of crimes by victims, in part because of publicity and in part because of expansion of theft-insurance coverage (auto theft has always, for this reason, been considered to be one of the most reliable crime statistics). Greater population mobility may also increase reporting, since an increasing proportion of crime is now being committed by strangers rather than by acquaintances or family members, and there is greater inclination to report the former.

CRIMES KNOWN TO THE POLICE

Despite flaws, certain conventional measurements continue to be used, including the basic *crimes-known-to-the-police* category.

This category includes all crimes reported to, and recorded by, the police. In general, this is the most reliable of the various devices used by criminal-justice agencies, since it is not based upon statistics of "disposition" of crime by various agencies (prosecutors, the judicial system). Such agency disposition may have little to do with the amount of actual crime.

Even these statistics, however, may be misleading. The police, who have great discretion to decide whether a given incident even appears to be a crime; simply may not record a report. Since the police discover only about 15 percent of the crime they deal with, they must sift citizen reports for the remainder of their work, and perhaps as many as 20 percent of those reports result in the police verdict of "unfounded." In part, this percentage is determined by various police-department practices, such as those determining the time when an incident becomes an official report (when the citizen complains or when the department investigates and reports). Police organization will affect the reporting rates. For example, agencies with more officers in the field during high crime periods will "report" more crime; organizations that are more "professional" will tend to make more arrests and to define more ambiguous conduct as criminal; agencies with specialized divisions, such as those on drugs and vice, will report more such crimes than agencies lacking such units. Of course, political decisions about police efficiency may affect crime reporting rates, at least where the police themselves initiate the reporting. In extreme cases, such political decisions may lead to police omission of citizens' reports where the resulting figures would be "too high."

Police classifications of reports will also significantly affect the "crime rate." Legal definitions of crimes may vary somewhat in different states, and there may be great ambiguity in those definitions: For instance, a "mugging" may be either robbery or larceny, depending upon the nature of the incident and the individual police officer's interpretation of it. Departmental policies may discourage attaching the label of "crime" to incidents regarded as too minor; this omission may even be more widespread than the practice of writing off some reports as "unfounded."

ARREST STATISTICS

The police claim that individuals arrested for a crime often admit the commission of other crimes (even crimes not originally reported or recorded). If the police are satisfied that persons charged with a crime have committed other known crimes, the police will "clear" * those crimes even though no arrest for them, or adjudication of them, may ever be made. Obviously, "clearance rates" are higher than "arrest rates," often twice as high for par-

---

* Crimes are *cleared* when the police are satisfied that they have acquired enough knowledge to believe that an arrestee has committed such crimes.

ticular crimes. Public and mass-media judgments about the effectiveness of particular police forces are often based on reported clearance rates. Clearance rates in the United States may be low (7 percent for burglary, 8 percent for theft, 12 percent for robbery) or high (40 percent for aggravated assault and 80 percent for murder), but almost always they reflect the willingness of police to believe what they are told. (Rarely in such instances will they conduct independent investigations.) Clearance rates do not necessarily reflect "good police work," since many crimes, especially crimes of violence against the person, involve offenders who are immediately identified to the police by victims.

PROSECUTION STATISTICS

Crimes known to the police are the most reliable sources of statistical measurements of the true crime rate. Crimes for which arrests are made (or that are "cleared" following arrests) are the next most reliable. Crimes actually prosecuted are almost no indicators of true criminality in a society. Certain crimes result in a trial or other formal disposition, including a finding of guilt after plea bargaining. But the percentage of persons actually tried decreases in accordance with various factors, such as public perception of the importance of certain categories of crime, and prosecutorial policies. "Conviction" and "imprisonment" statistics are the least reliable since cases may be dismissed before or at the beginning of trial for many reasons, or there may be an acquittal after trial. Moreover, many of those convicted (approximately 50 percent) receive probation or a suspended sentence or fine instead of imprisonment.

VICTIMIZATION SURVEYS

The Law Enforcement Assistance Administration (LEAA), an agency of the United States Department of Justice, in recent years conducted a series of intensive, widespread surveys of sample households and businesses to supplement official statistics. These studies have, not surprisingly, revealed significant underreporting of crimes to official agencies. In general, only about half the rapes, aggravated assaults, and robberies that probably were committed were reported to the police, as were only a third of burglaries and larcenies. Murder and automobile theft tended to be fairly accurately reported, the former because of its high "visibility" the latter because auto-insurance policies require reporting in order to file a claim. Businesses surveyed tended to report more of the crimes committed against them than did individuals. Among the reasons for underreporting were (1) victim belief that the police would be ineffective in solving the crime and (2) the often close relationship between victim and offender. The range of underreporting varied for different crimes. In general, the more serious the crime, the more public its commission, and the stronger the cultural norms stigmatizing it, the more likely it was to be reported. The studies showed that the relative patterns and intensity of crimes registered by official statistics (at least by region of the country) were accurate (see pp. 75–76). The surveys have also demonstrated that some of the statistical rise in crime rates could simply be attributed to more reporting of crimes.

The reliability not of the sample but of the substantive responses to the surveys has been undermined by (1) faulty memories of respondents, especially about minor crimes (often forgotten) and past crimes (the more distant the event, the less reliable the memory) and (2) respondents' feelings of humiliation, especially in rape cases and in intrafamily crimes. The reliability of the interviewers was also questioned in some research about the surveys. Perhaps as many as 50 percent of the criminal incidents alluded to by respondents were improperly classified as major crimes either by the respondents themselves or by the interviewers or both. Because of these and other serious methodological problems, the LEAA victimization surveys were suspended in 1978.

UNIFORM CRIME REPORTS

The main sources of criminal-justice statistics, of course, come from the agencies: the police, the courts, and the prisons. These agencies may either publish the statistics or report them to a state agency for general publication. These reports may or may not include material on trends and comparisons or on statistical interrelationships between crime and other factors such as race, age, and sex distribution in the general population.

The United States Department of Justice, through the FBI, has published the Uniform Crime Reports (UCR) since 1930. This compilation includes one section listing seven "index" (major) crimes: murder, rape, aggravated assault, burglary, robbery, larceny, and auto theft. Reports from the police of local jurisdictions (approximately three thousand) are the sources of this information. Another section of the UCR lists the total number of arrests for all crimes in the reporting jurisdictions. Only police departments that *voluntarily* cooperate with the Justice Department are included, so that cities and adjacent areas tend to be overrepresented, and rural ones underrepresented. Neither the Justice Department nor the FBI will vouch for the reliability of the statistics submitted to them, and, at times, both have refused to use statistics from agencies thought to be flagrantly abusing collection and recording procedures. Underreporting has sometimes been notorious, and corrections, when made, have often resulted in apparent crime rises (for example, between 1970 and 1972). The UCRs, once a monthly publication, have become an annual one (with brief interim quarterly reports).

Variations in Reporting Procedures Albuquerque, New Mexico, was for a time first in the nation for crimes in cities with more than one hundred thousand population, but in 1973, it fell to one hundred fifth place and then rose to twentieth a few years later, not because crime suddenly waned and then waxed again but because reporting procedures had changed. At times, the FBI has refused to accept figures from New York City and Chicago; and those and other cities were restored to the list only when their reporting procedures were changed (of course, crime "rates" thereupon grew dramatically). In Washington, D.C., in the early 1970s, the index crime rate fell rapidly, mainly because the national political administration (housed there) wanted to show the nation that "get tough" policies worked; many thefts became downgraded to "less than fifty dollars" and some burglaries and robberies were recorded as larcenies of under fifty dollars. While "playing politics" with criminal statistics is not unknown, honest and voluntary changes in reporting methods may also have a dramatic impact (usually upward) on crime rates. Thus changes in Kansas City in 1959 led to a reported increase of 20 percent in two years; in Buffalo, New York, of 95 percent in two years (after 1961); and, in Chicago, of 72 percent in one year (after 1960).

Percentage of Arrests. Most arrests, it should be noted, are not for the major index crimes. Generally, only 25 to 30 percent of all arrests involve such crimes. And of the index crimes reported, 80 to 85 percent were against property rather than persons. While many states no longer treat drunkenness (or appearing drunk in public) as a crime, arrests for this crime (where it is still a crime) and for driving under the influence of alcohol far exceed those for any index crime. Comparing arrest rates with known crime rates for particular index offenses, we find that they range from one third down to 10 percent. This is low, especially when unreported crime is so high and when a person may be arrested for a crime committed in a previous year, not for one committed in the year of the arrest.

FBI Interpretation. The role of the FBI, itself a crime-fighting agency, in gathering and disseminating these reports has been controversial, especially when the bureau "interprets" raw material. Such dramatic devices as "time clocks," which graphically note that X number of crimes will occur in Y minutes, are regarded by criminologists as misleading and potentially explosive in a society where fear of crime is rampant. The Bureau has also resorted to other dubious interpretations of the data; in one report, it claimed that 92 percent of those arrested in 1963 but later acquitted (or whose cases had been dismissed by a court) were rearrested within the next six years.

Judges, it was suggested, were obviously being too soft on offenders. Analysis of the data base for this startling finding revealed that 76 percent of all accused who had been released in that year were simply not included in the equation; 92 percent of a selected group, which were only 24 percent of the entire group, were subsequently rearrested. But if all of the group were placed in the data base, the percentage of rearrests would not be 92 percent but 22 percent.

Comparison with Victimization Surveys Comparison between LEAA victimization surveys and the Uniform Crime Reports is not valid for the following reasons: (1) The crime categories differ (simple assault, for instance, is a victimization-survey category but not a UCR one). (2) UCRs include general metropolitan areas, while LEAA surveys encompass only central cities. (3) UCRs divide the total number of index crimes by general population, while victimization surveys break general crime down into categories (personal victimization rates, household victimization rates from burglaries and larcenies, and commercial victimization rates from crimes against business establishments) and divide each category not by total population but by the number of persons, households, and businesses in the area. (4) While the UCRs record the number of crimes, the LEAA records the number of victims, so that crimes with more than one victim will inflate the LEAA survey rate. (5) Since the UCR reports crime within an area, and the LEAA surveys report crimes against permanent residents and businesses within an area, crime rates in resort areas (as well as those with high transiency rates) will be higher in UCRs and lower in the victimization surveys.

OTHER STATISTICAL SOURCES

Major statistical compilations include National Prisoner Statistics, published by the Justice Department; Federal Prisons, published by the Federal Bureau of Prisons; Vital Statistics of the United States, published by the Bureau of the Census (homicide rate statistics); Juvenile Court Statistics, published by the U.S. Department of Health and Human Services (containing representative statistical samples of cases disposed of by juvenile courts) and thirteen state reports. Some private groups, such as the American Bankers Association, also publish records about particular crimes.

Other sources of information are "self-report" surveys conducted by sociologists, often in middle-size cities, and often involving small samples of juveniles. Of course, self-reporting cannot be statistically accurate, but the surveys have been reliable for what they have measured: the incidence of true crime among the reporting groups. It appears that almost three quarters of those interviewed tell the complete truth, while less than 20 percent completely hide their criminal records. There is a greater inclination to disguise the truth when the surveys are "nonanonymous" (the interviewee is named), but this danger is diminished when the interviewer and interviewee are of the same ethnic background.

LIKELIHOOD OF APPREHENSION

Despite the low clearance rates for most crime, the probability that a particular habitual offender will be caught is much greater than one might suppose. Probability theory postulates that the chance of something happening in a series of events (such as the number of heads turning up when a coin is tossed several times) is the product of the individual probabilities for each event. Thus, the chance of being apprehended for a crime such as robbery in a given jurisdiction may be 10 percent. The commission of the first robbery will result in a 90 percent chance of nonapprehension; for the second robbery, the chance is no longer 90 percent, but 81 percent (.90 multiplied by .90); for the third robbery, it will decline to 72 percent (.90 multiplied by itself twice). Computing the likelihood by standard logarithmic methods, the chances of apprehension will rise to more than 50 percent for the sixth robbery, and 87 percent after the twentieth robbery. Thus, criminals who enjoy a "hot streak" at the beginning and who continue in crime are almost certain to be caught—and quickly, if they frequently commit the same kind of crime. While life does not always conform either to probability tables or to laboratory experiments of rewarding animals, it does so often enough to warrant acceptance of the foregoing as a reasonably valid generalization.

Behavioral psychologists have found that behavior that is always rewarded becomes habitual, but when the reward is withdrawn it will almost immediately cease (strangely, when behavior is only periodically rewarded, it will continue even after the rewards cease). Often, repeated success will lead to attitudes of personal invulnerability and carelessness, especially by new, young criminals. Professional criminals may not worry much about their chances of being apprehended; rather, they will do things (obtain good lawyers, threaten witnesses, shrewdly plea bargain) to reduce their chances of either conviction or long prison terms.

TRENDS IN AMERICAN CRIME

Crime has been a general historical phenomenon in the United States. American history is replete with instances of mass and individual criminality despite the lack of statistics for earlier periods. Before becoming a nation, Americans regularly disobeyed English prohibitions against colonial manufacture of certain competitive products and trade restrictions by smuggling. Among succeeding demonstrations of lawlessness were: (1)

Shays' Rebellion in 1786 in Massachusetts (which spurred the calling of the Constitutional Convention the following year); (2) the 1794 Whiskey Rebellion by Pennsylvania farmers protesting a federal tax on alcohol; (3) "nativist" riots against Irish immigrants in the 1830s; (4) numerous violations of slave laws (both by abolitionists and by slave owners); (5) "draft law" riots in major eastern cities during the Civil War; (6) wholesale southern lynchings of newly freed blacks after 1865; (7) warfare between employers and labor unions from 1880 through 1936; and (8) mass violations of national Prohibition in the 1920s. Contemporary widespread flouting of laws against gambling, drug possession and sale, and deviant sexual behavior is therefore not a departure from a previous law-abiding situation.

Recently, historians have begun to study the growth of crime and have used available (though incomplete) records to clarify the past. Often, the results of even inadequate record-keeping practices were mitigated by intense interest in crime within communities. One study of Boston, which grew from town to city during the nineteenth century, concluded that (1) major crime was high prior to the Civil War; (2) it declined during and after the Civil War; (3) it peaked between 1875 and 1878; and (4) it has steadily declined since then.

While murder continuously declined through the twentieth century (until the 1960s), manslaughter rose startlingly when the automobile became important; despite this factor, even manslaughter declined after 1934 (for no apparent reason). In general, rapes increased steadily during the twentieth century, but increased more rapidly during periods of prosperity and declined during wars and depressions. Robbery and burglary patterns have been on a long-term downward trend, though they dramatically increased during wars and depressions. The assault rate sharply increased during wars and depressions in the nineteenth century, but steadily decreased through all conditions in the twentieth century. This statistic may reflect contemporary police practices relating to noninvestigation of minor assaults; in the nineteenth century, the police simply arrested for any kind of assault. Prior to the Civil War, larceny rates rose dramatically, dropped during the war, rose rapidly during the depression of 1873–78, and then dramatically declined in the twentieth century; this statistic too may be a result of police investigative practices.

Crime waves are thus nothing new in American history, and further study of urban patterns may well reveal that nineteenth-century crime was greater (on a per-capita basis) than even the strife-ridden 1960s.

Some crimes go out of fashion because the social and technological conditions that fostered them have disappeared. Moreover, particular and particularly well-publicized crimes may spur imitators, and the fads (for example, kidnaping in the 1930s) come, go, and may spring up again.

CRIME TODAY

Self-report surveys indicate that crime is much more widespread, especially among "respectable" groups, than is commonly assumed. Most of the crimes commonly committed by middle-class youths and reported in in self-report surveys are less serious than the ones delinquents report. The former include public drunkenness, driving under the influence of alcohol, and shoplifting. Very few of the middle-class self-reported crimes were detected by the police. Moreover, middle-class criminals and delinquents often benefit from police discretion not to arrest even when they know of crimes. Whether this is because of the offender's status or because the crimes are relatively trivial (or both) is difficult to determine.

Street Crime. Street criminals often obtain very little from their crimes; it has been estimated that the average theft or robbery nets three hundred dollars, while the average burglary nets only eighty dollars (because goods will be fenced for only 20 to 30 percent of their true value). Young criminals probably obtain even less, since these amounts are composites of all types of crimes within each category (bank robbery and robbery from individuals are lumped together, for instance). Young criminals tend to have expensive tastes and indulge in conspicuous consumption and conspicuous generosity toward their friends. Young criminals often are more careless than their professional counterparts, believe that they are somehow immune from apprehension, and commit high-risk crimes to gain peer favor. Failure to achieve success at home or at school may make them more willing than older persons to take risks even when, by objective standards, they are more likely to be arrested. However, many young criminals are not committed to crime and will "mature" out of crime (or delinquency) when they marry or obtain a decent job.

White-Collar Crime. Criminologists define white-collar crimes as those committed by persons of respectability and relatively high social status by means of, or in the course of, their occupations. This definition does not include (but probably should) the range of crimes that respectable people can commit outside their occupations for the purpose of obtaining or retaining money or property or to gain a particular personal or business benefit. Such crimes include filing of false income-tax returns, concealment of assets in bankruptcy proceedings, credit-card fraud, fraudulent load applications, and misrepresentations on insurance, Social Security, and unemployment-benefit applications.

Business Crimes. White-collar criminals may commit crimes against their businesses, including violation of trust (bribery and kickbacks), embezzlement, "insider" stock trading by taking advantage of special knowledge, computer frauds to secretly take money from corporate assets for one's own use, and illegal self-aggrandizing by fiduciaries such as lawyers and trustees.

Many business crimes are committed not to benefit oneself primarily but one's company. Corporate tax and antitrust violations, truth-in-lending violations, bribery of another company's or government employees, or submitting false claims for payment to government under contracts are but a few of these crimes.

Fraud. Another type of white-collar crime, though it is often committed by members of organized crime (who may be locally, if not nationally, reputable), involves the establishment of businesses for the sole or primary purpose of engaging in fraud. Medical and health frauds, home-improvement schemes, merchandise swindles, charitable and religious frauds, fraudulent business and bank takeovers for the purpose of looting the enterprise, employment-agency fraud, and organized frauds against government are outstanding examples. Often, these frauds are perpetrated by respectable businessmen in combination with organized crime, often after the businessman has become beholden (for example by gambling debts or loanshark borrowing) to the criminal.

Fraud is probably the most prevalent crime in the United States. Misrepresentation, either by word or silence, is endemic to American business. Income-tax fraud is widespread and costly. There is considerable fraud committed by lawyers and other professionals and fiduciaries. Insurance fraud (both by and against insurance companies) is widespread. Violations are rarely detected and even more rarely prosecuted, in part because many such crimes have no individual victims, they rouse little public concern, and much fraud is intertwined with legal (or marginally legal) conduct. Also, many violations are handled by noncriminal agencies, so that the stigma of criminality is often avoided. Administrative agencies are assumed to have certain advantages because they (1) can act more quickly than the criminal courts, since their procedures involve fewer due-process protections; (2) have an expertise not possessed by courts; (3) are more flexible than courts and have more remedies at their disposal; and (4) can continually monitor the activities of the businesses involved. It has been argued, however, that agencies should be allowed or indeed be compelled to prosecute offenders in criminal courts, since discretion in this area is unwarranted. Studies have shown that some corporations are both habitual lawbreakers and recidivists and that businessses lose more to employee crime than to outside theft, larceny, or robbery.

The extent of white-collar crime, under the circumstances, is unknown and probably unknowable, although greater public concern for the problem has developed in recent years.

THEORIES OF CRIMINOLOGY

Part II

3. Methodology of Crime Study

Criminology has attempted to be a science. Science seeks to (1) discover consistencies and (2) find the causes of these consistencies by use of rigorous testing and verification procedures. When scientific analysis has been performed, a theory is formulated, and that theory must be stated so that it can be independently examined and tested by other scientists. Everyone knows that once-accepted (even sacrosanct) theories have been overturned, often after being believed for centuries. Criminology is not a "natural" science dealing with physical matter and energy but a "social science" dealing with behavior. The uncertainties of theorizing in the natural sciences are inevitably magnified when we deal with human beings in society, often a rapidly changing society. It should not be surprising that severe methodological problems exist in criminology and that virtually all theories of criminality contain substantial flaws. Criminology involves especially perplexing problems because crime is a bundle of different behaviors (involving different states of mind) that defy the attempt to find one underlying "cause." Also, criminology has been not only a "science" but also an attempt to deal with crime in society (or to find "answers" demanded by societies), so that criminologists often see their roles as social rather than scientific ones, and they may sacrifice their role as pure scientists to become shapers of social policy. (This problem is more acute when criminologists are part of a political establishment that adopts one or another theory of crime to gain or hold political power in a given society.)

AIMS OF CRIMINOLOGICAL THEORY

Criminological theory has been concerned with two main areas: first, the overall problem of crime and society, the patterns of crime, and broad consistencies (and changes) within a given society and, second, explanations for individual criminality. The first tends to be descriptive (What are the patterns?); the second tends to be explanatory (Why the crimes and the criminals?). Criminologists use explanatory theories to attempt to predict criminality in individuals (or groups), so that society may then attempt to redirect the lives of those vulnerable people to prevent criminality. Actually, it appears that general theorists have had more success in predicting overall crime rates and changes in societies (or in certain areas of society) than have scientists of the second category in dealing with smaller groups.

Much criminological research confuses the question of what is being studied (general criminality or causes of individual criminality) and what is being achieved by the experiment (description or prediction). Some criminologists have attempted to combine the two by seeking to isolate "causal" factors and to find which factors in which combinations will result in crime. The number of factors studied may be great (in one case, 170 were deemed related to crime) and the combinations could be almost infinite. Any resulting theory would thus be hopelessly complex and, in any event, would not account for *all* crime (or even noncrime) among those apparently subject to the same factors. It is, however, possible that such an explanation might account for the incidence of crime (the overall problem) without telling us much at all about individual criminality. Thus such an explanation might have a predictive value without having an explanatory one.

In recognition of these problems, most criminologists have attempted to demonstrate "cause" (again, on the second type of theory) by establishing (1) a frequency of association between crime and a single (or several) factors; (2) occurrence of an alleged "causal" factor or factors prior to the criminality; and (3) the irrelevance of other possible "causes." Failure to achieve all of these—or any of these—means failure to prove the "cause-effect" relationship. Criminologists, however, have agreed that proof need not be perfect; the effect need not always be present when the cause is, and a given "cause" may not produce the effect. If the statistical relationship between the cause and the effect (crime) remains strong, theory suggests that the cause is still important.

An *immutable* characteristic such as age, sex, race, or to an extent religion outside any social context cannot be the *sole* cause of crime or delinquency. If something else is necessary to produce criminality, then the original factor (especially an immutable one) cannot be the cause. Also, if an alleged "cause" can be measured (for example, family earnings, home ownership), it cannot be the true cause, since such attributes are usually the result of other social factors. If an alleged "cause" depends upon another (for example, substandard housing as a result of low income), then it cannot be *the* cause.

Fulfillment of these canons of research is difficult, and no one theory has been shown to account for all crime or to distinguish crime from noncrime.

The most that can be claimed for any theory is that it creates "probabilities" (perhaps only "possibilities") and that it may contain descriptive and predictive value.

TYPES OF METHODOLOGIES

Despite the label of "science," most criminological research has been intuitive rather than scientific. (Some would argue that the beginnings of most scientific research also commence with hunches.) The investigator takes data and materials that he believes to be significant. Since criminologists study what is available, they may well overlook phenomena such as white-collar crime, which, though widespread, is difficult to quantify.

The second general approach is to study known criminals to discover common factors in their lives. This method tends to be more scientific, since the sample is precise, and it attempts to isolate particular common factors.

Hypothesis Based on Data. A common methodology involves the creation of a hypothesis about criminality based upon available data, which may not be accurate or complete. This results in generalized findings and, often, the choice of a wrong factor (recurring factors are not necessarily significant ones). Also, this method does not, in itself, eliminate other factors that may also be present. A general "cause" may (1) itself be caused by something else that is more significant or (2) may cause something else that is more significant, and this method of study sheds no light on either possibility.

Personality Traits. Another common method isolates personality traits common to criminals (or particular types of criminals) and seeks to ascertain whether or not they are shared by law-abiding groups with the same general background. Many of these studies concentrate only upon one particular trait. This trait, if found prevalent, is labeled as a "cause." However, this method does not answer the question whether or not the trait actually *caused* criminal conduct. It is also hampered by its focus: prisoners, not criminals in general, are studied (what is true of the former may not be of the latter). It is also difficult to gather the relevant data, except for factors that are obvious (age, sex, and race); prisoners may not tell the truth about the trait involved or may have faulty memories or may be guilty of other misperceptions. Also, it is difficult to tell whether (1) the "general population" group used as a control group is truly noncriminal and (2) the factor studied is not also present in the general population. Most researchers take for granted the absence of (2). Again, those factors that seem important may only "cause" other factors that may be the true culprits. Many factors or traits studied are vague and cannot be specifically described. Also, mere statistical analysis cannot account for the particular case: for example, the child from a broken home who does not become delinquent, or the child from a happy home who does. (This defect is relevant to the individual explanation level of theory, but may be irrelevant to the overall descriptive type of theory.)

Study of Individuals.   Another method is to study the individual criminal. While the investigator may look for a particular trait (as he would do in the previous situation), he seeks to assess its particular causal significance to an individual. However, the "trait" investigated may not be the criminal's (or may be, though the criminal docs not recognize it). Also, there is a danger that a mere listing of factors will result. The role of the investigator may also be crucial. If he is employed by a government or private agency dealing with crime or delinquency (as he often is), he may well consciously or unconsciously focus upon a particular factor that is the employer's concern, though that factor may not be of major significance.

Case Study.   The limited case study method involves a rigorous attempt to study a given category of criminal behavior and a number of criminals who have behaved in that way, in order to find patterns. Once a pattern is discerned (it could be psychological or sociological or both), the investigator will then (1) identify it and (2) see whether it applies to new offenders. If, as has often happened, (2) fails, the theory must be reformulated to exclude incompatible new cases (or newly discovered "old cases"), or broadened to include those cases. The final theory should then include only those cases to which it applies and to exclude all others. This approach, also called the "typological" one, will be discussed in Chapter 11. Often, the theory does more to define particular behavior than to explain it.

Observer.   The observer (also called the participant-observer) method stresses the study of criminals in their natural environment rather than in prison or elsewhere in the criminal-justice system. Its success, of course, depends upon the willingness of criminals to allow themselves to be observed (some conduct may be changed because a criminal is being observed and knows it). Of course, particular findings cannot be duplicated by other social scientists, since new researchers may not have the willing consent of the subjects of the original study. Often, the result demonstrates not how one becomes a criminal but how he himself describes the process. This method more often describes how criminals operate rather than how they become criminals.

Change of Factors.   Another method is to experimentally change the factors believed to be "causes" of criminality, under the assumption that "background" factors are significant. On the individual level, clinical treatment of criminals, delinquents, or predelinquents will be undertaken; on social and economic levels, changing the environment—if environment is believed to be the significant cause—will be attempted (though, of course, this is expensive). However, it is hard to tell whether reduction in individual criminality or the general crime rate, if it occurs, can be attributed to the change or was the result of another factor existing prior to the change or itself caused by the change. Thus, if individual treatment leads (or apparently leads) to "maturation" out of crime, would that maturation have occurred anyway?

4. History and Development of Criminological Theories

The difficulties of theorizing about crime are best exemplified by study of the history of criminology. That history reveals (1) the existence of broad theories that have been discredited by later research; (2) the relevance of those theories to social, and sometimes political, demands to solve "the crime problem"; and (3) the persistence of parts of theories even today. Most theory has been of the "grand" variety, sweeping attempts to encompass all criminal behavior into one or a few magical formulas. Although the history is complex, it would be wise to keep in mind and to distinguish between the two levels of theorizing discussed earlier: the broad one, seeking to describe and at times explain crime patterns, and the individualistic one, seeking to explain individual criminality.

EARLY EXPLANATIONS OF CRIME

Generally, in Western thought between A.D. 500 and 1700, the world was viewed as divided into good and evil forces. Nature, by God's design, was a "great chain of being" wherein all human beings played a definite, predetermined role in society. Crime and other calamities were considered the result of man's sinful nature, the Devil's influence, or God's punishment. In this era felonies were regarded as mortal sins. In addition to religious crimes such as heresy and witchcraft, murder of a social superior was often punished by torture and death. Misdemeanors, it was thought, resulted from excessive passion and were violations of human rather than divine law. Punishment was invoked to preserve the peace rather than to maintain status privileges; payment of fines and penance were the chief penalties, and both were graded in accordance with the offender's social status. Corporal punishment became the substitute for fines when the poor could not afford to pay. Since criminology should be viewed as part of the history of ideas, it is clear that certain intellectual currents drifting through western Europe during the Age of the Enlightenment played a major role in redirecting and wholly changing the notion of crime as innate evil or God's punishment for violation of the social order.

THE CLASSICAL SCHOOL

The Enlightenment philosophy of the seventeenth and eighteenth centuries reflected the growth of new classes: merchants, bankers, and businessmen (the bourgeoisie). The "Protestant Ethic" arose to stress that personal success was the result of hard work, rational thought, and departure from tradition. The study of science encouraged attempts to discover natural laws, rather than merely to bow to God's often erratic ways. Man was seen to be capable of reason and of judging pain and pleasure. The state was viewed not as a divine entity but as a government that could no longer impose harsh and arbitrary punishment but was required to follow the dictates of reason.

The following generalizations encapsulate, in somewhat oversimplified form, the thought of several influential reformers who had similar attitudes toward crime. These reformers reacted against a system that permitted (1) the power of judges to interpret vague laws and often to interpret them inconsistently and arbitrarily; (2) secret trials, secret accusations, and secret sentences; (3) no right of defense at trial; and (4) torture to extort confessions. The abuses were more serious on the Continent: For instance, French judges maintained that law could not be enacted or interpreted uniformly because the country's different provinces had different traditions. In England, the law schools admitted only the nobility; justices of the peace were arbitrary; and kings could appoint and dismiss judges at will. Juries were subject to intimidation. The judges continually changed and expanded the definition of treason. Capital punishment was prescribed for between 225 and 300 crimes. Minor offenses were punished by methods such as the pillory and amputation of limbs. Whipping was a frequent punishment, especially for soldiers and sailors. Drawing and quartering the body (dismemberment of the limbs by teams of horses pulling in different directions) was a frequent penalty for serious crimes, sometimes before the offender had been put to death. Hanging occurred in public, and it often took a long and agonizing time for the felon to die. Classical reformers primarily sought to remedy abuses of the then "criminal-justice system" rather than understand crime per se.

The classical theory of a crime reflected concern for crime control (a general truism throughout history). Classical reform commenced in England and Italy in the last half of the eighteenth century and spread to western Europe and the United States thereafter. In 1764, an Italian nobleman named Cesare Beccaria (then only twenty-six years old) wrote *Dei Delitti e*

Delle Pene (Of Crimes and Punishments). He sought to (1) limit the scope of the criminal law to the minimum necessary to deter crime; (2) codify that law, to enable all to understand it and to limit the power of judges to interpret it, and (3) assure equality of all before the law. Beccaria influenced, among others, Sir William Blackstone, author of the classic *Commentaries on the Laws of England,* and Thomas Jefferson and Benjamin Franklin in the United States. Other late eighteenth-century and early nineteenth-century English reformers, notably Jeremy Bentham, argued that the law should be utilitarian in that it should serve "the greatest good of the greatest number." All men, Bentham argued, were blessed with reason and could logically determine what actions would increase their pleasure and diminish their pain. Lawlessness would end when society provided a series of logical, closely defined, and clearly stated penalties that would be minimally sufficient to ensure that people would not voluntarily commit crime and thereby suffer punishment. The classical reform movement sought (and largely achieved) limitation of capital punishment, arguing that it was irrational to inflict the same severe penalty for totally different acts.

Proportionality of punishment to the crime was a central tenet of classical philosophy. In addition, the reformers contended that criminal laws should be known to all (to inform everyone of the "pains" attached to various crimes) and should be inflexible, since all human beings were equally rational. Judicial discretion would thus be eliminated. Severity should be abolished in order to preserve both human dignity and proportionality, since the infliction of more pain than that which would deter a rational man would be cruelty and violative of man's natural freedom. Graded punishment would deter some crime. (The provision of the death penalty, for instance, for both robbery and murder encourages murder, since a robber has no incentive to refrain from murder.)

THE NEO-CLASSICAL SCHOOL

The classical reformers recognized that children and lunatics, by definition, could not "reason," so that lessening of punishment was appropriate for them. The neo-classicists argued that some flexibility, though not arbitrariness, should be reintroduced to mitigate the injustices of fixed punishments for all, irrespective of circumstances. The first recognition of these principles occurred in modifications of the punishment structure to exempt children under the age of seven from criminal responsibility, and to require proof of rationality of juveniles seven to fourteen before imposition of punishment. Both classical and neo-classical thinking are reflected in much contemporary criminological thought. Indeed, there has been somewhat of a return to emphasis upon fixed and inflexible punishment. The matter remains controversial.

THE CARTOGRAPHIC SCHOOL

In the midnineteenth century, certain scholars, led by A. M. Guerry and Adolphe Quetelet, argued that crime had roots in the physical and social environment. Using maps and statistical data, they sought to measure the variations in crime rates in different areas and to correlate criminal and other social data. They found that crime correlates closely to poverty and other factors. This school did not reject individual responsibility for crime, but sought to understand the conditions that, in their view, were in part responsible. Their research tended toward the descriptive. This approach is still extant (see pp. 75–77).

THE SOCIALIST SCHOOL

Socialists, building upon (and perhaps distorting) the ideas of Karl Marx, argued that economic conditions "caused" crime. Marx's general theory that the working class was exploited by a capitalist system of production became transformed into a theory that capitalist development created poverty and a sense of powerlessness that resulted in crime. Socialists argued that crime rates fluctuated with economic conditions. They tried to prove that crime increased when the business cycle declined, bringing widespread unemployment. William A. Bonger, a Dutch Marxist sociologist, argued in *Criminality and Economic Conditions* (1916) that capitalism produced a certain personality type, an egoist who recklessly pursued his own self-interest. Bonger thus viewed crime not only as the response of the oppressed poor but also as a consequence of disregard for social cooperation and an emphasis upon competitive relationships that weaken the social fabric.

THEORIES OF INNATE CRIMINAL TYPES

In the nineteenth century, the search for natural laws was extended to the study of man, and the sciences of human behavior including psychology, anthropology (initially an offshoot of biology), and sociology appeared. "Social Darwinism" was an attempt to fit Darwinian theories of natural selection and survival of the fittest to social and economic conditions. "Natural" deficiencies, especially intelligence, led to crime, it was argued, and those deficiencies were most often to be found in the crime-prone class of the poor.

This reasoning gave rise to several theories purporting to show that criminals inherently and innately differ from noncriminals, although how they differ was in dispute. The premise was that criminals were, in some respect, "weaker" than the law-abiding. Such theories emphasized clinical testing of particular criminals in order to validate the "scientific" knowledge of their behavior. Cesare Lombroso, an Italian physician, believed that criminals can be distinguished from noncriminals by certain physiological characteristics such as flat noses, longer jaws, and an asymmetrical cranium. While not all persons possessing these physical traits will be criminals, he believed that they are atavistic (resembling primitive man), and such physiological degeneracy will predispose toward criminal behavior. Lombroso himself later admitted that deficient physiognomy could account for only 40 percent of known criminals. He made no systematic analysis of the physiology of noncriminals, and early twentieth-century research disproved his basic hypothesis. Recently, there has been a mild revival of the Lombrosian approach, as research into chromosomal imbalance has increased.

Positivism. This approach gave rise to another theory of criminology (or more accurately, crime control). The "positivist" approach (see p. 14) stressed that science has shown that classical free will was either a myth or irrelevant. In this view the sole function of the criminal law is to defend society from predatory conduct. That is, irrespective of intent or even mental state and capacity, government has the right to incarcerate or otherwise remove the dangerous elements in society—perhaps to hospitals, perhaps to prisons. In modern times, there has been a revival of this notion.

Mental Retardation. As inherent physical notions of criminality waned, other similar theories surfaced. In the early twentieth century mental retardation, "feeblemindedness," was thought by many to be a major cause of crime. Attempts to prove that all or most criminals were unable to control their conduct because of genetic predispositions, while law-abiding people were genetically superior, have foundered on the rock of increasingly sophisticated research.

Psychological Determinism. The theory that criminals are psychologically sick has largely replaced these older notions of inherent depravity. Early Freudian emphasis upon the "unconscious" and "frustration-aggression" stressed the role of infantile experience and socialization upon later personality. In this view retarded ego development will keep growing children at the infantile stage and prevent maturity. Adherents of this approach differ about (1) the precise nature of psychological deprivation and (2) the relative frequency of psychological problems among criminals, but the psychological approach has played a major role in "treatment" approaches to criminality (see Chapter 13).

THE SOCIOLOGICAL SCHOOL

The cartographic and Socialist perspectives about society were the antecedents to the growth of modern criminology's emphasis on the social causes of crime. Gabriel Tarde, a French sociologist and justice official who was a contemporary of Lombroso, believed that criminality is learned conduct. Tarde found that example was the elementary fact of social life and imitation of others was the primary method of learning in society. He argued that (1) people imitate other people, primarily those with whom they are in close contact; (2) inferiors imitate superiors; and (3) when different customs converge, the newer one will be substituted for the older one. To an extent, modern sociological theory has drawn heavily on Tarde.

Sociological analysis flourished first in the United States and, indeed, was called the American School. It took the form of "macrocriminology" (study of large social forces). Various early theories went beyond description (see chapters 7–10) and found that crime rates were linked to (1) economic developments (a view especially characteristic of the Marxists), (2) social mobility and stratification, (3) culture conflict, or (4) population density and movements (this factor derived in part from the cartographic school). This approach was discarded when criminologists found that crime statistics were not particularly reliable, but the general view, and some of the specific forms, have revived in the past twenty years.

MULTIFACETED APPROACHES

The United States has led the way in what might be called "microcriminology," the study of criminals and the process by which they became criminal. This has involved heavy empirical research, often with individuals and small groups. The approach encompasses both sociology (the elements in society that conduce toward criminality) and social psychology (the process by which these elements influence the individual). Some scholars cross old boundary lines to study such purely psychological factors as imitation, frustration-aggression, and reinforcement and learning theory. Modern sociology, in contrast, attempts to define crime-inducing cultures and "criminogenic" social situations. Theories of "culture" and "personality" are notoriously difficult to reconcile; theories that combine both are difficult to test.

Many criminologists, often combining sociological, social psychological, and psychological concepts have argued that crime cannot be understood by any one theory but that it comprises many events with many causes. As noted, adherents of this contend that only study of individuals will reveal the various "causes" of their criminal conduct. This approach has been criticized because it logically confuses "single factors" with "single theories"; a single theory may include more than one factor. The main criticism of multifactor approaches is that they yield long "laundry lists" and so many possibilities of combination of factors that they are useless as explanations. That may be true, but it may be irrelevant if the purpose of the study is either descriptive or predictive.

5. Factors Correlating with Crime

Before analyzing criminological theories, it is necessary to comment upon the factors that are correlated with crime and delinquency, for any valid theory must account for these factors. Also, the presence and extent of these factors provide an indication about crime in the future. It must be emphasized that these factors do not "cause" crime (for example, not all males are criminals), but their presence raises significant questions for criminological theory, the subject of the next chapters.

AGE FACTORS

Certain correlates are so strong that they are essential to any theory about crime. Statistics have consistently and accurately indicated that young people commit much more crime than do adults. Young people are "overrepresented" (in terms of proportion) in the criminal population. While some adults may escape being recorded as criminals, more very young people will be given "breaks," so that statistical significance is not diminished by social factors. The age of maximum criminality is during or shortly before adolescence, and this is true in virtually all countries that maintain statistics (although the specific age of maximum criminality may vary slightly in different nations). The age of crime-prone youth in America has been declining. In 1976, young people between 11 and 25, though constituting only 25 percent of the population, accounted for 73.7 percent of the arrests for serious crimes: 74.5 percent for arson, 84.7 percent for vandalism, 83.5 percent for auto theft, 84.3 percent for burglary, and 76.1 percent for drug violations.

Several factors qualify the importance of age. The nature of the crime is one; while teenagers may commit burglary and auto theft, murders tend to be committed primarily by somewhat older people. The "age range" for crimes is significant. Most of those arrested for serious crime other than homicide and assault are under 25. Median ages, which divide in half those arrested (thus one half are older than that age and one half younger), are low for those crimes that juveniles tend to commit (24.1 has been the age in recent years for robbery).

Age also correlates with sex. Males tend to commit most of their crimes at earlier ages than do females, although one violent offense (homicide) and most nonviolent offenses are committed at earlier ages by females than by males. As shall be seen, women commit many fewer crimes than do men.

The age of first contact with the criminal-justice system, usually in a delinquency proceeding, also varies according to geographic area. High crime and delinquency areas tend to produce younger criminals than do low-crime areas. The younger the person is when he commits his first crime, the more likely it will be that he will quickly commit a second one. The type of crime committed by people of particular ages varies by area (high crime-low crime, urban-rural).

By definition, the crime rate among an age group decreases once the age of maximum criminality (the age at which most offenses are committed) has passed; in general, the crime rate tends to decrease after age 19 in the United States. The rate of decrease is not the same for all crimes, and the crime rate itself (as well as the age of decrease) will change over time.

There may be some relationship between delinquency and adult criminality, although comparatively few delinquents go on to become adult criminals. While many criminals under 25 have had juvenile records, new criminals over 25 tend to commit their first crimes at later ages. Indeed, the crime rate for some crimes, such as drunkenness, increases after age 35. It appears that juveniles tend to get arrested for offenses they frequently commit and that older adults (over 35) tend to commit different types of crime.

There is no adequate explanation of why young people commit a disproportionate amount of crime. While they may be stronger and more vigorous than older people, this theory cannot account for the *variations* in age ratios and *particular* kinds of crime. The evidence, however, does point to one important "social fact": The higher the proportion of young people to the population as a whole, the greater the crime rate. Between 25 and 30 percent of the great increase in crime in America during the 1960s can be attributed to the increased proportion of teen-agers in the population.

SEX FACTORS

Sex status, even more than age, is the critical variable in criminality and its incidence. Men commit greater numbers of crimes than do women at all times, at all ages, in all communities. The arrest rate for males in the United States is five times greater than for females; the conviction rate is ten times greater; the institutional rate (commitment to prison and other correctional institutions) is fifteen to twenty times greater. (The latter figures may tell more about institutional responses to female criminality than about female criminality as such.) About 80 percent of all delinquents are

male, although this percentage is somewhat lower when self-report delinquency studies are analyzed.

Sex status tends to be less important where women have greater social
and political equality. The sex ratio may also vary in accordance with the
social standing of various groups: For instance, American black males and
females, who are closer in social status than are their white counterparts,
also have a narrower sex ratio. Variations also occur when geographic area
is taken into account; the ratio is narrower in cities than in rural areas. The
ratios tend to shrink as the sexes get older, so that the numbers become
more nearly equal for older offenders. The higher the crime rate in a given
area, the lower the variation in sex ratio. Family factors are relevant; the ratio is lower when delinquents come from broken rather than stable homes.

The sex ratio has been narrowing in recent times. Between 1960 and
1975, the arrest rate for females increased by 374 percent, while for males,
the increase was only 119 percent. Females were being increasingly arrested
for drug possession, property theft, fraud, robbery, and forgery. It is important to note however, that the ratios are not now anywhere near equal; the
percentage increase of females commenced from a much lower baseline.

The explanation that women's liberation has caused the disproportionate
increase is not convincing. Increased labor-force participation by women
(for economic rather than ideological reasons) may simply have given them
the opportunity to commit more crime; this suggestion is partially borne out
by an analysis of the crimes actually committed. In truth, until recently, female criminality was seldom studied. Female crime was thought to be the
result of rare individual psychological or physiological aberrations. This
view was probably related to general social beliefs about women's inferiority
to men. Freud, for instance, considered female crime to be the result of an
aberrant refusal to face "women's true role," and the presence of "masculinity complexes" and "penis envy." Traditional law-abiding female behavior was equated with passivity and masochism.

One recent American criminologist, Otto Pollack, argued that (1) women
commit as much crime as men; (2) crimes by women are less likely to be detected; and (3) women are likely to be the beneficiaries of a "double standard" of law enforcement even when detected. He believed that women are
biologically weaker than men and that their sexual socialization conduces
toward greater cunning and secrecy. The peculiar nature of women's crimes
thus was a blend of the social and the biological.

RACE FACTORS

Race in America is difficult to determine; perhaps as many as 80 percent of
American blacks are of mixed racial parentage. National statistics also do

not clearly furnish information about the racial composition of areas where blacks tend to be arrested. The proportion of blacks to whites in those areas is probably greater than the general black presence in a given state or in the United States as a whole (about 12 percent). Black crime rates should be based upon the proportion of blacks in a given area, not in the general population. Also, it is likely, though statistical analysis is difficult, that blacks are more often arrested for acts that, if committed by whites, would not result in arrest. Offsetting this may be the propensity of criminal-justice agencies to overlook crimes committed by blacks against each other (by far, the greatest percentage of black crime) because of a belief that the poor-black "subculture" does not condemn such crime. This view, if valid, is rapidly changing.

Underreporting of black crime may occur because criminal-justice personnel believe that blacks (and other groups) are particularly crime-prone. On the other hand, the clash between black cultural mores (for example, hostility of young blacks toward the police, lack of deferential demeanor when stopped) and police emphasis upon the "right" attitudes may result in arrests of blacks more frequently when police discretion is involved (as it often is in police-juvenile confrontations). However, while racial variations in manner may contribute to disproportionately more arrests of blacks for "lesser crimes," studies have shown that demeanor is unimportant in police arrests for serious crimes.

Even correcting for these possible statistical distortions, there appears to be a great difference in the black-white crime rate. Blacks commit three to four times as many crimes as whites, and the black commitment rate to prison is six times that of whites. In 1976, 53.5 percent of murder and negligent manslaughter arrest rates were of blacks; for forcible rape, 46.6 percent; and for robbery, 59.2 percent. For other crimes, including arson, vandalism, and drug-law violations, the percentage arrested was much closer to the black proportion of the population.

As might be expected, there are variations in black crime rates. Black crime rates are closest to white ones in the South, somewhat greater in the North, and greatest in the West. Black female criminality is much greater than white female criminality, the ratios between black male and white male criminality are much smaller. Studies have shown that place of residence of blacks has little relationship to black crime rates, although cities with high black populations tend to have high murder rates. In the South, cities with large black populations tend to have both high black *and* high white homicide rates. Over time, the variation between black and white crime rates has fluctuated; the rate of increase for blacks for certain crimes has slowed while for whites it has grown. Studies have shown that newly arrived blacks, even in slum areas, have low delinquency rates at the beginning, but the rate increases over time to match the general-area crime rate (at about the five-year mark). Education is another variable: Well-educated blacks in cities have a lower crime rate than do poorly educated whites.

Minority, especially black, criminality may be explained by discrimination, but this explanation is not all-inclusive because some minority groups, long the victims of discrimination, have low criminality (Japanese, for instance). Also, while some minority groups have higher crime rates than do whites (Puerto Ricans, Mexican Americans, native Indians, and Chinese Americans, for instance), those rates are not nearly so high as black ones.

One psychological theory argues that high frustration leads to crime, but the evidence for groups (as well as for individuals, see p. 56) is inconclusive. This theory contends that black frustration led to much intraracial crime (since whites could not be chosen as victims) and that various social changes have led to more true "acting out" against whites.

The economic status of minorities may be as important as their racial status (and more important than what might be called their "psychological status"). Blacks have traditionally been poor; although blacks comprise only 12 percent of the national population, 25 percent of American families living in poverty are black. The precentage of black families that are poor is more than four times as great as that of white families (although because of their low numbers, there are fewer poorer blacks than whites in the total population). In addition, it must be noted that American history has been unique for blacks in two respects: First, the legacy of slavery was a peculiar one applicable only to American blacks and creating a particular combination of social and economic discrimination not faced by any other group. Second, in many places in the nineteenth century, blacks were pushed out of reasonably well-paying secure jobs (with the opportunity for social and economic mobility) in favor of new white immigrant groups. Such an explanation, of course, cannot be substantiated by any known method of investigation or experimentation.

As will be seen, modern sociological theory accounts for racial variations by stressing that different races have different exposure rates to criminal patterns. Being of the "wrong" race may condemn individuals to social and economic levels that feature certain types of crimes (though not others, such as white-collar crime). The process of segregation or "ghettoization" may have the same effect.

IMMIGRATION

In the late nineteenth century and the early twentieth century, vast numbers of immigrants came to the United States, and many native Americans raised serious questions about immigrant criminality. Although large-scale immigration has ceased except for increasing numbers of illegal aliens from Mexico and Latin America, the issue is still important. Despite certain beliefs that immigrants are (1) "naturally" inferior, (b) unsocialized into native values, (3) poor, and (4) highly mobile, thus free from general cultural restraints, the simple truth is that immigrants had lower crime rates in America (indeed, in most countries) than native inhabitants. The crime rate of immigrants is even lower when other factors are taken into account—for instance, the fact that many youngsters are among arriving immigrants.

As might be expected, the variations between native and immigrant crime rates differ by type of crime. Variations are also affected by the cultural traditions of different immigrant groups, especially cultural patterns of alcoholism. Criminal patterns among immigrants tend to reflect the criminal patterns of societies from which they come.

Immigrant groups differ from each other in rates of crime. The first native-born generation crime rates will tend to resemble the parents', but in the second generation, crime rates will rise to match rates in the general area. On the whole, immigrants from eastern and southern Europe tended to have higher crime rates than those from western Europe. Immigrants who are young when they arrive have higher crime rates than middle-aged immigrants. Indeed, young-immigrant crime rates tend to approximate those of natives in the areas in which settlement occurs, and this similarity extends to types of crimes committed. Immigrants who have settled in their own enclaves tend to have lower crime rates than those who settled within, or at the borders of, native areas. In time, immigrant groups tend to adopt the crime rates of the new area, whether high or low. Sociological explantions of culture contact and adoption of learning patterns seem to account best for immigrant crime.

6. "Personality" and Psychological Theories

The data in the previous chapter would be dismissed by a psychoanalytically oriented scholar, who would maintain that criminality is a property of individuals and not groups. Perhaps he would concede that some social conditions might exaggerate some individuals' problems or give them means to act out their problems. But he would argue that crime is specifically caused by individual defects. This chapter will trace the modern development of various theories of personality and psychology.

Of course, attribution of crime to specific personality defects is a continuation of the Lombrosian theory of "innate" criminality; as was true with Lombroso, there is dispute about the frequency of these defects among criminals.

MENTAL DEFECTS THEORY

The assumptions of the 1920s and 30s about "feeblemindedness" of criminals have been invalidated by findings that (1) many noncriminals have low IQs and (2) there is no great incidence of crime among mentally retarded people. Those who are both mentally retarded and offenders have about as much difficulty coping with the criminal-justice system as do their "normal" peers. More recently, adherents of this theory have stressed the "social consequences" of retardation, especially the inability to adjust to society, rather than the inherent characteristics of the defect itself.

PSYCHOANALYTIC THEORY

The origins of psychoanalytic theory, as previously noted, are found in the works of Sigmund Freud. He theorized that the human personality is a function of the interaction among the "id," the "ego," and the "superego"; the "id" being the primitive impulses present in all human beings from birth, the "superego" being the dictates and demands of society, and the "ego" being the internal mechanism that directs and controls the "id" to satisfy the "superego." The id's impulsiveness is channeled by the ego toward socially acceptable ways. Various mechanisms and results are possible, some of them neurotic. Repression of the id occurs when the ego forces its drives to remain unconscious. The battle between the id and the ego creates anxiety, which is relieved when the impulse is stifled. But the impulse still exists and seeks to "break out" in other forms. One form is "displacement," a transference of blocked feelings to another object, which arouses less anxiety. Thus, aggressive feelings toward the father (which Freud said were inevitable) may become aggression directed against authority figures or may, because of guilt, lead to identification with the father, who may be a criminal. Other mechanisms for the reduction of anxiety include *projection,* attribution of one's own impulses to others; *reaction formation,* replacement of an impulse by its opposite; *fixation,* failure to develop beyond a certain stage of personality; *regression,* a return to a previous level of personality development; and *denial,* refusal to recognize and admit what is painful and unacceptable. If the id triumphs over the superego, the ego may feel guilty and seek to be punished. To obtain that punishment, a crime may be committed (to ensure punishment, the criminal may leave clues). Of course, not all id-ego battles are neurotic (else we would all be at least neurotics and perhaps criminals). *Sublimation* involves transferring the id's impulses into socially acceptable behavior.

Since Freud, other analysts have argued that failure to form ego identity is critical. They believe that human beings go through stages of maturation involving (1) the development of trust (stemming from the infant's dependency on the mother); (2) the development of autonomy (toilet training); (3) the learning of initiative (the child sees its ability to manipulate situations); (4) the beginning of industriousness (mastering tasks) in the prepubic period; (5) acquisition of a sense of identity in adolescence; (6) learning of patterns of intimacy in young adulthood; (7) productivity and creativity in adult life; and (8) during maturity, a final ego integration involving acceptance of the past and present and confidence in the future. In this view, individuals may commit crimes because of shame, guilt, inferiority feelings, confusion, isolation, and despair brought about by failure at any one of these steps.

Other psychoanalytic theories such as the popular "transactional analysis" stress the inability of people to "role play" well as adults and a tendency to revert to the child's role when frustrated.

All analytic theories claim that the drives they discover are not known to the actor and can become known only by the help of a professional analyst. It has been argued by opponents of analytic theories that they are untesta-

ble, provide no basis for prediction, and are usually provable only in unusual
cases that have been extensively analyzed.

PSYCHOSES

There are numerous, often conflicting, definitions of mental disorders, and
there are no reliable methods of ascertaining the extent of such disorder in
either the general or the known criminal population. Different mental disorders may have different causes. There may even be a relationship between
social disorder and the frequency of certain psychoses, since some environments and social classes seem to produce (or correlate with) certain disorders. There may even be social "epidemiology," whereby mental disorders
may be transferred by people to others in close contact, but this phenomenon has not been verified.

Psychosis has been blamed for crime on the basis that psychosis is a mental disease wherein individuals lose a sense of reality (become delusional)
and often withdraw from social contacts. However, very few offenders (perhaps 5 percent of those admitted to prison) are psychotic. Many offenders
have alcoholic psychoses that are not permanently disabling. Medical diagnoses of psychoses often reflect the bias of the examiner. As with drug dependency (see p. 65), the psychosis may not necessarily be the cause of
criminal conduct. There is some evidence that a pattern of law-abiding conduct, followed by the onset of psychosis, results in a continuation of the lawful conduct.

THE PSYCHOPATHIC PERSONALITY

Those who are emotionally abnormal though not psychotic have been labeled "psychopaths" or "psychopathic personalities." Because of termino-
logical vagueness, this personality type is now called by the American Psychiatric Association the "antisocial" personality. This personality is
unsocialized, selfish, callous, irresponsible, impulsive; is unable to feel guilt
or learn from experience and punishment; blames others for his misfortunes;
rationalizes his crimes and deviance; and has low frustration tolerance. Psychopaths are hyperactive, cannot plan ahead or delay gratification, and fail
to identify with others.

In recent years, scientists have studied psychopathology by analysis of the
nervous system. Offenders thought to be psychopaths may send out emotional "distress signals" more slowly than other individuals when danger
threatens, and the galvanic skin responses of these offenders (measurement
of "nervousness" in lie-detector tests, for instance) do not increase as rapidly as those of "normal" people. Because of this slower "learning" ability,

some scientists have hypothesized that psychopaths cannot quickly learn to avoid punishment. However, this theory is highly controversial because there have been few studies on the extent of this characteristic in the general population. Fear responses may be slow to develop and to dissipate, so that the "normal" child's fear of committing a wrong (because of family disapproval) and reward for not committing the wrong (in the form of a reduction of the fear) are absent in the psychopath.

It is believed that some criminal psychopaths might be aided by injection of hormones (adrenalin) to speed up both arousal and relaxation rates, though the evidence indicates that only nonaggressive psychopaths seem to have benefited from this experimental treatment.

Brain-wave abnormality studies have shown that many criminals have high rates of EEG (electroencephalograph) abnormalities. But such abnormalities vary among different criminals; they are not present in all criminals; and their frequency in the population at large is not known. Some criminality may be due to psychopathic search for arousal, but it should be noted that psychopathic personalities in general tend to commit property crimes rather than personal ones involving passion.

There appear to be different types of psychopaths: (1) the *egocentric,* who will have abnormal brain-wave shape and commit violent crime; (2) the *inadequate personality,* who will have a slow brain wave pattern and commit property crime; and (3) the *vagabond,* or lone-wolf type, who may share the brain-wave pattern of the inadequate personality but commit no, or little, crime. Psychopaths may also be classified in accordance with their dominant psychological characteristic, such as paranoia, schizophrenia, sexual deviation, and alcoholic or drug addiction. While all psychopaths presumably share the major characteristics of social alienation mentioned earlier, the forms of demonstrating that alienation will differ.

Despite these descriptions, there remains substantial disagreement about the degree of conflict and anxiety manifested by psychopaths. Some have argued that body type and other hereditary factors are significant (even to the point of claiming that psychopathology runs in families). Other explanations include the theory that some psychopaths are merely unsocialized people, that guilt and anxiety are socially conditioned reactions. Thus, many apparent psychopaths only act like true psychopaths, because of various personality disorders, and they can be successfully treated. This approach might lead to treatment such as group therapy whereby hostility can be expressed, especially to psychoanalysts who are not threatening to the patients (used with some success in the Patuxent Institution for Adult Offenders in Maryland and in some British hospitals). Other scientists have claimed that heredity accounts for nervous-system deficiencies and that those deficiencies cannot be altered by treatment.

Laws attempting to define psychopathology, especially the "sexual psychopath" laws once popular in the United States, tend to be overly broad and eventually to be applied to many nonpsychopathic criminals.

PHYSIOLOGICAL IMBALANCE

For a time many thought that the presence of XYY chromosomal imbalance "caused" violent crime. Further studies have shown that (1) the imbalance is rare, both in the population at large and among criminals, and (2) known criminals with the deficiency commit property, rather than violent, crimes. Moreover, this explanation would not account for statistically high violence among blacks, who rarely manifest the abnormality.

Hormonal imbalance, in the form of female secretion of estrogen and male secretion of androgen (both believed to stimulate aggression), may play some role in female crime. Many women are uncomfortable during the four days preceding and the four days of menstruation, and half the assaults committed by women occur during this period. At this time, the woman produces low levels of progesterone (a hormone resembling male androgen). But few women commit assaults anyway, and some female assaults, of course, are committed outside the menstrual period. There are no data on the presence or absence of other hormones during crime, including crimes directly related to aggression and irritability.

FRUSTRATION-AGGRESSION THEORY

Some psychoanalysts have argued that persons subject to an unusual amount of frustration will become aggressive and hence delinquent or criminal. This position has been refuted by studies demonstrating that most human conduct is learned, that behavior is variable, and that language and history greatly modify conduct. Reactive behavior to frustration (which all of us experience) is learned. Often, aggression may create greater disquiet rather than discharging existing unease. Of course, if particularly aggressive behavior is rewarded, it will continue to occur; if not, then another outlet will be found.

In general, violence may be found in two personality types (although, of course, very few persons of these types will become aggressive): the "overcontrolled" and the "undercontrolled." It has been widely assumed that the "overcontrolled" person will "blow up" after lengthy efforts at self-control, but most overcontrolled people do not perform violent acts. If they do, it is because they have not learned to cope moderately with frustration; the result may well be suicide rather than aggression toward others. Also, many who are thought to be overcontrolled have a previous, though unknown, history of violence. Undercontrolled people more typically are violent toward others; indeed, they often provoke or manipulate situations to justify violence.

PERSONALITY STUDIES

One famous personality study concluded that juvenile delinquents fall into three categories: (1) the "overinhibited," who exhibit tendencies such as reclusiveness, shyness, apathy, submissiveness, extreme sensitivity, and a tendency to worry; (2) the "unsocialized aggressives," who commit assault, are cruel, and defy authority; and (3) the "socialized delinquents," who join gangs and engage in cooperative stealing, school truancy, and loss of contact with the home. Unfortunately, most delinquents do not fall into any clearly defined category. In general, psychologists have argued that there are (1) neurotic delinquents, who can be cured, (2) psychopathic delinquents, who are self-centered and cruel, and (3) gang-type delinquents, whose conduct often indicates a desire to conform. Again, the definitions of these types often differ, and many delinquents share other characteristics with nondelinquents that may be more important to the delinquents' lives than the differences. All "personality theory" studies are deficient, and no single test or trait seems to be more characteristic of delinquents than of nondelinquents.

Studies of identical twins have attempted to define relevant emotional variables. About forty years ago, a major study of twins (identical and fraternal) comparing 105 delinquents with 105 of their siblings seemed to confirm the "emotional disturbance" theory of criminality. But the investigator-psychologists may have been influenced by their own predispositions, may have interacted more frequently with the delinquents than with the control group, and may have erroneously concluded that the disturbance caused the delinquency rather than vice versa. Since some nondelinquents were also emotionally disturbed, the question of cause remains unanswered.

ALCOHOLISM

Is there an "alcoholic personality" that is prone to commit crime? There are millions of alcoholics in the United States. Alcoholism may be termed a crime or may be a constituent factor in crime (drunk driving, for instance). It appears that about 30 percent of all arrests in a given year may be for conduct caused or heavily influenced by alcohol consumption. In general, those who admit to heavy drinking also admit to more, and more serious, criminality than other persons, and many admitted criminals have acknowledged use—often heavy use—of alcohol. Thus the correlation between crime and alcohol seems strong. But correlation, of course, is not cause.

A brief history of alcohol consumption in the United States may shed light on the question of cause. During Colonial times, drinking of alcohol was taken for granted within family circles and during community events. These habits developed when wine and beer were popular, but manufacturers soon turned to hard liquor because it was easier to transport and did not spoil as readily as the other beverages. Drinking habits changed so that, by 1800, about 90 percent of all alcohol consumed was in the form of hard liquor. The place of drinking also changed from the family table to the saloon and tavern, attracting young, single men. Between 1750 and 1830, drunkenness became a major phenomenon of American life, and it often caused rowdy behavior. For various reasons, including both a general fear of disorder and apprehension of danger to property, many reformers joined the temperance movement. In part, temperance was an attempt to control the masses. Ironically, the early goal of the temperance movement—moderation in drinking—changed to a demand for abstinence just at the time when newer immigrants from southern, central, and eastern Europe were influencing national consumption patterns back to wine and beer. Laws were changed to make single incidents of drunkenness, rather than habitual intoxication, criminal. Thus, in the guise of "helping" the lower classes, middle-class reformers used the criminal law and an expanded police role to control the allegedly dangerous classes. Medical and, later, psychiatric opinion was enlisted to show that even moderate drinking caused physical and mental breakdown, as well as, of course, criminality.

Since alcohol consumption is a social event, the legal reaction to alcohol consumption differentially affected different cultures. For instance, Italians in Italy have high rates of alcohol consumption but have little alcoholism because drinking is not regarded as a sign of masculinity.

Prohibition and its aftermath led to the situation that until the 1970s, the greatest numbers of arrests in any given year were for public drunkenness. Today, because of either decriminalization or lessened law enforcement, only about 10 to 13 percent of all arrests fall into this category. Other crimes specifically related to alcohol are "driving under the influence" (the third crime in the United States in frequency of arrest) and disorderly conduct, often involving alcohol (the fourth crime in frequency). While arrests for public drunkenness have sharply declined, those for drunk driving have doubled in recent years. Although most arrests for these crimes involve older men, it appears that the greatest social problem involves younger ones (twenty-one- to twenty-five-year-olds), who, because of physiological factors, can normally exhibit more self-control over their actions than their older counterparts. It has been estimated that more than 40 percent of all prison inmates had been drinking at the time of their crime.

There are several types of alcoholic pathologies, each of which may result in criminality, though of differing sorts. Young men who drink to excess do so primarily to express feelings of manliness. Most of those who commit assaults while drunk are young men (although, on occasion, an older man seeking to demonstrate his virility may also commit assault). Young alcoholics tend to (1) drink in groups, at least at first and until a strong dependency emerges, (2) come from various social classes, (3) exhibit conflicts between the need for autonomy and a need for group support, and (4) use the social setting of drink to exhibit power and dominance needs.

Skid-row alcoholics tend to be older. Skid rows originally were employment centers for temporary laborers; their environment includes low-rent rooming houses, saloons, pawn shops, and missionary centers. The area attracts transients who go on binges, poor men with no attachments, "winos," and older welfare clients (who may not be alcoholics). Skid-row alcoholics commit many crimes against each other; they are also often the victims of juvenile delinquents.

Alcoholic forgers are another type of alcoholic criminal. They are older, better educated, and middle-class. They commit forgeries of small amounts by using checks and credit cards belonging to family and friends; the crime tends to be compulsive, and the recidivism rate is high. They have certain verbal skills (many have been salesmen) and use them to convince victims to drop charges or to talk strangers into cashing checks.

The existence of these typologies does not demonstrate that people, otherwise innocent, will commit crimes solely because of the influence of alcohol. Drinking and fighting are characteristic of certain, but not all, subcultures. Also, in certain groups, drunkenness may lead to violence because of social expectations; for instance, it appears that American Indians (who, in general, did not drink until they met European whites) adapted white behavior, especially "holidays" from traditional morality, to their own customs and learned that whites would excuse disorder on the grounds of drunkenness and would fear drunken Indians.

Alcoholism is not always a form of "vagabond" personality disorder or associated with certain personality traits. Indeed, the success rate of Alcoholics Anonymous indicates that there are no inherent personality defects that stimulate alcoholism. This organization was founded in 1935 on the principles of (1) group support of alcoholics to cure each other; (2) mutual admission that members are alcoholics; (3) confessions of misdeeds committed under the influence; and (4) continual availability to help each other. There are at least five hundred thousand members of AA, and they continually proselytize each other as well as outsiders. AA's undoubted success may be attributable to its ability to encourage dependent personalities to become protective ones. AA tends to attract middle-class alcoholics who have

verbal abilities and to "turn off" skid-row drunks because of what they consider its "preachiness." Although coercive methods of treating alcoholism
rarely succeed, one study found that many alcoholics treated in clinics (by
methods such as giving unpleasant drugs along with alcohol to "condition"
recipients to find both distasteful) are cured.

It appears that alcoholism in the United States has declined considerably
in the last century. Insofar as the problem of alcoholic crime exists as a
matter of legal definition, it has also lessened because of a successful decriminalization movement fostered by (1) the failure of law-enforcement officials to rehabilitate drunks, (2) unfair arrest procedures in cases of drunkenness, and (3) changing social attitudes.

NARCOTICS ADDICTION

If there is no proof that alcohol creates either crime-prone personalities or
crime itself, is the same true about narcotic drugs? Again, a brief history of
drug-control efforts is necessary not only to shed light on this problem but
also to demonstrate some truisms about the sociology of law.

Opium.   Since ancient times, opium has been cultivated in the Middle
East and India and has been widely used to kill pain. It has been eaten, then
smoked, and, more recently, chemically treated to create "opiates," which,
in turn, have become popular. Opium's first commercial form in the United
States was called laudanum (opium and alcohol) and was a popular pain-
killing home remedy sold in general stores at the end of the nineteenth century. Morphine, a derivative, was extensively used during the Civil War,
and many soldiers became addicted, often after self-administering the drug
to relieve the pain of wounds. Heroin, another derivative, developed in 1898,
was taken orally in small doses and was thought to be both more quick-
acting and less addictive than morphine.

Legal attack on opium and its derivatives commenced in 1909, when the
United States banned importation, perhaps because of prejudice against
Chinese immigrants who favored it. State and local efforts to ban opiate derivatives (often because their use offended the Puritan work ethic) foundered since it was simple to purchase the products elsewhere. The United
States then signed a series of treaties to limit importation and, pursuant to
one treaty, enacted the Harrison Act in 1914. This law both taxed opiate
sales and required records to be kept of such sales; commercial sales of
home remedies containing small amounts of opiates were exempted because
of manufacturers' lobbying. Prior to the Harrison Act, the average opiate
user had been a white, middle-class woman between thirty-five and fifty
years of age. Many of these women then switched from opiates to sedatives,
especially barbiturates. After the Harrison Act, opium use shifted to lower-

class ghetto residents (primarily blacks, Puerto Ricans, and Mexicans).

Early enforcement of the laws was sporadic, but in 1920, the Prohibition Bureau of the Treasury Department, under the leadership of Harry J. Anslinger and influenced by the Prohibition movement, began vigorous enforcement. In 1929, Anslinger became Assistant Commissioner of Prohibition and, in 1930, head of the Bureau of Narcotics in the Treasury Department. Although the Harrison Act permitted medical use of opiates and was interpreted by the U.S. Supreme Court not to apply to physicians' prescriptions, enforcement threats against doctors led to increasing caution about prescribing opiates to maintain addiction. In 1924, a federal law banned importation of heroin. Anslinger thereafter carried on a vigorous campaign against opiates and demanded that addicts be treated as dangerous criminals. He was the most powerful government official in the field between 1930 and his retirement in 1962, and he chose his successor, Henry L. Giordano, who continued his punitive policies.

While there was a certain amount of lower-class opiate addiction in the 1930s, some middle-aged women living in the South and doctors and other medical personnel with access to drugs were also addicted. But despite Anslinger's crusade, upper-class and medical addicts were rarely prosecuted. Drugs were regularly smuggled into American port cities; often European firms sold their legal surpluses to the smugglers. During World War II, when the armed forces requisitioned available supplies of opiates, domestic growing of the opium poppy began; it was promptly banned. After the war, there was an increase in opium smuggling, much of it directed by organized crime. New addicts tended to be male, young, and members of minority groups in cities; many new addicts had committed crime prior to opiate use. In order to pay for expensively smuggled heroin, these young people committed crimes—usually property crimes rather than violent crimes. They also sold drugs to raise money, and those sales began patterns of contagion (as friends were "turned on"). "Hustling" to raise money requires both energy and resourcefulness, values prized by many delinquents.

The Nature of Addiction. Addiction to opium and its derivatives means (1) tolerance for increasing amounts to achieve the same high and (2) withdrawal symptoms when drugs are removed. Some scientists have claimed that true addiction does not exist, but that users of drugs partake in a strong social ritual that gives meaning to their lives. People, it has been shown, can become "conditioned" to addiction when (1) drugs relieve pain and when (2) pleasure, under the social circumstances, increases. Whether or not physiological addiction occurs, psychological habituation does develop when drug takers (1) find the ritual of injection habit-forming, (2) attain some standing in the drug culture, and (3) become convinced that they need drugs. This is true even of many street users who obtain only very diluted heroin and who can, when persuaded, readily go off drugs without painful withdrawal symptoms. Many "weekenders" use drugs without losing jobs or showing withdrawal symptoms, and, indeed, few of these users become addicts. Very few members of the armed forces who became addicted during the Vietnam War used drugs after their return to the United States. Insofar as drug users commit crimes to feed their habits, they do so, of course, in part from necessity and perhaps, in part, because they have adopted prevalent cultural myths about themselves; "marginal" addicts tend to hold jobs *and* not commit crime. Since there is no sharp dividing line between "marginal" and "committed," it may be that, for the latter, crime is a self-fulfilling prophecy encouraged by both their own and the larger culture. Of course, popular assumptions about addicts and crime also compel addicts (at least lower-class ones) to participate in a criminal culture and to learn the values of that culture. Countries that do not treat their drug users as criminals report no particular criminal pattern among drug users.

Addiction and Present Law.   Criminal jurisdiction over drug offenses (and other crimes) may be exercised by either the states or the federal government or both. The states, which have general authority to protect the lives, property, and welfare of their residents, have the broadest legislative latitude. The federal government has no such general jurisdiction, but may pass laws pursuant to its constitutional powers to tax, to regulate interstate and foreign commerce, and to make treaties. In the realm of drugs, such constitutional powers are broad, and it is not unusual for the federal government to penalize exactly the same conduct (possession and sale of certain drugs) as that subject to state law.

After World War II, penalties for drug crimes increased, largely because of the activity of the Bureau of Narcotics. The Harrison Act of 1914 had prescribed a maximum of ten years for violations, but the Boggs Act of 1951 created a penalty structure that ranged from two to five years for a first offense of drug sale, five to ten years for a second offense, and ten to twenty years for a third offense (plus a large fine for any sale). Probation was permitted only for a first offense. In 1956, the Narcotics Control Act further revised penalties upward to ten years for a first offense, twenty for a second, and forty for a third; any sale to a minor was punished as if it were a third offense. Probation and parole were absolutely prohibited. The same penalties applied to sales of cocaine and marijuana. The Bureau of Narcotics lobbied the states to adopt a uniform law (resembling the federal statute), and most did. In 1970, Congress passed (1) the Comprehensive Drug Abuse Prevention and Control Act and (2) the Controlled Substances Act, which gave the Food and Drug Administration (FDA) the power to define dangerous drugs and drugs subject to abuse, and to restrict shipment of such drugs in interstate commerce. A uniform state law on the subject of drug classification was recommended and forty states adopted it. The maximum penalties were lowered, although they were still severe for sales of certain types of drugs, including the opiates. In addition, the Bureau of Narcotics and Dangerous Drugs (in the Justice Department) replaced the Bureau of Narcotics in the Treasury Department, and the Drug Enforcement Administration (with international and some domestic jurisdiction) was created.

Treatment of Addiction. In recent times, partly because of the rapid changes in the criminal laws described in the preceding section and a growing dissatisfaction with the use of criminal law, treatment alternatives have increased. This policy resembles an earlier one: Between 1917 and 1925 addicts were often maintained on morphine in clinics. After the clinics were closed, psychological treatment of addicts to "cure" both the addiction and the underlying neuroses and anxieties was provided. The United States Public Health Service opened treatment facilities in the 1930s at Lexington, Kentucky, and Fort Worth, Texas, for this purpose. These hospital detoxification programs became the prototypes for many other public and private programs designed to reduce opiate dependence. The success rate, once praised by Harry Anslinger, was in truth less than 10 percent. Many of these facilities changed in the 1960s and 1970s to other forms of treatment.

Civil commitment of addicts involves a determination that they are, in essence, mentally ill. While mere possession of narcotics can be made a crime, addiction per se cannot (according to the U.S. Supreme Court). Civil commitment often follows a charge of crime, and a judge, under certain circumstances, may impose such a commitment in lieu of punishment. Although, in theory, at some point, trial and sentence for the crime itself can occur, in practice this is rare once civil commitment has been mandated. Most civil-commitment programs are carried out within state correctional institutions, usually in prison wings. Many civil-commitment laws permit "voluntary" proceedings instituted by noncriminally accused addicts. Despite vast amounts of money spent on such programs, and often adequate staffing of facilities, they have had high failure rates, even for voluntary entrants.

New York State's program used a variety of private, city, and county agencies for care and aftercare of addicts. Approximately twenty thousand addicts passed through with little success. In 1973, the "Rockefeller drug laws" were enacted; they established the harshest sentences in the nation for drug possession and also for sale of opiates (fifteen years to life for possession of two ounces or sale of one ounce) and severe limitations on plea bargaining. This law was meant to supplement, not to replace, civil commitment. Although more narcotics cases went to trial as a result, the law was of little benefit and was substantially revamped in 1979 to lessen the penalties.

California had greater success with civil commitment, at least for those completing the full seven-year program. Perhaps as many as half of those admitted succeeded (though the definition of success changed, so that even return to use of opiates was not a ground for recommitment if the person was employed). Also, the availability of methadone maintenance helped to increase success rates.

Synanon and Similar Programs. Synanon, founded in Los Angeles in 1958, resembles Alcoholics Anonymous, but has the following distinctive features: (1) Members must reside on the organization's premises; (2) initially, members must perform degrading work to test their commitment; (3) group discussions mix harsh criticism of addict rationalizations with group support for newer members trying to "kick"; (4) absolute prohibition of drugs, including alcohol; (5) graded steps of job improvement, subject to demotion and even expulsion for backsliding. The success rate is difficult to assess, since Synanon excludes from its figures those who leave the program. However, studies indicate that such groups retain only 30 percent of their members for one year, and approximately 80 percent of those admitted relapsed into drug use within five years (the same rate as for those in other drug-detoxification centers). In 1978, Synanon came under heavy criticism as a cult after its leadership allegedly sought to kill an ex-member.

Methadone Maintenance. Methadone is a synthetic opiate first used in the United States at the Lexington, Kentucky, detoxification center. It was popularized by Rockefeller University physicians Vincent P. Dole and Marie E. Nyswander, who claimed great initial success at weaning addicts away from heroin. The methadone user at some point reaches a tolerance toward a peak dosage and neither wants nor needs more methadone or heroin. Methadone can be taken orally and its effects last for twenty-four hours. Since it metabolizes slowly, an addict can work successfully. It is also cheap (about twenty-five cents per day), and it has few harmful effects. As many as one hundred thousand (a quarter to a third of the nation's addict population) have gone through the program, and success rates at first were about 80 percent (perhaps owing to the high motivation of the first group). They fell somewhat as the program was extended to "average" addicts. Falling success rates can be attributed to (1) broadening of admission standards (some entrants come only for temporary relief and are still committed to heroin); (2) reduction of ancillary counseling services (to counter the addict lifestyle) when programs became overcrowded; and (3) expulsion of many who did not wish to lessen their dependence upon methadone, in part because of federal regulations that envisioned termination of dependency. Although retention rates (the percentage of those who remain in the program for its prescribed period) in methadone programs compared favorably with those in therapeutic community programs (fourteen months vs. six and one-half months) and outpatient detoxification centers (fourteen months vs. two months), those leaving the program had the same rate of arrest, unemployment, and return to opiates as did former therapeutic-community-program members. Also, many methadone users sell the drug to buy heroin or use methadone to supplement heroin.

Maintenance on Opiates.   In England and western European countries, addicts are maintained on heroin, a practice that ended in the United States around 1925. Before 1968, any English doctor could prescribe heroin for addicts, but after the number of known addicts rose from 437 in 1960 to 1,729 in 1967 (because doctors, by prescribing more than was needed, created a black market), England required that heroin be dispensed only at designated clinics. Many of these clinics persuaded addicts to switch to methadone (about 95 percent did). The clinics also successfully assisted patients in employment, housing, and counseling needs. The official number of addicts in England then stabilized at about 3,000, or 1 percent of the number in the United States (England has 25 percent of the population of the United States). Even if there are twice or four times "real" addicts, as some claim, except for smuggling opiates these addicts rarely commit crime. Although it has been argued that English addicts differ from Americans—English addicts are likely to be "secret" (at home) users and their lifestyles differ—there is reason to believe that the English system, suitably modified to account for the greater variety of addicts and treatment programs, could be successful in America.

Relation of Drug Use to Criminality.   The belief that drug use creates criminality because it weakens personality controls is less likely to be true than the belief that criminals become drug users because of previously deranged personalities. Drug users are often passive and dependent people, and petty criminality, followed by drug use, followed by more frequent (and increasingly serious) criminality are major characteristics of lower-class addiction. Of course, many dependent persons do not become addicts, and many addicts have virtually no criminal record prior to or during addiction. It may be that many addicts "kick the habit" as a result of prison and parole, in part because they have less contact with other addicts and the drug subculture. The lower-class addict whose career commences in his juvenile years does find life stressful and difficult; ties to parents are often absent and, after a time, his only peer-group association is with other addicts. Although slum conditions contribute to addict lifestyles, the critical variable appears to be a disordered and inadequate family life, which either causes (or brings to the surface) certain personality traits such as narcissism, ego and superego pathologies, and sexual-identity difficulties. The addict subculture provides addicts with support and information and an identity (as an addict, not a criminal), but these generalizations are simply too broad to account for the differences between addict and nonaddict personalities.

CONTAINMENT THEORY

Containment theory seeks to account for delinquency that is neither clearly psychologically caused nor the result of a cultural or subcultural explanation; it also seeks to account for the presence of nondeliquents in delinquency areas. It is a theory of personality that argues that all people have two control systems that inhibit tendencies toward criminality: (1) the outer control system of the environment and (2) an inner control system of conscience, a strong self-concept (self-esteem), and a high ability to tolerate frustration. Failure to form, or a breakdown of, strong self-concept leads to crime. Questionnaires and interviews have attempted to define, measure, and test "self-concept" in individuals and groups. One study demonstrated that those teen-agers (1) thought to be potential delinquents by teachers and (2) who had unfavorable self-concepts had more police contacts than a control group chosen by teachers as law-abiding. This theory attempts to account for delinquency not caused by unusual family situations. However, the term "self-concept" is vague and difficult to measure. Since not all delinquents have a poor self-concept and since there is no necessary connection between even a poor self-concept and a behavioral outlet into crime, the theory contains some fundamental flaws. It also has little predictive value, since it does not state when, how, or why any control (and which control) will break down under what particular circumstances to create what kind of criminal conduct.

7. Theories of Family Influence

Much early sociological work concentrated on the family as a criminogenic factor. The family has traditionally been the primary agency for shaping early behavior. In earlier times, it is thought, the values of society were unambiguously reflected in family values. Increasingly, it is argued, there is a conflict among those who socialize children; that conflict may be within the family or between the family and other social institutions. The culture itself may have become ambiguous and therefore offer little guidance to parents. In addition, the culture may have reduced the prestige of parents in the eyes of children.

Certainly, delinquency has often been accompanied by one or more of the following family factors: (1) alcoholism or criminality among family members, (2) absence of one or more parents, (3) diminution of family control because of either parental physical illness or psychological indifference or hostility, (4) unhappiness in the home, (5) intrafamily religious and cultural conflicts, and (6) poverty and associated economic conditions. Some have argued that (1) weak bonds between parents and children and (2) the child's belief that the parents are fundamentally dishonest strongly correlate with delinquency. Children who believe that home discipline is unfair, partial, excessive, or permissive also may become delinquent. This theory may be too general, but it does emphasize that parent-child conflict has something to do with delinquency—whether it causes delinquency or results from delinquency is still an open question.

Early use of scales and ratings of stability in the home reflected the prejudices of the investigator more often than the actual role of the home in contributing to delinquency. This method of analysis also failed to predict who would become delinquent. Evaluations of the effect upon individuals of the aforementioned conditions also tended to reflect (1) investigators' prejudices and (2) prevalent "moral" notions of the times. Thus, when strict child-rearing practices were socially approved, any laxity in discipline was interpreted as contributing to delinquency; when permissiveness was in social vogue, the opposite was true. The most popular scientific method has been the statistical, the measurement of which home variables occur most often in the lives of delinquents (again, this is not proof of cause).

STATISTICAL CORRELATIONS

Criminality in the home statistically correlates with delinquency; sons of criminals have higher delinquency rates than do sons of noncriminals. Significantly, sons rejected by criminal fathers are highly likely to be delinquent (perhaps because the father serves two contradictory functions, as criminal role-model and as the object of aggression). While the sons in these circumstances may not specifically be influenced toward imitation of conduct, they may well be influenced toward imitation of attitudes toward crime. Believers in the "subculture of violence" theory argue that it is manifested in the home as well as the community at large. One study confusingly concluded that *increasing* contact with increasing criminality correlated with increased delinquency but that *initially high* contact with high criminality had the opposite effect.

THE BROKEN HOME

At least 40 percent of known delinquents came from broken homes, but this statistic may, in part, be due to juvenile-court practices that single out children from these homes for either treatment or confinement. The factor may be more significant for females and blacks. It has been surmised that broken homes also lead to more serious forms of delinquency, but general poverty may be more important than the status of the home.

HOME DISCIPLINE AND TRAINING

Parental discipline is probably more important than the status of the home. As noted, punitive discipline seems to be correlated with both lower-class family life and delinquency. Children of working mothers may be undisciplined. Parental neglect may be combined with a lack of respect for parents; this is probably truer of lower-class than of middle-class homes. Parents who charge their children in court with being unmanageable are likely to lose (or have lost) their influence. Children charged as "incorrigible" may be labeled as "delinquents" or even "criminals" (although, in theory, juvenile court is not a criminal court) and will then adopt expected behavior patterns. Since immigrant children in cities more readily adapt to neighborhood behavior patterns than do their parents, contempt for parents may result.

DELINQUENCY PATTERNS WITHIN THE FAMILY

Since each child may experience both the home and the outside world differently, the presence of a delinquent sibling does not necessarily predict delinquency. Birth-order studies that found an abnormal amount of delinquency in first-born children have been discredited. There may, however, be a correlation between delinquency and intermediate position in the family, since parents may lavish affection on oldest and youngest children. Only children are not necessarily more delinquent than children with siblings.

THE DELINQUENCY PROCESS

A child may learn delinquency in the home in various ways: He may (1) absorb and imitate criminal conduct; (2) learn to respect certain persons, and that pattern of respect may be transferred either then or in later life to criminals (or, of course, to noncriminals); or (3) be alienated from the home by his experiences and readily associate with delinquents. He may prematurely "grow up," and interact more with delinquent peers and less with the family. Thus, for many reasons, delinquent associations will overcome family norms (if any). The psychological explanation that disobedience in the home will lead to general disobedience is probably not valid, for such explanations, which stress home tensions and individual emotional disturbance, cannot demonstrate that these factors prevail in the homes of delinquents or are absent in the homes of nondelinquents. These explanations also fail to demonstrate the process by which unhappiness becomes translated into delinquency.

MARITAL STATUS

Married people have the lowest crime rate, widowed the next lowest, single the next, and divorced people the highest. The differences among these groups are somewhat less in the twenty to twenty-four-year age bracket, but, at later ages, fewer married men become criminals. The results are more mixed for females; married women have a slightly higher rate of commitment to prison at all ages, except between twenty-five and thirty-four. These statistics parallel those for other countries (except Greece, where most crimes are committed by married men). It appears that marital status tends to reinforce commitment to noncriminal conduct; indeed, for many (probably most) juvenile delinquents, marriage is the critical event that changes them.

8. Theories of Intimate Associational Patterns

This chapter will discuss sociological theories of criminality that assume that criminal conduct is learned in intimate, though not necessarily family, settings. None of the theories says anything about the larger society. Rather they involve experiences close to the individual criminal or delinquent and are variations of "learning" theory. Sociologists believe that the present moment can be interpreted by the individual only in accordance with what he has learned, either in general or specifically. The meaning of "facts" lies not so much in their existence but in the "definition" given them by the individual.

DIFFERENTIAL ASSOCIATION

Differential association is a major, though controversial theory, propounded originally by American sociologist Edwin H. Sutherland. In general, the theory is descriptive and argues that conduct is based upon the receipt and acceptance by individuals of information and values. The theory specifically contends that (1) criminal conduct is learned behavior; (2) the learning occurs by communication from others, usually in close, intimate groups; (3) the learning communicated is not only about specific means of committing crimes but also about general attitudes toward crime and means of transforming "personality" and psychological drives, motives, and attitudes into behavior; (4) specifically, an individual who learns more information that is favorable to criminality than information that is not, will become a criminal (if a particular culture emphasizes criminal conduct, it will produce more criminals); (5) since all individuals learn at least some codes of lawful conduct, in order to predominate, the information favoring criminal behavior must be communicated more frequently than noncriminal information, must be of longer duration, must be given in a more intense form, and even perhaps have been given at an earlier age than competing information; and (6) learning can occur in many ways.

This theory does not attribute crime to personal characteristics, many of which, as we have seen, may be present in noncriminals as well as criminals. The theory does not explain anything about the source of the information. The theory holds that whatever the source, when the learning factors are present and are influential, crime will be approved in general, and criminal behavior will follow. The theory does not argue that criminals "associate" with criminals (or even noncriminals who approve criminal behavior patterns); rather, it holds that criminal associations (learning associations, not necessarily ones involving immediate criminal conduct) occur more frequently than noncriminal ones. Since different people will have different experiences with criminal and noncriminal attitudes, their "association" with those attitudes will be different; hence the term "differential association."

Arguments for and against the Theory. The differential-association theory has been criticized on several grounds. Among the major criticisms are (1) the theory does not account for certain types of crime that have nothing to do with "learned behavior" (such as rural criminality, naïve check forgery, white-collar crime, and even some delinquency); (2) the theory does not take into account personality and psychological traits; (3) the theory does not inform us about the "receptivity" of individuals exposed to the information; (4) many key terms are vague (for instance: What are "definitions favorable to law" or to "law violation"? What does "intensity" of contact mean? How can one measure "excess"?); and (5) the theory oversimplifies the process of learning and, in essence, negates free will.

Defenders of the theory argue that (1) "learning" may well be applicable to the kinds of crimes mentioned, but researchers simply have not studied the possibility; (2) personality and psychological traits do not themselves determine behavior, but may influence how and whether the information communicated is received and accepted (this is a "learning" question not relevant to the theory); (3) "receptivity" is not important, for the person has previously "learned" to be receptive; (4) definitions of key words may not be important if the theory is generally correct as an explanation of crime (even if nothing is proved about individual criminality, presumably better research methods will enable the theory to be applied to this problem); and (5) sociology cannot accept the notion of free will per se. Also, since nothing we know contradicts the theory, it should at least serve as a general explanation.

Although the theory does not answer at least one essential question— How did the first criminal start?—it focuses attention on certain fundamental issues. Conflict within society is the basis for different cultures and different cultural experiences related to crime. Generalizations such as poverty, broken homes, and other single explanations of crime are too broad. The meaning of various experiences to the particular person, based upon his intimate associations, is important. The focus on the "meaning" of experience, however, does overlook some criminality; people suddenly exposed to unemployment, for instance, may commit crimes without either any previous criminal background or association with criminal attitudes.

Elaborations of the Theory.   Some sociologists who agree with the thrust though not the specific formulation of the differential-association theory have added refinements. One is the "value added" notion, which argues that "background" factors "prime" criminal conduct and that situational factors then "trigger" it. This theory would investigate the steps or stages that precede an outcome and distinguish between those stages that make the outcome likely (though not inevitable) and those that are critical to the outcome. This is difficult to ascertain: When does a process go from likely to necessary? Does that "process" apply to anyone but the particular person studied?

Another variant of differential-association theory adds to the equation the factor that criminality is determined by one's anticipation (expectation) of the consequences of future acts. While social ties and differential learning will shape expectations, it is the expectations themselves that determine the individual's conduct. Expectations are defined as perception of the risks and rewards of future criminal conduct. This elaboration is called *differential anticipation.*

LABELING THEORY (SYMBOLIC INTERACTIONISM)

Labeling theory, another variant of learning theory, argues that criminality, at least after the first crime, and perhaps at times prior to it, is the result of the individual's experiences with criminal-justice and other social agencies that "define" his conduct. Criminality is, in this view, created by society, which labels the individual as a criminal; the individual then accepts the label and begins to shape his future conduct in accordance with society's perception of him. Thus it is the interaction between the individual and society ("symbolic" because of the affixing of the label) that creates criminals and crime.

The Process of Labeling.   The process occurs when an individual is labeled an offender. Official reaction is supplemented by unofficial responses from neighbors, employers, and others. Originally, the theory distinguished between psychologically caused individual deviance, and systematic deviance, caused by persistent, organized, and collective forms of behavior. Deviant subcultures arose, it was argued, because of the existence of pluralistic values in a society. Individual deviance may become systemic if (1) despised conduct is caused by internal psychological processes and (2) disapproval is so prevalent that it forces the deviant to seek out others like himself. Deviant subcultures, it must be noted, have the same values—apart from the deviant ones—as the main culture.

Labeling theory emphasizes the process that changes people and thus does not rely on a simple stimulus-response learning model. The theory regards much initial deviance as "risk-taking," a temptation to which many succumb. Only if this initial behavior is (1) socially noticed and (2) socially acted upon, in the form of labeling, does the deviant himself begin to change his self-image. Thus "primary deviance" involves the commission of a deviant act but not a perception by the offender that he is a deviant. "Secondary deviance" occurs when the person accepts and defines himself in terms of his deviant characteristics and conduct. It may occur when (1) the act is repeated or (2) society reacts to the primary deviance, or both. It may become engrained when there is a cycle of deviant acts and increasingly harsh social reaction to them. Society not only punishes deviance but also puts distance between itself and the deviant (virtually making him an outcast), and thus reinforces the deviance.

Mitigation of Labeling. Labeling theory does not take into account cases where (1) deviance is met not with hostility but with concern by family, friends, and relatives and where (2) especially in the case of many first offenders, the shock of confrontation with the criminal-justice system often results in immediate cessation of crime. Labeling may not be as serious as many criminologists believe when those labeled (1) are not committed to crime, (2) are not publicly labeled, (3) are labeled by persons they hold in high regard, (4) may readily lose the label when they do not repeat their conduct, or (5) are helped to become reintegrated into the community.

OTHER INTERACTIONIST PERSPECTIVES

Interactionism may occur under the following circumstances: (1) Law enforcers who rigidly believe in upholding rules interact with offenders who are compulsively rebellious; the tendency is for rigidity and cruelty to predominate and for opposing attitudes to escalate until polarization occurs. (2) People who are submissive law supporters (bureaucrats) interact with offenders who are passive; the tendency is for both to withdraw from conflict because the offender will become evasive rather than or more hostile. (3) People who are passive (law enforcers or the law-abiding) interact with a highly antagonistic or rebellious opposite; the active person becomes more antagonized, and his attitudes (but only *his* attitudes) become polarized. The greatest social danger occurs in the first situation, since polarization is greatest. Polarization may be avoided by (1) refusal to treat the offender as an outcast, (2) tolerance of minor offenses, (3) helping the offender help himself into greater conformity, (4) showing patience with the offender's hostility, and (5) granting rewards to offenders who conform. Unfortunately, few offenders and few law enforcers act in these constructive ways. However, where criminality occurs after a period of interaction rather than merely after a specific event, this analysis may be valuable. It is also in accordance with psychotherapeutic analysis and has been used by those who attempt to cure crime by modifying behavior.

LEARNING BY REINFORCEMENT

Differential association is, in part, a learning theory. Labeling and interactionist theories are also attempts to interpret learning and its consequences. A general learning theory has been constructed by natural scientists and psychologists from laboratory experiments. The most famous experiments were those performed about 1900 by Russian physiologist Ivan Pavlov, who stimulated animal responses by substituting artifical mechanisms for natural ones—ringing a bell instead of sight or smell of food to induce an animal to find food. The bell became a substituted stimulus, which reinforced the satisfaction of the animal because it was associated with pleasure, the finding of food. Other scientists then found that any "secondary" reinforcer (a buzzer instead of a bell, for instance) would continue to reinforce the animal's behavior. This simple type of conditioning is called respondent conditioning. American psychologist B. F. Skinner later devised a theory of operant conditioning that took a given response, then controlled the consequences of the behavior caused by the response in order to elicit new responses. A particular response was "reinforced" by pleasant consequences, so the response recurred. If not reinforced, the response did not recur. Once a particular stimulus elicited a particular response, a similar stimulus can elicit the same response. As responses become more regularized (learned), they will recur earlier in anticipation of the stimulus. Applied to criminological theory, learning notions show that reinforcement of past criminal behavior will stimulate such behavior in the future.

9. Cultural-Structural Explanations of Crime and Delinquency

The theories discussed in the previous chapter might be called "near theories"; they attempt to explain the process by which particular individuals become criminals. The theories presented in this chapter might be called "distant theories"; they attempt to find in the culture general explanations of criminality. They do not try to explain or even describe any process. They study the social structure of and historical developments in American society in order to identify its criminogenic elements. Many of these theories derive from the cartographic school, which, it should be remembered, aimed to describe crime correlates rather than to discover causes.

CRIME AND DEMOGRAPHIC FACTORS

The most obvious influence of the cartographic school comes from its study of geographic dimensions of crime; again, this is descriptive. In some countries, including the United States, more crime is committed in and around central cities than elsewhere. Crime patterns are regional, so that people migrating from low to high crime areas tend to take on the characteristics of the new area. In the United States, crime patterns vary significantly by region. New England tends to have the lowest rates for homicide, rape, and serious assault; the Southeastern states the lowest for burglary, larceny, and auto theft; the highest rates for rape, burglary, and larceny tend to occur in Pacific Coast states; in the East murder and serious assault occur most frequently in those states south of Pennsylvania; New York, New Jersey, and Pennsylvania have the highest robbery rates. The New England states, though, having low rates for many crimes, have the highest incidence of auto theft. Crimes against the person are highly correlated with region, but crimes against property are not. Certain types of towns tend to have higher crime rates than others, at least for certain periods; in the United States the best examples are frontier, river, and resort towns. Regions have tended to maintain their crime rates through time, but no particular accompanying demographic characteristics (age, race, sex) can be shown. Thus, while murder predominates in the South, any racial explanation is misleading; the white murder rate is five times greater in the South than in New England, while the black homicide rate in New England is lower than the white rate. These persistent characteristics of regions can be best explained by patterns of community organization and other traditions.

Urban-Rural Patterns.   Traditionally, crime has been an urban phenomenon. But the crime rates for the largest cities, at least for certain crimes, are not as high as those for middle-sized cities (self-report studies confirm this). Although it may be true that much rural crime is unreported, the same is true for much urban crime, so that recorded figures probably parallel the "dark figures." It also appears that the variation in crime rate decreases in proportion to the distance between urban and rural areas. The difficult variable (at least for property crime) is the difference between the amounts of property available to be criminalized in either urban or rural areas. In the United States, rural murder rates are slightly higher than urban ones, but crime rates for other offenses are lower in rural areas. As might be expected, there are also regional variations; in some regions rural crime rates resemble urban ones. Also, as communications between urban and rural areas have grown closer over time, so have the rural-urban crime rates. Such factors as rapid social and geographical change, value conflicts, and the substitution of formal for informal social controls in cities account for the remaining differences.

Historic and Current Trends.   Another method of studying crime is to analyze historic changes and current trends in patterns of particular crimes. Despite the known inadequacies of crime statistics, homicide trends can be measured because the U.S. Office of Vital Statistics has published records on all causes of death for a much longer period than have the Uniform Crime Reports. Between 1900 and 1930, the number of homicides in the United States per 100,000 population steadily increased from a low of 1.3 to 8.8. After 1930, the rate steadily decreased from 8.3 in 1935 to 4.7 in 1960. In the 1960s, the rate rose rapidly so that, by 1975 it was 10.2, the highest figure in the twentieth century. Although, as previously mentioned, homicide rates vary by region, regional differences have narrowed. Sex is another important variable; although females murder much more than they used to, the male murder rate increase still exceeds the female. Since police clearance rates for murder are still quite high (though they declined from 90 percent in the early 1960s to 78 percent in 1975), generalizations about the identity of known to unknown murderers are probably accurate. Race is, or course, a critical variable; blacks constituted 62.2 percent of all those arrested for homicide in 1971 (the figure has declined slightly since then), and they commit homicides far out of their proportion to the general population (four to six times as many). Mexican Americans in California had a homicide rate twice as great as that of whites, but only one fifth that of blacks. However, most homicides continue to be intraracial.

Most murders now occur in large cities (rural areas predominated before the 1960s). Age became an important variable as the median age of killers declined from 30 (before 1965) to 25.4 (1965 to 1975). The peak age for most persons arrested for murder declined from 25 to 29 before 1965 to 18 to 24 in 1980. The 1970s saw a leveling off of the rapid growth of urban homicide by young males so characteristic of the 1960s. While murders of kin declined from 31 percent of homicides in 1965 to 22 percent in 1975, in 45 percent of the 1975 killings the victim and the offender probably knew each other. Felony murders (usually stranger-to-stranger ones) rose from about 21 percent of all murders in 1965 to 32 percent a decade later. Thus it remains true that personal relationships are the settings for most killing. Studies have confirmed that as many as 40 percent of all murders are, in part, victim-precipitated.

Specialized Geographic Studies. The most intensive study of urban crime was conducted in the Chicago Area Project during the early 1930s. It dealt with juvenile delinquency, and it concluded that juvenile delinquency is prevalent in the low-rent areas in the center of the city and in industrial and commercial areas, but decreased with geographic distance from these areas. Truancy was also highly correlated with delinquency. Delinquency rates tended to remain stable no matter what ethnic or racial group inhabited any particular area. The delinquency rates for all groups within the area resembled that of the area generally. Delinquency areas also produced more recidivism. Although poor people may be generally overrepresented both in proportion of population in these areas and in official statistics, place of residence was a more significant factor than was poverty. The study also found that delinquents tended to commit crimes in their neighborhoods against members of the same social class and race.

General observations about the urban-crime relationship have stimulated much theorizing. The theories range from broad generalizations about historical trends in society to analysis of American culture and its impact upon urban life. The attempts to "explain" geographic data are controversial, often flawed, and ultimately unprovable. However, as with most theory in criminology, they simultaneously call attention to significant factors and dispel popular myths.

THE ADOLESCENT ROLE IN MODERN SOCIETY

In primitive societies, youngsters had definite, unambiguous, and well-understood roles. Today, society regards the adolescent as part boy or girl and part man or women. Also, modern adolescence is prolonged and filled with "identity crises," while, in primitive society, youngsters passed into "manhood" at a prescribed time and by rituals that clearly differentiated them from children. Modern "rites of passage" such as religious confirmation have less meaning than did primitive ones.

The process of differentiation means that children are segregated from adults by age. Formerly, children and adults worked together both in and out of the home, and youngsters frequently left school at an early age to become unskilled laborers or apprentices to craftsmen. Now, schooling is much longer. Whereas in 1940 only about one half of American adults had finished elementary school, by 1970 a majority had graduated from high school. Other social processes have virtually eliminated the family business, increased parental employment (often of both parents) outside the home, and increased time spent in school and at organized recreational activities with other juveniles. Thus adult ties (and controls) have weakened. Today there is no rapid entry into occupations; adolescents remain financially dependent upon their parents and become segregated in their own social world. Many fail to see that school has much meaning for their futures. They develop their own lifestyles, in part because of this separation. Thus crime may be fostered not so much by peer-group contact or by imitation of neighborhood criminals as by the adolescent's simple rejection of all groups in the community that traditionally uphold law-abiding values.

SOCIAL DISORGANIZATION

Modern society, in contrast to at least some primitive ones, is characterized by cultural conflicts. Neither parents nor other social institutions that mold the child have consistent roles. People in industrialized urban society play many roles (parent, worker, social-organization member), and these roles may have differing norms of right and wrong, giving rise to inconsistency and conflict. A society marked by such conflicts is, to some extent, "disorganized." Its individual members will either learn several norms or become confused and withdraw into *anomie* (a sociological term for lack or loss of norms). Current conflicting norms about crime mean that, especially in the area of delinquency, the individual will move between criminality and legality.

Historical and Cultural Developments.   Social disorganization has been caused by certain historical developments since the Middle Ages. Feudal patterns of static land ownership and mutual loyalty between classes and statuses gave way to, first, free trade and, later, capitalism. Accompanying these developments were new norms of individualism and competition and a basic belief that individual acquisitiveness (even greed) would result in more efficient production and distribution of goods and services, hence of wealth, and ultimately of social happiness. These revolutionary economic developments were accompanied by a political revolution that stressed individual dignity and rights and shunned government interference in economic, social, and personal life. The promise of greater wealth and satisfaction for all by limitation of government (and of law, which is "produced" by government) became widely accepted in the belief that all would ultimately benefit.

One result was, of course, a great stimulation of economic activity. Other results were (1) the attachment of a moral value to wealth; (2) an ideology that stressed that there were no natural limitations upon desire and ambition; (3) an inability to satisfy the appetites so stimulated; and (4) a situation that in practice meant that those who became wealthy at the beginning of the capitalist period sought to limit the opportunities of others in the race to acquire wealth. The newly wealthy often acquired a natural monopoly of production or distribution and used existing law or sought government aid in the form of new law to maintain their position. Thus the social and economic structure of society could not satisfy the demands stimulated by that very structure and its accompanying ideology.

These twin phenomena—the changing role of youth and the social structure of society—have either separately or together provided the basis for the theories to be discussed in this chapter. Changing role theories will inevitably stress disorganization and normlessness, while social-structure analysis will concentrate upon economic inequality, but the elements of each may be intertwined in a particular theory. Both perspectives have been applied to studies of delinquency in urban areas in an attempt to "explain" the geographic patterns noted here, especially the tendency of the areas to produce lower-class gang delinquency.

Social Disorganization. The original Chicago Area Project concluded that criminality was caused by a pattern of social disorganization. That pattern (based upon some of the historic developments noted previously) consisted of economic hardship, lack of community institutions, population decrease, transiency of population, and a high percentage of rental rather than owned property. "Social disorganization" theory, beginning in Chicago, argued that certain urban areas have not developed vital social and community roots. Such areas may be populated by recent immigrants and older people who have not been able to leave; these groups can afford the area's low rent (which indicates substandard housing). According to some, social "losers" are also attracted to this area, thus increasing the incidence of petty and often serious crime. The lack of social organization supposedly imbues residents with attitudes that life is corrupt, immoral, and criminal.

The theory of "social disorganization" has been severely criticized on the following grounds: All areas seem to have some form of social organization, perhaps indeed fostered by organized crime (which may be the largest employer). Even allegedly disorganized areas produce more law-abiding than lawless people. Female delinquency is lower than male, despite the conditions. Some residents may avoid crime and delinquency because of fear of apprehension (justified by the high arrest rates of delinquents and criminals that may prevail). And many residents are positively drawn toward law-abiding patterns.

THE THEORY OF CRIMINOGENIC SOCIAL STRUCTURE

Robert M. Merton, a prominent American sociologist, published *Social Structure and Anomie* in 1939. He contended that the discrepancy between cultural success norms of wealth and actual opportunities to acquire wealth resulted in five different methods of adaptation. People could (1) "conform," or accept both the goals and the approved means of reaching the goals; (2) "innovate," or accept the goals but not the methods and thus create new means (some of which may be deemed criminal); (3) abandon any hope of reaching the goals and reduce aspirations accordingly ("ritualistic" was Merton's term for this attitude); (4) "retreat," or abandon hope and not conform to accepted means (the solution of drug addicts, alcoholics, and vagrants); or (5) "rebel," and thereby deny both goals and means. Large-scale deviant behavior occurs because (1) social values define success in material terms; (2) social structure does not permit many to attain success as so defined; and (3) questions of morality are less important than those of accomplishment. Means for accomplishing the goals become flexible and expedient rather than moral. Many groups, at least of the innovative category, who feel deprived of any true opportunity to succeed and who perceive existing means of achievement as illegitimate may then use other means, often criminal ones, to overcome failure. Of course, if this theory were entirely true, we would expect only lower-class delinquent subcultures rather than middle- and upper-class counterparts. Also, as will be seen, there is some evidence that delinquents do not necessarily feel deprived.

Richard Cloward and Lloyd Ohlin in *Delinquency and Opportunity* (1965) extended Merton's analysis. They contended that a delinquent subculture will develop when "failures" begin to question the means provided by society for attainment of norms. If they feel that they are personally qualified but are denied opportunities for illegitimate reasons (such as race), further believe that collective action will permit attainment of valued goals, and can find acceptable rationalizations for delinquency, they will create a subculture. The ability of this subculture to survive will then depend upon the overall social system of the neighborhood. Criticisms of this form of what has been called structure-opportunity theory are: (1) The analysis confuses cause with rationalization, motivation with justification; (2) The analysis disregards the individual life histories of delinquents; (3) There is no proof that delinquents would in fact be able and be qualified to participate in middle-class patterns of conduct, whether or not they are denied legitimate opportunities.

THEORIES OF JUVENILE GANGS

The structure-opportunity theory is primarily a theory of delinquency, based upon a broader theory of social change. The theory attempts to explain the presence of juvenile gangs in lower-class delinquency areas. Most delinquent acts are produced by at least two juveniles acting together. Social psychologists have accepted the notion that people will embrace more deviant attitudes and commit more deviant acts if these are endorsed by others, and will take more chances in groups than alone. Taking of "risks" may be an important way for an insecure adolescent to demonstrate his "character," especially in the presence of others. Delinquents are most anxious to exhibit "maturity" by means such as smoking, dating, and owning cars; and these activities, unlike school success, require money. Also, immediate rewards from peers is more important than long-term rewards from society (this theory is, of course, most compatible with that of the adolescent-role-in-modern-society analysis mentioned previously.)

The major criminological generalization on gangs is that having one or two delinquent "best friends" will enhance the prospects for delinquency. Yet there is some evidence that ties to friends may actually be stronger for nondelinquents than for delinquents. However, the meaning of friendship may be different for delinquents. Weakness of attachment to law-abiding persons may increase the importance of peer influences toward delinquency so that these associations become substitutes for family ties (thus confirming much of differential-association theory). The nature of the delinquency may be relevant to the question of the role of friendship; some have argued that prodelinquency attitudes, followed by delinquent associations, will lead to the commission of crimes such as assault and vandalism, while theft often precedes delinquent associations (although, after theft and delinquent associations, there will be more and larger-scale theft). It has also been surmised that most delinquents do value legal means of acquiring wealth and status, and are in conflict about illegal means (thus tending to confirm Matza's "drift" theory discussed below).

Many, if not most, young people will congregate in groups, and they may (or may not) call those groups "gangs." Childhood gangs are loosely organized. Later delinquent gangs have a greater degree of organization and may persist for long periods of time. Whether called "clubs" (by members) or "near groups" (by criminologists), these gangs do not necessarily attract only one kind of person. Even highly organized gangs may have a short life-span because membership is unstable. Delinquent gangs may be classified according to their primary activities: criminal, conflict and violence, and drug use.

The critical question about delinquent gangs is their relationship to broader cultural and social values. There is profound disagreement about whether or not gangs reject cultural norms and whether they are really subcultures with different values (or, perhaps, reflections of adult subcultures with different values).

Gangs as Frustrated Middle-Class-Value Seekers.   One criminologist, Albert K. Cohen,* partially confirming Merton's analysis, studied lower-class delinquent gangs and found that they are formed when (1) some lower-class youngsters seek middle-class status but cannot attain it and (2) there exist alternative means of achieving success. Often that success will not be financial but will involve status, and status may derive from "symbolic" conduct, such as vandalism, as much as from obtaining money. ("Symbolic" attainment has been called "nonutilitarian.")

Professors Cloward and Ohlin, in line with their general theory, maintain that the disparity between cultural promise and real opportunity affects lower-class youth in three ways. One type of delinquent subculture will be "criminal," using theft and fraud to obtain wealth. Another will be "conflict," using force or threats to gain wealth. A third will be "retreatist," consisting of dropouts, often users of drugs and alcohol, in the race for wealth. Criminal subcultural values are stable and are passed on because of strong bonds between and among different age groups. The conflict subculture is not as strong, so that most of its members leave it when they reach early adulthood. Socialization into the retreatist subculture means, of course, a pattern of addiction that may persist through life.

Juvenile Drifters.   David Matza's† theory of "drift," another major theory, fundamentally agrees with Merton's notion, but carries it farther. Matza's theory argues that some juveniles episodically fall away from middle-class norms to which they are otherwise committed. The theory does not attempt to explain just why this may happen but concentrates upon the con-

---

* *Delinquent Boys: The Culture of the Gang* (Free Press, 1955).

† *Becoming Deviant* (Prentice-Hall, 1969).

sequences. Drifting delinquents tend to rationalize their conduct by (1) maintaining that the deviance was only an accident or the result of some temporary mental state; (2) denying that anyone was hurt; (3) denying that the injured party was really a victim (victims deserve their fates); (4) regarding authority figures as hypocrites; and (5) justifying actions on the ground of higher loyalties or other moral duties (such as maintaining the group to which they belong).

Delinquency and School Experience. One possible means of testing theories on delinquency would be to ascertain the relationship between delinquency and school success. There is no question that delinquency is highly correlated with poor performance at, and a dislike for, school. As with all correlations, however, there is no necessary causal relationship. It is difficult to determine whether school failure causes delinquency or vice versa, or whether the two factors interact to "cause" each other. Failure of educational expectations (not finishing high school, not going to college) also significantly correlate with delinquency. Again, cause may or may not be present. There is some evidence that if the delinquent can define something other than school experience as "success," he may refrain from delinquency. While delinquency may forecast dropping out of school, dropping out reduces delinquency (or, again, at least correlates with its reduction). The greatest reduction of delinquency occurs after the child is freed from the obligation to attend school. The acquisition of an adult role, especially for lower-class youth, may be a substitute for school "success" and restore a dropout's sense of esteem. This theory, if true, would tend to confirm that juvenile delinquents do not deny middle-class values.

Delinquency and Culture Conflict. The previously discussed theories depict the delinquent as either a failure or just confused but fundamentally as one who accepts prevalent cultural values. But another criminologist, Walter B. Miller,* has argued that working-class (or lower-class) culture contains the seedbed for delinquent values; he does not attempt to find the origin of the lower-class culture values. The lower class is thus depicted as having values of its own (often, though not always, opposed to middle-class values). These are transmitted to lower-class youth. Toughness, masculinity, risk-taking, and other "symbolic" conduct are not reactions to frustration but themselves a set of positively prized norms. This is a true "subcultural" theory, and the subculture is one of violence.

One possible explanation for the origins of this delinquent subculture can be found in the writings of sociologist Talcott Parsons, who suggests that

* "Lower-class Culture as a Generating Milieu of Gang Delinquency," *Journal of Social Issues,* Vol. 14 pp. 5–19 (1958).

modern technological work requirements (1) remove the father from the home; (2) create female-centered households; (3) foster drift by boys toward the mother; and (4) create confusion, because the culture stresses masculinity and thus leads to aggressive conduct designed to overcome tendencies toward femininity. If this pattern is valid, it is more characteristic of lower-class than of middle-class households.

SUBCULTURAL THEORY

Miller's work has given rise to the "subcultural" theory of violence. In this view different subcultures are characterized by different social and economic opportunities and by different social histories. These in turn create (1) varying norms and (2) powerful internal socializing forces for those born into such cultures. A "violent" subculture will (1) have high rates of violence, (2) stress preparation for violence, (3) use violence where other groups will not, (4) have high youth violence rates, (5) involve much victim-precipitated crime, and (6) have many members with criminal or violent records. Patterns of violence within such groups will be fairly predictable.

   Since the American South has always been more violent than other sections of the country and such violence has been independent of other correlations such as urban-rural, schooling, income, and employment, subcultural explanations for it abound. Some statistics about assault and self-reporting studies about assault in Milwaukee, Wisconsin (the locus of much southern black and white migration), indicate that the southern code of gentility may preclude fighting over minor matters but demand violence for grievous insults and other wrongs. It should be noted that southern states also inflicted the lowest rates of punishment (except for capital punishment in a few) for homicide and that most southern murders are of the interpersonal kind, not the results of felony murder. Northern murder rates may have increased because of the heavy population migration from the South. In addition, changes within the South (including a reverse migration in recent years) may have made its subculture more diffuse.

STRUCTURAL THEORY

In contrast to the subculture explanation, the National Commission on the Causes and Prevention of Violence in 1970 attributed violence to certain structural conditions: neighborhoods with low income, physical deterioration, dependency, racial and ethnic concentrations, broken homes, working mothers, low levels of educational and vocational skills, high unemployment, high proportion of single males, overcrowded and substandard housing, low rates of home ownership or single-family dwellings, mixed land use, and high population density. These findings replicated the social-disorganization theory of the Chicago Area Project. The Commission also argued that violent crime is (1) a function of large-city life, (2) primarily committed by young males (fifteen to twenty-four), (3) committed by poor people, (4) caused by the conditions of ghetto life, (5) intraracial, except for robbery, which is often committed by black youths against older whites, (6) often the result of passionate encounters (again except for robbery), (7) committed by recidivists, and (8) very high in the United States. This analysis is, of course, descriptive rather than explanatory. It may be that violent crime can be explained by both subcultural and structural theories. Indeed, the *cultural-adaptation* theory combines the two to argue that structural conditions may create certain behavior patterns but that those patterns persist even after the original structural conditions have been eliminated or modified.

THEORY OF CULTURE CONFLICT

All subcultural theories are actually culture-conflict theories. Traditional culture-conflict theories concentrate upon the clash of two distinctive cultures, a clash that may occur, for instance, during immigration or conquest after a war. While subcultural theories discuss conflicts *within* a culture, conflict theory analyzes "border" meetings between cultures (such as that of white Europeans and Indians in eighteenth-century America) and even nongeographic exposures of cultures to each other (more sophisticated communication enables cultures to confront each other without personal contact).

MOBILITY THEORY

The theory that increased geographic mobility has contributed to modern crime may be viewed as either a derivative of "culture conflict" (since mobility increases contacts with other cultures) or an extension of *anomie* theory. Under modern industrial capitalism, families grew smaller, ties within families weakened, people readily moved from one neighborhood to another, if not from one city to another. The result was that traditional social organizations could not perform their functions. Movement to large cities, small ones, and even suburbs permitted anonymity, and anonymity itself hampered the ability of social organizations to perform their functions. Thus mores (social beliefs in right and wrong) may change, develop slowly, or not develop at all while law increases. Law not supported by a true consensus will then lose its legitimacy. It is difficult to measure the long-term effects of such mobility, but some local studies have confirmed that families who are more mobile produce greater numbers of delinquent children.

FUNCTIONALIST THEORY

"Functionalist" theories argue that crime is an adaptation to the conditions of society and therefore criminal conduct is "functional," that is, useful, at least to the criminal and perhaps even to society. They differ from conflict theories in four significant ways: (1) Functionalist theories tend to be less historically based than conflict theories (functionalists tend to see contemporary social conditions as universal); (2) functionalists see society as having certain fundamental social needs that must be met, while conflict theorists find conflicting social needs, some of which cannot be met; (3) functionalists are "scientists" who attempt to fit theory to fact, while some conflict theorists (Marxists, for instance) believe that criminologists should be agents to change the facts; and (4) functionalist theorists presume consensus and presume that the law (even when disobeyed) reflects that consensus, while conflict theorists assume that either there is no consensus or that those in power have manipulated or forced others to accept the consensus.

THE PROCESS OF DELINQUENCY

All the previously discussed theories have been used to explain the origin of urban gang delinquency. To complete the picture, the process by which gang membership contributes to continuing delinquency and adult crime must be understood. The gang provides the means by which certain values are transmitted to members; in turn, acceptance of these values by members reinforces the values. Values such as "honor," "heart," and the learning of certain skills are encouraged or even demanded by gang life. Many gang activities, including the most violent ones, are symbolic means of acting out of gang codes.

General learning theory (see p. 74) supports this analysis of the gang's function. If it is true that (1) behavior that is rewarded in certain situations will tend to be repeated in those situations; (2) behavior that is not rewarded will soon cease; and (3) behavior that is first rewarded but later punished will tend to reappear when punishment ends (unless new behavior is rewarded), then gang support for delinquency is a critical form of reward. Of course, people do not perform in laboratories, and many delinquents, even when rewarded rather than punished for delinqency, abandon it.

Delinquent conduct tends to recur more frequently with each offense, as gang members become more fully socialized into the value system of the group. In turn, the group reinforces the behavior until the behavior becomes characteristic of most members, so that norms of the outside world gradually disappear. Although some members of delinquent gangs form internal cliques for "professional"-type crime (burglary, theft, extortion), the primary focus of gang life is status, not financial gain. Gang members come to share and accept not only mutual values, but also mutual ways of doing things and mutual skills.

This "ideal typology" of the delinquent gang cannot be taken as universal. Not all gangs become delinquent gangs; they may live in an area where accepted neighborhood (though not middle-class) values may discourage delinquency or influence the type of delinquency chosen. Where juveniles still respect important people (such as parents or community leaders), delinquent conduct may cease; many students in self-report questionnaires admit that they shoplifted small amounts from the ages of twelve to fifteen, but about half ceased when fear of apprehension prevailed over the joys of theft (about a third experienced moral qualms). Although alienated delinquents took risks in the form of "dares," even for them participation in crime may have been sporadic and casual. Many delinquents have a stake in conformity, and those not caught and "labeled" may soon drop out. Moreover, many juveniles living in high-crime neighborhoods never participate in delinquency.

These generalizations must qualify the theories discussed in this chapter. The "structure-opportunity" thesis seems not to apply to many delinquents who feel no sense of deprivation and who commit "symbolic" crimes for hedonistic rather than financial satisfaction. "Labeling" theory may not always be applicable either.

DELINQUENCY AND THE NEIGHBORHOOD

As noted previously, the neighborhood may powerfully influence the presence and form of delinquency. An area, for example, may contain many "fences" and other individuals or groups dealing with stolen goods. The presence of bookies, loansharks, and other criminal services may indicate that an area desires the services afforded. At times, certain businesses, such as brothels, are placed in a neighborhood that does not have the political power to resist their presence. In turn, these businesses reinforce the neighborhood's undesirability. The presence of prostitutes and pimps may create "role models" for area youth. Organized crime may be behind many of these operations, and local boys may compete for recognition of, and affiliation with, organized crime. The presence of organized crime is a constant reminder that crime does pay, that politics and law enforcement are corrupt, and that the neighborhood is undesirable (though lucrative for some). The notion that "healthy" recreation facilities (for example, pool rooms, dance halls) will alleviate delinquency is not necessarily true, since those facilities may not negate delinquent attitudes and merely provide another meeting place for those who have them.

CURRENT DEVELOPMENTS

Since all cultural theories can be related to the general historical ones mentioned at the beginning of this chapter, today's significant developments may over time affect criminality and delinquency. In modern America, the individualistic ethic has lost much real meaning, although it still theoretically predominates. Large corporations and other collective groups outside the home dominate national life. Thus what might be called a new feudalism, in the form of private collective action, has largely supplanted free enterprise and individualism. The process has restored some social integration in the form of loyalty, for example, to the corporation or the trade union. This in turn has fostered the creation and growth of special-interest groups that have exerted increasingly greater influence over government. The mass media have also contributed to a form of social integration by publicizing lifestyles and affording a greater degree of popular identification (at least in dress and manners). The rise of the welfare state has stimulated some social organization in the United States (other nations have sought to compel nationalism and patriotism, as occurred in Nazi Germany and Communist Russia). The trend toward suburban living, the virtual elimination of immigration, and a lower birth rate may foster the development of new cultural norms that are stronger than present ones. The spread of the scientific attitude, calling for rationality and honesty, may also help create new norms.

10. Theories of Institutions and Crime

The previous chapter discussed cultural theories of crime. This chapter will concentrate upon the relationship to crime of existing American institutions, irrespective of the culture in which they operate. While many of these institutions are thought necessary to our society, they may, in themselves, contribute to crime. Again, the distinction between description and explanation should be kept in mind. While, in general, it appears that (1) the existence of and (2) changes in social institutions have some relationship to the existence of and changes in crime patterns, it is difficult to do anything beyond describing the apparent correlations.

ECONOMIC INSTITUTIONS

When measured by such criteria as social class and economic status, there can be little doubt that poverty correlates with crime. Of course, criminal-justice agencies have been established primarily to fight the kinds of crime most likely to be committed by the poor and are not geared to discover, much less contend with, white-collar crime. Probably crime is not concentrated in any one economic class, although, as previously mentioned, certain types of crime are. Studies have shown that minor forms of delinquency are prevalent in every social and economic class. There appears to be little bias within the criminal-justice system against the poor when serious predatory street crime is committed; sentences for such crimes in the same jurisdiction are uniform irrespective of the class of the offender. It remains true, however, that lower and working classes contribute disproportionately to serious "street" crime.

Within the lower class, specific crime ratios do vary. The rural poor and certain ethnic groups (such as the Japanese) have lower rates than do poor people generally. During depressions, there may be little correlation between class and street crime, especially when other factors, such as degree of urbanization and community social disorganization, are taken into account. The crime rate appears to be more affected by geographic area than by class, although it is highest in poverty areas. In those areas, middle-class delinquency virtually parallels lower-class crime rates. Also, as previously noted, the female delinquency rate is generally much lower than the male rate, even in poor areas and among poor people. Homicide and crimes against property tend to be concentrated among the poor; sex offenses (except for rape) are not.

The role of "pure" poverty in crime is minimized during depressions. In general, the crime rate does not tend to rise during the depth of the business cycle, though the incarceration rate of those arrested does. During depressions, serious crimes may rise, though inconsistently with each other. Property crimes involving violence tend to increase somewhat. While arrests of adults rise during unemployment, teen-age arrests decline (they rise rapidly during prosperity), perhaps because parents are at home and can provide greater control during depressions and because juveniles may be more independent during prosperity. Drunkenness appears not to correlate at all with the business cycle. Crimes against the person seem not to be related to depressions. Thus generalizations about poverty and crime must be viewed skeptically. It may be that urban poverty is so endemic that depressions have little effect.

GOVERNMENT

It has been said that democracies have more crime than do dictatorships and that capitalist democracies have more crime that socialist governments or other forms. This assertion is difficult to prove, since dictatorships customarily do not furnish crime figures and high-crime capitalist America is counterbalanced by low-crime capitalist Japan. It is also hard to ascertain whether the dominance of a particular political party correlates with crime, in part because political administrations tend to "politicize" crime rates for their own purposes.

While the long-term effect of group differentiation may tend toward social integration (see p. 17), the short-term effect may be a loss of respect for a government that seems to legislate in favor of certain groups and against others. This may foster a general cynicism toward law and contempt for the general political process even by nonlawbreakers. Criminal-justice agencies may be perceived as inefficient, biased, and corrupt. The vast proliferation of law, much of which touches on subjects for which no real majority support exists, may lead to widespread lawbreaking and selective enforcement of the law.

Public demands may be inconsistent: Control crime but do not eliminate the services it provides. The public will often tolerate gambling but condemn corruption without perceiving that the two factors are integrally related. Where political machines run cities (a phenomenon declining in the United States) and even when they do not, many political "services" (for example, "ticket fixing" and dismissal of drunk-driving charges) are illegal though common among normally law-abiding groups. Political machines may provide patronage and the "licensing" of such illegal and corrupt activities as prostitution, gambling, loansharking, and liquor-law violations. Political campaign contributions often buy immunity from the law, as do business payoffs to permit violations of fire, health, safety, and environmental laws. Fraudulent bidding for city contracts such as bus routes and for other services is a source of illegal income for many public officials. Some groups can buy advance immunity from law to ensure that new laws adverse to their interests are not passed. Although vote fraud has declined, it still remains endemic in certain states and localities.

RELIGION

The alleged lack of religious training in modern society is thought to be a cause of crime, but if true, this is not documentable. Indeed, some studies suggest that delinquents are more favorably inclined toward religion than are nondelinquents. While many who commit crimes attend church, there is no evidence about the number of church attendees who commit crime. The fact that Baptists and Catholics are the religions most represented in prisons probably reflects the lower-class origins of such prisoners rather than any religious variable. Jews tend to consistently have the lowest delinquency rates.

EDUCATION

School relationships are probably the most important ones in any individual's life after family and peer group. It may even be true that school is the most significant factor in delinquency, although the evidence does not clarify whether school failure precedes (and causes) or follows (and is caused by) delinquency. Again, it is not education per se but the individual's experience of that education that is probably important. Crime, apart from white collar crime, tends to decrease with an increase in education. In one American study, it was found that 99 percent of those incarcerated had not completed college, 61 percent had not finished high school, and 26 percent had not finished the eighth grade (in contrast to much higher educational levels of the general population). Although delinquency may be more frequent among school dropouts than among graduates, the evidence is, as noted, mixed.

Truancy often precedes delinquency (though, of course, not all truants become delinquents). Educational failure may, of course, be caused by home and neighborhood factors that also contribute to delinquency.

The process by which educational experience contributes to delinquency may commence with the presence of a group of lower- or working-class students who have not developed certain skills and attitudes compatible with the norms of the school. This deviation may, in turn, lead teachers and other students to "label" them as troublemakers or stupid. The teachers' attention then is concentrated upon those students who cooperate with the system. Truancy and alienation of other students may follow. While family and peer-group influences may "save" even some of the labeled students, many will find comfort and meaning in delinquent associations. In-school delinquency and crime have dramatically increased in the past few years. A lack of available jobs for dropouts or mediocre students may contribute to increased delinquency. It appears that much delinquency is generated by the school environment, and even the delinquency of many who drop out may have commenced in school.

WAR

There is probably an increase of juvenile delinquency during wartime. War may breed permissive attitudes toward violence generally, as many have claimed, but this fact would not account for property-crime increases. Some have contended that war increases economic hardship and thus delinquency, but hardship has not accompanied all wars. The theory that emotional strains increase during wartime does not account for the variations in delinquency increase (much less for the actual decreases that sometimes occur). A more likely explanation is that wartime disruption of family and community institutions lead to increased neglect of children. In addition, social-service agencies may be cut back on personnel and funding. The delinquency trends may extend into the immediate postwar period to affect those who were predelinquents during the war. Although the crime rate for adults drops during wartime, it remains constant when measured as a proportion of adults not in military service. Adult female crimes rise because women perform formerly male functions. Wartime regulations, such as food and gasoline rationing, are frequently violated. The crime rate rises dramatically in those countries suffering great internal social dislocations and rises least in countries that do not undergo such stresses. Returning servicemen, as a whole, do not commit more violent crimes because of their experiences, although they may commit more fraud and embezzlement. The homicide rate, especially in nations actually engaged in wartime fighting, tends to rise during the postwar years. Perhaps homicide rates are independent of both general crime rates and even the amount of social dislocation in a given country. They may also be independent of economic factors, since those nations whose wartime economies improve *and* those whose economies suffer experience increases.

THE MASS MEDIA

Although many people suspect that mass-media preoccupation with crime leads to an increase, no one can explain just how this happens or how the media cancel out other influences. The prominence of crime reporting may lead to the belief that crime is widespread, and this, in turn, may engender public indifference. Another possible result is to stimulate demands for more severe punishment for particularly atrocious crimes. The mass media also may create "crime waves" by the choice of matters to report. Criminals who are the subjects of prolonged curiosity may gain social esteem. Coverage of charges against particular defendants may create problems of "trial by newspaper" or "trial by television," but this rare occurrence should not be overstated. (Several official agencies, including the American Bar Association, have tried to curb the dissemination of pretrial information by police and prosecutors.) Newspapers that give distorted versions of various aspects of crime also influence public attitudes on crime and punishment.

Violence and the Media.   Some research indicates that people, especially lower-class youth, will model their conduct upon media portrayals of those who use violence to achieve their own ends. Movies or television shows that emphasize aggression seem to increase aggressiveness in the audience, at least the young audience. Some short-run stimulation in either triggering violence or in learning violent techniques (such as making weapons) may result. Toleration of violence after repeated exposure to it may increase; some galvanic skin-response tests rates seem to confirm this possibility. Whether initial feelings of violence are reinforced by adolescent exposure to media violence, or whether media violence stimulates the otherwise nonviolent is not known.

Familiarity with the locale of media-depicted violence may be a significant factor. Violence presented (1) as unfamiliar, (2) in stylized patterns (cartoons), (3) in other unfamiliar settings, (4) as harmful to "bad" people but not to "good" ones, (5) as "make-believe," and (6) as irrelevant to children's desire to "identify" may have little effect, but violence shown in (1) ordinary situations, (2) situations where "good" people are victimized, especially brutally, and (3) situations where this can be easily accomplished (for instance, with a gun) may have different effects. It is possible that the nature of the time spent watching violent depictions and the circumstances under which violence is communicated to juveniles, as well as the "messages," influence later conduct. It is startling to realize that a major national newspaper's decision to limit reporting of violence in 1970 in a small west European country led to (or correlated with) a falloff in violent crimes except in one city, where a local newspaper continued to flamboyantly report violence.

Riots and the Media. Riots often reflect a situation of escalating emotions, much like family fights. Riots often occur on weekends or holidays when other routines that divert attention are absent. Anger feeds upon anger shared by others, and the mass media may abet such intensification by showing that the anger is widespread. This situation apparently occurred in the 1960s, when police brutality and assassinations of civil-rights workers and leaders led to some violence. Much of the anger reflected the belief that real improvements had not been made. Publicity about the riots that flared up in the Watts section of Los Angeles in 1965 and later in Detroit, Gary, Cleveland, Newark, Philadelphia, and other northern cities attracted official attention and concern. Many ghetto residents claimed to have become more militant as a result of the riots though they denied that they would participate in riots. This period also witnessed the greatest recorded increase in black teen-age urban homicide rates. As some opportunities for blacks opened up, the relative deprivation felt by youths falling behind may have been enhanced by media-depicted riots in which lawbreakers achieved some success. Publicity may also have stimulated delinquents to travel to riot-torn areas to join in looting and to re-create gang structures. Since homicides have always tended to increase after wars, executions, and well-publicized instances of mass murder, it would not be surprising that riots abetted by publicity produced the same results. In riot situations it appears that widespread publicity and deliberate acceptance and adoption of the "message" presented (usually after some contact with others who are strongly influential) will lead to disorderly behavior. There has been little scientific research about the contagious effect of calamitous events and surrounding publicity.

Of course, the major medium for presentations that "count" is television. Television's ability to influence style and fashion may well extend to behavior and may contribute to a philosophy that violence is an acceptable means of coping with life's problems. Furthermore, television may influence not only behavior but also attitudes toward crime, most often in the direction of fatalistic acceptance of crime as a norm in itself.

11. Criminal Typology

The previous four chapters dealt with attempts to "explain" the origins of crime, although many of the theories discussed are descriptive rather than explanatory. This chapter will deal with *typology,* the attempt to describe particular types of offenders and the crimes they are likely to commit. Criminologists who believe there is no one cause or causal theory (even one comprising many factors) and who are not content to merely find correlates have developed typological theory. Broadly, typologies study the behavior patterns of known criminals and attempt to make generalizations about personal and environmental factors from the mass of available data. Typologies are models of the "typical" person who commits one or another crime. These models are applied to later known criminals who commit the same kind of crime in order to ascertain if the model holds true and has at least some predictive value. Because so much delinquency is "unspecialized," criminologists tend to apply their models to adult criminality. For young delinquents, the study is of the "maturation" process by which they proceed from delinquency to delinquency. Since early maturation precedes later specialization, early maturation will be discussed prior to later behavioral typologies.

MATURATION

It is crucial to remember that most delinquents do not follow any maturation pattern, since they terminate delinquency before forming a pattern. For those who do not, it appears that such "maturity" occurs at an early age because lifestyle has been adapted to criminality. On the other hand, an older criminal who begins his career later may not be as fixed in that career and may never truly "mature" into a condition of what might be called permanent criminality.

The age at which crime or delinquency commences and the type of crime committed are critical aspects of the process of criminal maturation. For crimes such as burglary or robbery, the pattern proceeds from trivial crimes to serious crimes and from occasional to frequent criminality. Crimes perhaps undertaken for "fun" reasons then become a business, and individual criminality may lead to small-group criminality and then to tightly organized small-group criminality. Ex-delinquents who persist in crime as young adults often change the types of crimes they commit. As teen-agers their crimes tend to be unspecialized; when they grow up, they tend to commit more property crimes. Early association with gang criminality gives way to either working alone or with only a few associates. Most become specialists in the sense that they commit one general *form* of crime (for example, property crime). They also tend to take risks, especially if the first few crimes do not result in arrest. The negative effects of jail or prison (if they are caught) are minimized when compared to (1) the offender's lack of ability to hold more than the lowest-paying legitimate job and (2) the lack of stigma in the circles to which he has turned to gain esteem. Many released offenders both work at low-paying jobs and commit crime. It has been argued that improved job training in prison plus cash aid at release or in emergencies might break this pattern.

SEGREGATION

Segregation is the process by which criminals are separated from the law-abiding, either because the criminal himself voluntarily separates or because he becomes "labeled" by official agencies. (It appears that public opinion about the odiousness of crime is less important than official labeling.) Segregation may not be complete—for example, organized-crime figures who become rich may well blend in with the upperworld, though they may not be socially acceptable to it.

Segregation tends to lead to an escalation of conflict between criminals and law enforcers. In the United States, violence characterizes both groups (in England, until recently, use of guns by both police and criminals was discouraged by the "rules of the game"). Increasing violence has led to an increasing number of deaths of both police and criminals—and occasional bystanders. Conflict also escalates because more and more law leads to more and more arrests, especially in minority communities, and to intensified animosity. Technological improvements in police work lead to greater sophistication by criminals. When fingerprinting became accepted, criminals began to wear gloves; the advent of police radios was accompanied by criminal monitoring of police calls; improved methods of making safes more resistant to forced entry led to newer entry techniques and, eventually, to kidnaping of bank managers. Certain developments, such as increased security for banks and bank practices or keeping little money on hand, have, in turn, changed the nature of the perpetrator. Bank robberies are now most often committed by a lone amateur rather than by professionals.

CRIMINAL-TYPOLOGY THEORY

Typology represents an attempt by criminologists to study crime in ways intermediate between the study of individual criminals and of general social patterns. The criminologist who studies behavior and process may find that people with certain personality types and processes (life experiences) seem to commit one particular crime or, more likely, a "category" of crime. Conversely, he may find that one legally defined crime may be committed by several distinct personality types; he will then break down the broad crime into subunits.

The formulation of typologies presents confusing questions. For instance, what is a "pattern"? Robbery may be committed by professionals or by impulsive youths using different methods. Burglary may be professional or amateur, and within both categories subpatterns may be discerned. Teenage delinquents may be unspecialized. To classify offenders in legal categories may be misleading since, because of the prevalence of plea bargaining in our criminal-justice system, many offenders are convicted of crimes they did not commit rather than the ones they did commit. Also, many typologies reflect the perceptions of the criminologist, who may choose certain factors that he believes to be important but that in fact are not. This is more likely to be true where he first creates a theory and then tries to fit known facts to it than when he lets the facts form the basis of the theory. The level of generalization is important for the criminologist; if he finds too many exceptions to a particular typology, he may create subbranches to account for those perceptions. He may, for instance, end up finding fifty or sixty "patterns" of robbers, and this study, in effect, tells us nothing. Typological analysis cannot explain the occasional criminal, the truly pathological criminal (who may adopt a pattern because he has learned something about it), and the variable-pattern criminal. It is conceivable that many "typological" explanations account for only a small number of offenders.

Factors in Typology. Two requirements of any "typological theory" are that (1) the information should be accurate for most of those "typed" and (2) the categories created by the typology should be broad enough to encompass the actual behavior of most individuals within that category. (Unfortunately, the latter criterion will lead toward too much generality.) There is also a danger that a particular typology will include noncareer offenders. Among the factors commonly used in typological analysis are (1) social class; (2) family background; (3) peer contacts; (4) contacts with the criminal-justice system and other social agencies that define deviance; (5) the existence of a pattern; (6) the pattern of social interaction with others at the time of the offense (Is it committed in concert with others?); (7) the offender's self-concept (Does he believe himself to be a criminal?); (8) general pro- or antisocial attitudes; and (9) career history, if any.

Thus criminologists attempt to narrow from a field of possibly thousands of factors those that seem to closely relate to actual, observable criminal conduct. The factors mentioned reinforce the sociological truth that people play different roles in society, perhaps based on social status, prestige, and assessment of how others view the role. A role consists of both behavior and expectations based upon that behavior. Behavior alone may not say very much, but the context of that behavior, especially the expectations of the individual himself or of others, will make the behavior "socially meaningful."

Limitations of Typology.   It is necessary to remember that typological theories are only descriptive, not analytical or predictive. Since there are no control groups, it is impossible to determine whether the characteristics described significantly differ from those in the general population or the portion of the population from which the offender comes. If everyone with the characteristics of a particular typology could be identified, probably most would not even be criminals. To use typology to predict would lead to "overprediction"; that is, many more persons predicted to be criminals would become noncriminal than criminal. Also, of course, typology theories do not even pretend to explain causation.

Methods of Classification.   One form of typological analysis classifies different types of criminals; thus one well-known theory* finds nine "criminal types": (1) the violent personal criminal, (2) the occasional property offender, (3) the organized criminal who functions in a highly developed organization, (4) the political criminal, (5) the criminal who violates only public-order laws, (6) the conventional criminal, (7) the occupational criminal, (8) the corporate criminal, and (9) the professional criminal. Other typologies break down certain categories, such as the professional criminal, into different subbranches.

THE PROFESSIONAL CRIMINAL

A profession may be defined as an occupation that has the following attributes: (1) standards of competence and ethics, (2) characteristic terminology, (3) a justifying ideology, (4) a process by which new members enter and gain acceptance and prestige from their colleagues, and (5) pride in status and ability that are known to colleagues and accepted by them.

* Marshall B. Clinard and Richard Quinney, *Criminal Behavior Systems: A Typology* (Holt, Rinehart & Winston, 1967).

Professionalism in crime means a commitment to crime, sophistication in participating in crime, and infrequent arrest. Professionals tend to be ruthless toward enemies and traitors and on the whole loyal to fellow workers. Professionals are not in conflict about their criminal lives and manipulate those who would help them.

Professional Thieves. Criminologists are interested in where professional thieves come from and how they perpetuate themselves as a group. Professional thieves share the same attributes of "straight" professionals: a regular vocational pursuit, development of skills and techniques, and ability to plan and carry out their objectives. The pattern often begins in youth when some delinquents learn elementary skills in theft, avoidance of capture, and how to act if captured. At some point, they may specialize (though not exclusively) in elite forms of theft, such as safecracking, pickpocketing, shoplifting, and confidence games. Except for shoplifters, pickpockets, and forgers, most thieves do not specialize, because this would mean loss of anonymity and immediate identification by the police (or even misidentification if another thief uses a professional's *modus operandi* "m.o." to confuse police). As skills develop, the professional thief will learn to plan more carefully, make advance preparations to avoid or minimize punishment if caught (preparation for bail, legal services, and perhaps bribery). His crude code of ethics stresses the duty not to inform on his partners and to be honest with them (violators may be dealt with by their partners, but only organized crime has an organized system of punishment). Professional thieves are not showoffs, sentimental, or cruel. They associate with each other, although they may work alone, and are made uncomfortable by amateur competition, which, in their view often only inflames the public and the police. Professional thieves' techniques differ from those of burglars and robbers and, because of a reliance on their wits, most often resemble the talents of a salesman. They will usually (1) select crimes presenting minimal risks, (2) learn from their teachers, and (3) employ professional "fixers" to corruptly terminate any legal case brought against them. The fixer may return stolen goods to victims in exchange for promises not to prosecute or testify, or bribe policemen to induce them to persuade victims to drop charges, forego filing of formal complaints, or commit perjury at trial. Eventually it may be possible to "fix" a prosecutor or judge. Professional theft gives rise to operations such as fencing, which involve many legitimate businessmen as eventual customers for stolen goods.

Professional Robbers. Banditry and robbery have existed from the beginning of history. Some social historians have contended that professionals in these fields started as displaced soldiers and sailors hired either to fight on behalf of landlords against peasants or vice versa. In early classbound societies with many social conflicts, robbers were "social bandits" who often switched allegiances. Banditry has often been used by ideological movements; when those movements fail, bandits often become bandits "without a cause." In the United States, banditry spread in the West after the Civil War by recruitment of ex-soldiers (especially Confederates), unemployed cowboys, and youngsters from recently arrived settler families. Another period of banditry occurred during the Depression of the 1930s, when for all of the presumed success by the FBI and other police agencies against John Dillinger and Bonnie and Clyde, many less flamboyant bank robbers were never apprehended.

Professional robbers and some burglars rarely are hostile to the police. These robbers and burglers often come from lower-class urban areas, have a history of predatory gang delinquency, and have acquired skills from elder teachers. Their careers last into middle age. If successful, they may move into middle-class neighborhoods but retain working-class ties. Although their intrafamily relations have often been good, they were "often" unsupervised as children. Many had family members, including parents, who were criminals. Their own marriages tend to be unstable. Although they associate with other criminals, they rarely form gangs. They are likely to have had contact with police and juvenile courts, and some adult contact with imprisonment, but are seldom imprisoned as they grow older. Although most robbery is committed by amateurs, professionals are often responsible for "big scores." Their activities are planned and organized (three to five people may play different roles in committing a crime); they steal cars (or may rent them, using false identities); and they use such professional techniques as surprise, intimidation, and quick collection of loot. Career robbers are somewhat more loosely organized than professional thieves (the career robbers' alliances break up easily). Career robbers are impulsive, high livers, free spenders, and may choose relatively easy, even unplanned targets rather than more lucrative but also more difficult jobs.

Semiprofessional Robbers.   Semiprofessional robbers engage in direct assaults on people or their property. These robbers' skills are simple, and they often use physical force. They frequently commit crimes alone or with one other person. They view themselves as criminals and believe that the "system" is phony and corrupt. They are often hostile toward police and bitter about their parents, social agencies, and schools. They have engaged in predatory gang delinquency and have often been caught. They spend much time in prison and are relatively invulnerable to prison treatment programs. They are likely to withdraw from crime in early middle age. Like professional robbers, they usually come from lower-class urban backgrounds, and their peers tend to be other unskilled professionals. They have noncriminal contacts as adults; since they spend so much time in the criminal-justice system, they develop a great hostility to it. Semiprofessionals (or even rank amateurs) have tended to take over certain crimes such as auto theft and bank robbery from professionals; semiprofessionals also interact with marginal types such as bookies, gamblers, and pimps.

Professional Burglars.   Although most burglars are juveniles, there are some professional ones. Professionals often rely on others ("tipsters") who line up targets and work with confederates such as lookouts (who may monitor police radio calls) and others to help remove the loot. Associations frequently change, and newer members of burglary teams are recruited through sources such as bartenders, deliverymen, and fences. Like other professionals, these burglars have lawyers and bail bondsmen "on call" to reduce the pains of being caught. Since most property stolen is merchandise rather than cash, burglars also make advance arrangements with fences, who are often otherwise legitimate businessmen with the ability to move goods quickly. Professionals receive more from fences than do amateurs or semiprofessionals. Professionals frequently commit offenses in different cities to avoid detection.

Professional Pickpockets.   Pickpockets tend to work in cities, at public events, in the evenings; they dress well but not showily. Often they work in pairs, one to distract the victim ("mark"), the other to perform the crime. Pickpocketing has declined as social patterns changed (for instance, the private car has largely replaced public transportation).

Professional Defrauders.   Professional fraud involves obtaining other people's money or property by trick rather than by force or fear. Professionals do not commit most forgery, which is naïve, impulsive, and usually detected by police, but professional check forgery is sophisticated. Professional activities have expanded from "laying paper" (large-scale check forgery, often engaged in while traveling from city to city) to counterfeiting and stealing credit cards and drivers' licenses in order to obtain cash. Most forgers have no juvenile records and experience severe anxiety when they are apprehended. They are likely to be arrested, though they travel and change names frequently, because their patterns and activities can be readily traced through computerized criminal-justice-system processes. Once caught, they usually face numerous charges in many states.

Professional swindling is another major form of fraud. One type of swindle involves a pattern whereby (1) a gullible "mark" is found (the swindle may either be personal, involving a passerby, or impersonal, involving a newspaper advertisement for a good "business opportunity"); (2) a third person who seems respectable is used to gain the mark's confidence; (3) the mark is allowed to make some money; (4) the mark is persuaded to cash in his assets and give them to the swindler (often, accomplices also pretend to give the swindler their assets); (5) when the swindle has been completed, the mark must be "cooled out" (the swindler's accomplices try to convince the mark that they too have been victimized, suggest acceptable rationalizations for nonprosecution, and argue that the mark himself is guilty of a crime); and (6) the police or a witness may be bribed, also to forestall prosecution.

While most confidence games involve marks who are greedy as well as gullible, many involve deception of average people by apparently legitimate businessmen. Furnace-cleaning services offered at bargain rates, sales of aluminum siding, training courses for certain trades, and phony representations to small-town banks that the swindler is a bank examiner are only a few of the apparently legitimate enterprises that are often fronts for swindles. Many swindles resemble other forms of doing business and are difficult to detect, especially when the customer receives something for his money.

THE NONPROFESSIONAL CRIMINAL

Nonprofessionalism or a low degree of professionalism in crime involves ambivalence between criminal and legitimate activities, impulsive illegality, and frequent apprehension.

Embezzlers. Embezzlers are persons in a position of financial trust who abuse this trust for financial gain. They are usually older than most other criminals and work for a respectable business; most embezzlers have been employed for a long period before the onset of embezzlement. Personal background and social-class factors are usually irrelevant to this crime. Situational ones are critical: (1) The situation may rapidly change (for example, gambling debts pile up); (2) the person defines it as a unique and unshareable problem; (3) he then begins to use his skills for illegal purposes; (4) the crime is rationalized as either noncriminal (the money is only "borrowed") or justified (the person is being underpaid); (5) small amounts are taken periodically; (6) at some point, the embezzler realizes that the sums cannot be replaced and that he is a "criminal"; (7) that realization will trigger one (or more) of several responses: emotional breakdown, surrender to the police, an attempt to get the money back by gambling, suicide, or the onset of criminal recklessness and the continued embezzlement of even larger amounts. Convicted embezzlers tend to become model prisoners and rarely recidivate (in part because they are not trusted with money again).

The only open question about this pattern of embezzlement is the issue of whether "rationalization" of illegality precedes or follows the crime. Since the only evidence comes from convicted criminals themselves, it is hard to know. If the rationalization preceded the crime, then the embezzler's general attitudes are more important than some have thought—that is, the matter is not entirely "situational." It should be noted that pre-existing rationales are important for employee theft generally, since most thieves distinguish between personal property belonging to others and corporate property (or property of no known ownership); theft of the latter is viewed as permissible when theft of the former is condemned, even by the perpetrator. The matter of what a thief or even delinquent choses to steal should be studied since, undoubtedly, that choice is dictated by some learning experiences.

Naïve Check Forgers.   This criminal in general (1) commits an unsophisticated offense with little skill; (2) repeats his conduct often; (3) has no significant juvenile offense record and does not commit other types of adult crime; (4) has no self-concept as a real criminal and believes that the act is situationally required or justified; (5) has on the whole prosocial attitudes but experiences difficulties in work and/or marriage and believes himself to be a failure; (6) comes from a middle-class background; (7) has a conventional family background; and (8) has no criminal peer-group associations. The first offense usually results in probation, and this may enhance the feeling that he can get away with future crimes. It has been suggested that this offender might well be positively benefited by early labeling as a deviant.

Occasional Petty Offenders.   As previously noted, much crime is situational, involving impulsive "risk taking" or an escalation of behavior that is not criminal at the outset. Some have argued that lower-class culture conduces to boredom in weekday work followed by weekend "release" in revelry (often accompanied by drink), frequently in crime. Many forms of petty theft and occasional shoplifting manifest this sudden behavioral outburst.

SEX OFFENDERS

Contrary to myth, sex offenders tend to be petty criminals with fairly normal personalities. Several major studies have shown that only a small percentage use force and even fewer are psychopathic. More than half were inhibited as children; this proportion is greater for exhibitionists and child molesters. Most are lower class, of low intelligence, and economically unsuccessful (again, it can be questioned whether these particular "traits" are truly relevant, especially since they are shared with many noncriminals). Most sexual offenders do not have extensive criminal records, and their parole-violation rates are lower than that of the average prisoner. The acts committed are usually socially repellent but rarely dangerous. Of course, those committing heinous crimes are quite emotionally disturbed.

Rapists.   Aggressive rapists use force to compel sexual activity. Often, a social encounter will turn violent when the female has attempted to withdraw either from an explicit agreement to have intercourse or from circumstances indicating such an agreement. Rape may also occur between strangers. Rapists do not define themselves as criminals, often blame the victim, and view the rape as alien to their true characters. Rapists usually have a background of no, little, or petty criminality. Most are from lower- or lower-middle-class backgrounds and are accustomed to the use of force. Although some rapists have been alienated from family ties at early ages, many have no unusual background. Peer pressures to commit rape are usually not present. Interaction with the criminal-justice system does not appear to significantly change them (except for high sentences, which apparently lead to diminished sexual needs when they are released). Rape is usually an intraracial crime, with high rape rates among blacks. One study showed that rape victims had records for minor crimes; that study also confirmed that a bare majority of rapists had known their victims prior to the attack.

Violent sexual offenders, distinguished only by degree from aggressive rapists, often use extreme and disgusting violence against their victims. They do not have a prior relationship with their victims, as do many conventional rapists. Although they know they are "different" from others, they perceive themselves as generally law-abiding (indeed, in matters apart from sex, they are conventional). They have little prior history of delinquency or criminality. The problem of recidivism rarely arises, since they are often caught and imprisoned for long periods. They come from no one class and their family backgrounds often involve either sexual repression and/or seductive interaction with mothers. They do not become more criminal because of their contact with the criminal-justice system.

Child Molesters.   Exhibitionists and child molesters rarely harm children but engage in minor fondling, usually with little lasting psychological effect on the child (who may regard the conduct as nothing more than excessive affection). While exhibitionists commit their crimes in public, where women are present, molesters rarely choose their victims randomly but rather become involved with children they know or with relatives. Molesters do not perceive themselves to be criminals; in fact, molesters often claim they were seduced. They do not have marked criminal attitudes or delinquency or criminal records. Although when apprehended and convicted they usually receive long prison terms, those who are released may recidivate. These offenders come from no particular social class, and their timid personalities may result from early family experiences but are more likely to stem from feelings of adult sexual inadequacy, often because of a dominant wife. Contact with the criminal-justice system often convinces these offenders that they are not normal, and they are reviled by both the public and the prison population.

FEMALE OFFENDERS

One of the few extant typologies about women's crime is that of the amateur shoplifter. The pattern of the crime is inconsistent. Some may use sophisticated apparatus to steal, while others use none. The amateur steals for personal use, while the professional steals for resale. Amateur shoplifters steal alone, usually in large department stores in urban areas. They perceive themselves as honest and are generally prosocial. Apprehension by store personnel usually results in a cessation of criminal activity. Until then, they probably have stolen regularly. This form of shoplifting is not class-based, and there is nothing unusual in the family patterns of offenders. There is also no peer-group involvement or support for these activities. Although professionals steal greater amounts, amateurs, because of their much greater numbers, account for more total theft and loss, though less than is taken by store employees (shoplifting accounts for only 25 percent of total store losses). Women tend to steal more items than men. Black shoplifters are more likely to be referred to the police and to receive higher sentences upon conviction.

OFFENSE TYPOLOGIES

While the previous discussion has been of particular types of offenders, this classification may not be feasible for all crimes since (1) like murder, the crime may be comparatively rare or (2) like robbery, the crime may be so frequent as to make generalization hazardous. Some interesting data can be provided by a broad analysis of two crimes.

Murder. Studies of individual murderers tend to stress the psychological aspects of the crime and are speculative and intuitive. One study of "sudden murderers" concluded that the killers were young, members of closely knit families, dominated by the mother, who stressed conformity, and had been unaggressive children. Tensions to make further conformist adjustments were present, and the killers tried to relieve those tensions for long periods prior to homicide. Those efforts at self-control (and underlying feelings of inadequacy) resulted in stress, feelings of helplessness, and finally a "blow-up." One study of 588 homicides in Philadelphia between 1948 and 1952 found that (1) both black males and females had higher rates than whites; (2) killing was intraracial; (3) killers were younger than their victims; (4) blacks were more likely to stab and whites more likely to beat (since then, the availability of firearms has probably changed this pattern); (5) weekends, especially Saturday night, were the most dangerous times, irrespective of month and season; (6) alcohol was a significant factor in two thirds of the homicides and was particularly significant for blacks; and (7) killers, especially blacks, had significant prior-arrest records. A major study of juvenile murderers found low IQs, severe psychological problems (for example, organic brain damage, schizophrenia), and reading deficiencies as significant variables. Other studies have correlated juvenile homicide with such family factors as instability in the parent-child or the parent-parent relationship, and with emotional rigidity in the parents.

Robbery. Robbery is the taking of property from a person by use or threat of force. It is a predominantly urban crime (about two thirds of all reported robberies in the United States occur in the fifty or sixty largest cities). Robbery has rapidly increased in recent times; in 1960, the reported rate was 60 per 100,000; in 1965, it rose to 72; in 1970, to 172; and by 1975, the rate was 218. Victimization surveys indicate that there are as many unreported robberies as reported ones. About 65 percent of robberies are armed, 45 percent with guns and 12 percent with knives; the remainder consist of force perpetrated because of the offender's physical dominance. Most armed robberies by gun involve minimal violence; victims are struck with the weapon rather than shot. Most robberies committed with knives and most unarmed robberies involve physical attacks rather than threats. Violence occurs in 70 percent of unresisted muggings and 90 percent of resisted ones. Physical injuries occur in about one third of all robberies. Robbery is a classical "stranger-to-stranger" crime; more than 90 percent of reported robberies are so classified. It is the "street crime" par excellence since about 60 percent occur in the open.

Robberies are predominantly committed by male juveniles (although the juvenile female robbery rate has increased at a greater rate in recent years). Males are more than twice as likely as females to be victims. Robbery victims are most likely to be other juveniles, although juvenile-juvenile types of robbery are least likely to be reported to the police. One major robbery typology suggests the existence of the following types of offenders: (1) the professional robber, who has a major long-term commitment to crime; (2) the opportunist robber, who infrequently robs, but commits a variety of crimes usually involving purse snatchings and muggings, often with little, if any, planning (these robbers may be unemployed); (3) the addict robber, who often (though not exclusively) steals to support his habit and views robbery as dangerous to himself (perhaps as many as one fourth of adult robbers are addicts); and (4) the alcoholic robber, whose robbery often follows the commission of an assault. The alcoholic robber belongs to a violent, rather than a theft subculture (the reverse is true of juvenile robbers). Juveniles tend to commit unarmed muggings, usually in the company of another juvenile; most juvenile arrests are for purse snatching.

One study of victims claimed that robbery occurs most frequently against (1) people who handle money as part of a business, (2) people caught unaware out in the open, (3) people present on premises during a break-in, (4) people with whom the robber has come into short association (a prostitute, a fellow drinker at a bar or party), and (5) people known to the robber. Most robberies are of the first or second variety.

ORGANIZED CRIME

Organized crime is a behavior system unto itself; while its typology often is similar to that of professional criminals, it goes far beyond them. Specialization is more pronounced; all organized-crime organizations (notably the Mafia) have assigned positions. There is a code of silence (called *omerta* in the Mafia) and other codes of conduct that more often bind the lower elements in the structure than the higher ones. There may be different codes in different organized-crime groups; those sharing kinship ties (like the Mafia) may emphasize acting so as not to disgrace the family, while newer organized-crime groups may stress personal qualities such as courage or competence. Of course, all organized-crime groups stress secrecy and loyalty. A cadre of staff officials (financiers, lawyers, accountants) perform specialized functions for extensive operations. While the Mafia is not the only organized-crime group, and indeed some say that its influence in organized crime is passing, it has been the group most extensively studied.

The exact nature of the Mafia is a matter of controversy. Some have likened it to a large corporation with a centralized management; others have found a loose confederation of organizations that cooperate with each other; some have found that the cooperation is so minimal that the term "confederation" is improper. The most widely accepted theory is that since 1931 a nationwide confederation has existed for the purposes of engaging in profitable crime, catering to the illegal needs of a number of people, and corrupting law enforcement.

Early History. In the nineteenth century, Irish youth gangs, children of recent immigrants, began to operate in the slums of big eastern cities and then gradually expanded westward with other elements of the population. They used force to overcome poverty and discrimination. Many graduated into more "professional" activities such as extortion and violence against often illegal businesses. With money came power, and that power was both economic and political: economic, for example, when businessmen used gangs to break early worker drives toward unionization; political when machine politicians recruited gangs to ensure election victories. Control over certain areas of city life, such as docks, guaranteed that only fellow Irishmen would predominate in these areas. Many of these bands moved into city jobs. After the Irish, other immigrant groups duplicated this pattern, which constituted the start of organized crime.

Origin of the Mafia.   While these events were occurring in America, the Sicilian Mafia grew. Mafia was originally not the name of a specific organization but rather a code word for a cluster of values and virtues: self-reliance, antipathy toward governmental authority (especially foreign authority), and willingness to combat enemies. Small bands of outcasts who stole cattle and committed extortion but often gave to the poor came to be called "Mafia." A Sicilian Mafioso was a man, often of humble origins, who gained power by cunning and developed a network of dependents. This web of followers (often blood or ritual kin) and others (businessmen for whom favors were performed) created a complex set of reciprocal relationships. When peasants became rebellious, Mafiosi often worked for landlords and provided small armies to discourage radical social change. When formal democracy came to Italy, Mafiosi delivered blocs of voters to candidates in return for later favors. The rise of the Mafia (and its continuing presence today) has often been attributed to the absence of a middle class in Sicily.

The Mafia in the United States.   Although no formal Mafia groups came to the United States in the late nineteenth and early twentieth centuries (2.1 million Italians arrived in the 1900–10 decade alone), a few newly arrived immigrants formed local gangs and committed extortion in certain cities. In 1890, the New Orleans chief of police was murdered in the midst of a grim battle between two Sicilian gangs for domination of the docks. Without real proof the police department and local newspapers attributed this crime to Mafia conspiracy. Eleven Italian prisoners were lynched after a jury acquitted the defendants in the murder trial; the lynchers and their supporters claimed that the jurors had been bribed. This led to the first of many charges that an international Mafia was operating in America. The rumors were renewed in the early twentieth century by an upsurge of "Black Hand" murders, kidnapings, and extortions (generally directed against wealthy or middle-class Italians). The "Black Hand" was a generic name adopted by various gangs and individuals to frighten victims. In reality, the rise of Italian gangs was caused primarily by anti-Italian discrimination, simple social need, and a rudimentary tradition (at least among immigrants from western Sicily and Naples) of secret societies. Southern Italians knew of the older Mafia tradition, and former Neapolitans were familiar with Camorra secret societies; many such immigrants mistrusted government and believed that disputes must be settled within a community. Prior to Prohibition, these gangs remained small, in part because (1) immigrants had arrived individually or in small families; (2) the American emphasis upon individualism clashed with immigrant traditions; and (3) there was insufficient time to permit natural growth.

Prohibition changed the pattern. It presented new opportunities for bootleggers and other illegal merchants and the experience of Italians working in Irish and Jewish gangs helped the Italians to expand existing gang structures. Legitimate and quasilegitimate businessmen (involved in alcohol distribution) were threatened by these gangs, who demanded protection and payoffs. In turn, the businessmen used the gangs to eliminate competition. Gangsters bribed or otherwise rewarded police and other governmental officials. Unions were taken over and their funds gutted by gangsters. In time, gangs merged and coalesced on an areawide basis, and they wielded enough political influence to ensure that law enforcement would break up would-be rivals and competitors. A series of gangland wars settled the question of competition, and predominantly Sicilian forces won. The "balance of power" among these forces (called "families") was established in about 1931 and has largely continued.

Organized Crime Today. Organized crime controls most illegal gambling, loansharking, and importation and wholesaling of heroin; it is heavily involved in cargo theft and bankruptcy fraud as well as labor-union corruption. Its legal enterprises include real-estate companies, restaurants, bars, hotels, trucking companies, private garbage companies, food distribution, and linen-supply businesses—all characterized by formerly heavy competition, service as their "product," and high labor input.

There have been periodic exposes of organized crime, often in sensational settings. In 1939, an ex-mob lawyer described the 1931 creation of alliances. In 1951, a United States Senate committee chaired by Tennessee Senator Estes Kefauver concluded that the Mafia was a "nationwide crime syndicate." In 1957, an apparent high-level mob meeting at Apalachin, New York, was disrupted by the police. It is believed that certain territorial decisions were made and certain murders approved at this gathering, although there is little hard evidence. In 1963, as the Kennedy administration made a major effort to investigate organized crime, another Senate committee, chaired by Senator John McClellan of Arkansas, unveiled Joseph Valachi, a low-level mobster. Valachi called the organization (or organizations) "Cosa Nostra." He described a loose federation of twenty-four families controlling various territories and criminal enterprises subject to the decisions of a nine-to-twelve-member commission that refereed territorial disputes and occasionally dealt with intrafamily disputes that might disrupt the smooth functioning of organized crime. It is now thought that this commission does not represent "families" equally; it is composed of the most powerful individual figures in organized crime, and is itself probably a collection of men of unequal influence.

Each "family" is led by a "boss"; in the larger families an "underboss" relays orders and collects information. Each family has a counselor (*consigliore*) who functions as a political adviser (even resident philosopher) and as a "buffer" who relays orders to working members of the family and re-mits both money and lower-level organizational complaints to the family's upper-management level. Basic decisions are transmitted to the "buffer," who relays them to the lieutenants (*caporegime*), the operating field offi-cers. In large families, lieutenants may have section chiefs who run one or more particular enterprises, and section chiefs (or lieutenants themselves in the smaller families) in turn control the activities of a small group of "but-ton men." These soldiers may be employees of a particular activity. They work on a commission basis, run independent "franchise" operations that share profits with the family, are partners with other soldiers (or even up-per-echelon members of a family), or operate in all these ways simulta-neously in different activities. The soldiers are the lowest-ranking members of the families, and are all Sicilian or Italian (there may be five thousand in the United States). They in turn employ street people: numbers runners, bettakers, narcotics sellers, who are not members of the family and are not protected by it. Soldiers may "license" activities to others. This basic struc-ture might be called "line" (the productive activities of an organization); in contrast are "staff" (support) activities and those of "outsiders": lawyers, accountants, corrupt law enforcers.

Organized crime continually attempts to nullify the law by bribery of public officials and by influencing legislative officials and bodies. Every family employs a corrupter whose duty it is to identify, seek out, and bribe public officials. The corrupter may be a person on any of the previously mentioned levels of the family or may be a supporting staff member or even an outsider.

Organized crime's ability to foil the law stems largely from its partial quasilegitimate role as supplier of goods and services to society. Suppliers may commence as independents but then discover that organized crime wishes to become a partner. Merger solves several problems: Costs are cut; markets are stabilized and extended; and protection from law enforcement is facilitated. Even in the legal side of business, fraud, threats, and occasion-ally force are used to ensure profit. As profits soar, organized crime has spread from blue- to white-collar criminality. The latter may be directly criminal (crime committed by the businessman) or indirect, as when legiti-mate businessmen-gamblers or borrowers from loansharks are pressured to facilitate or even to commit crimes against their companies. Organized crime has now attained, often insidiously, marginal legality in many of its enterprises.

SOCIAL REACTIONS
TO CRIME

Part III

12. Punishment

Just as crime has had a history, so has social reaction to crime. Criminologists have begun to study not only "crime" as evil but also the kinds of societies that define—and, because they define, in a sense, create—that evil. The notion of a general social reaction is itself unique; early societies treated much of what we call crime as merely personal wrongs to another family. The ideas that ordinary crime affects the society and that society has a responsibility to combat it developed along with increasing social complexity and the growth of the nation-state. The predominant theme of most social reaction, at least since the early Middle Ages, has been "punishment." Only recently has the notion of treatment of the offender made some headway. The development of a professional criminal-justice system complicates matters, since the system may merely mirror public attitudes or may shape them or both. While "punishment" has been the predominant theme of modern social reaction, the nature and purposes of the punishment have changed and reflect other social developments.

Criminological punishment may be defined as the deliberate decision of society to inflict pain upon individuals under its jurisdiction for the purpose of some presumed social good. It can be characterized as (1) the infliction of coercion (2) by the state acting through specified agencies (3) in the name of the state and for its defense (4) in accordance with designated and communicated norms that the state and society believe are just, (5) for the purpose of harming only the individual offender, (6) by disadvantaging him. How punishment is interpreted in a given society can perhaps best be demonstrated by a brief history of punishment in Western society.

HISTORY OF PUNISHMENT

As previously mentioned, punishment was not the response to most crime in primitive society. For crimes against the person, considered dangerous because they provoked socially disruptive feuds, first vengeance ("blood feud"), then civil damages were the preferred methods of settlement. For crimes within a family (the common crimes), the penalty was contempt or ridicule. Thus, even the murder of a father was regarded not as a crime against society but as a social wrong evoking disgust. Punishment of disobedient children usually consisted of requiring them to fast. However, crimes such as treason and sacrilege were severely punished, by death or exile, as wrongs against society. Such punishments were regarded as a "cleansing" of the tribe against pollution.

The rise of the nation-state and the centralization of power in kings, who created "courts" to act in their name, radically changed the notion of common crime from that of a personal wrong to a matter of state. Punishment initially took the form of (1) removing the offender (a continuation of the "feud" notion), (2) mutilating him both to impair his ability to commit further crime and to identify him to others as untrustworthy, or (3) imposing a fine upon him to satisfy victims, who received the proceeds. (Eventually, the King kept the fine, and victims of crimes were required to sue in civil courts in order to obtain financial satisfaction.) All these were highly pragmatic—though often cruel—solutions based upon simplistic religious notions of sin.

Only in modern times have societies believed that pain should be inflicted as a "deserved" punishment that will either reform the offender or deter others. As previously noted, the classical school's theories about crime were, in reality, theories of punishment that emphasized man's rational ability to calculate his pleasures and pains and to control his behavior accordingly. Although classicists wished to make punishment less arbitrary, they clearly viewed punishment as pain or as threat of pain. The neo-classicists, in effect, agreed with this theory, but wished to exempt from punishment those offenders who could not reason. Later, the positivists believed that no criminal was responsible for his actions, so that punishment as the infliction of pain was wrong, but "social defense" might require incapacitation (even death) for the socially dangerous.

TYPES OF PUNISHMENT

Different types of punishment have characterized different societies. Theories about crime, its causes, and its frequency affect social policies toward crime; and punishment varies today because modern society is somewhat schizophrenic about its underlying beliefs. Also, all social reactions are part of a society's "national character," which itself may change over time. In the United States, the prevalent, somewhat contradictory beliefs are (1) crime is "evil" and should be punished, so that any proposals for abolition of punishment per se will not be adopted; (2) the state cannot use punishment indiscriminately or establish institutions that might be more effective in fighting crime because government itself is dangerous and its powers are capable of abuse. While crime reduction is a major social goal in Western societies, the means are limited because of certain notions of the value of human liberty. The history of punishment must be read in this context.

The Death Penalty.   The death penalty was most prevalent during the Middle Ages, when it was carried out by techniques including drowning, impaling, boiling in oil, and burning at the stake. Powerful social and economic groups persuaded government to penalize by the ultimate penalty crimes that they believed horrendous. In early days religious groups fostered enactment of the death penalty for crimes against religion, but as ideas of separation of church and state grew, punishment for these crimes eased. Instead, rising aristocracies (based on land ownership) and the bourgeoisie (merchants and early industrialists) sought enactment of the death penalty for many property crimes that offended them. Classical reformers considered the penalty irrational (some thought it inhumane), and in the late nineteenth century they succeeded in drastically limiting the number of crimes for which it could be imposed. Today, eleven countries have entirely abolished capital punishment, while it has been eliminated for nonmilitary crimes in about another twenty-five nations. In many countries where it still exists, it can be imposed only for a small number of crimes. In the United States, the movement to abolish capital punishment has measured its greatest success in limiting the type of crime to which the penalty is applicable.

Indeed, the practice of capital punishment in the United States has varied widely. In some states, few of those eligible for it were even sentenced to death, while in others more than 50 percent of those eligible were sentenced and executed. In all states, in recent years, far fewer eligible offenders have paid the ultimate price. Public attitudes toward the death penalty have varied; after a decline in public approval in the 1960s, an upswing has occurred in recent years (but usually favoring it only for murder). Public opinion, as measured by jury recommendations, indicates that death is acceptable only for murder (for rape, also, until the U.S. Supreme Court outlawed the death penalty for this crime). Public opinion has also modified the manner of execution, each modification favoring the newest short and painless method. Although the southern and southwestern states of the United States contain only a third of the nation's population, they carry out 60 percent or more of the executions.

Torture.   The incidence of corporal punishment (for example, whipping, branding, mutilation) has significantly decreased in the Western world in modern times. The only form of torture that has survived in the United States, whipping in Delaware, is (1) now rarely imposed and (2) probably unconstitutional as a "cruel and unusual punishment."

Shame and Humiliation.   Infliction of social versions of personal shame is always present in punishment but was the primary form of punishment only from the sixteenth to the seventeenth centuries. The pillory, imprisonment in stocks, and other forms of the punishment were used for minor crimes. Physical torture that resembled humiliation (such as branding) passed into disfavor when it was discovered that permanent scarring tended to lead to a life of crime.

Loss of Rights.   The Roman device of deprivation of status and of civil, political, and property rights as penalties for infamous crimes was transmuted during the Middle Ages into the infamous bill of attainder. This imposed loss of property and legal rights, often by a legislative decree rather than after a judicial conviction. (Bills of attainder are specifically forbidden by the United States Constitution.) The infliction of humiliation continues, in attenuated form, in many places: For instance, in most American states, a convicted felon loses the right to vote and to hold public office and perhaps the right to serve on a jury or to be a witness, though these deprivations can be removed in various ways, most often by a gubernatorial order. Conviction also may disqualify an offender from admission to certain state-regulated professions.

Banishment and Transportation.   Banishment, in either the positive (exile) or negative (prohibition against entering certain areas) sense, has long and frequently been practiced. After being abandoned in the Middle Ages, it was revived in England in the late sixteenth century. The founding of the American colonies led to the Transportation Act of 1718, which permitted mass exile of convicted felons both as punishment and to fill labor shortages. Between 1783, when the American Revolution was successfully completed, and 1867, transportation to Australia for serious offenders became English policy. This practice ended because it was too expensive, did not reform the criminal, and was politically opposed by Australia. Other western European countries continue to use this method of punishment. Individual banishment is still employed, even in the United States, where people may be informally told to "leave town" after conviction for minor crimes.

Imprisonment.   Until fairly recent times, imprisonment was rarely used as a penalty. In France and other countries during the Middle Ages, it was occasionally imposed to enforce payment of fines or in lieu of the death penalty. Short-term imprisonment, for purposes of temporary discipline, occurred in Rome and during the Middle Ages. In the fourteenth century certain Italian municipal laws permitted imprisonment for a six-month maximum. In England, during the late thirteenth century it became a popular method of ensuring that fines were paid. The Church employed it more extensively since it had been deprived of its power to inflict the death penalty. Imprisonment was frequently imposed by the Inquisition of the thirteenth century; imprisonment was considered a valuable and effective method of encouraging the sinner's reformation. Galley labor for prisoners, enforced in the sixteenth century, was as much a device to secure otherwise scarce labor as it was a punishment. (Often, the prisoners died within a short period of time.) This practice was abandoned in the eighteenth century, when galleys were found to be inefficient means of transporation in comparison with larger sailing vessels.

In the mid-sixteenth century in England, houses of correction were built (or, like Bridewell, converted from other uses) to house the unemployed or idle. Soon thereafter Parliament required each county to maintain such an establishment; it housed both criminals and vagabonds and other possible objects of public welfare. The goal of Bridewell and similar institutions was to induce vagrants, beggars, expelled students, unlicensed actors, and other disliked vagabonds to learn constructive work. The building had spinning rooms, nail houses, and other facilities, and the products were sold to pay for the institution's upkeep. In some countries, lunatics, orphans, and other unfortunates were housed with criminals.

In Amsterdam, in 1589, separate houses to hold male and female youthful offenders were operated on the labor principle. Soon, what today would be called "incorrigible" children were brought there. Because of its financial success, and the benefits to the children of good food and educational facilities, this form of workhouse spread to certain German cities.

In Italy in the early eighteenth century, the Catholic Church created a "prison" for young people (both criminals and incorrigibles) that combined hard work (textile spinning) with reforming religious education and silence during work.

In 1711, a three-year maximum term of incarceration at the Bridewell-type prisons was fixed by Parliament, but the number of offenses subject to the penalty was greatly increased. In theory, houses of correction were part of the penal system, and workhouses were part of the welfare system; in practice, there was little distinction between the two. Imprisonment was adopted in Germany and other European countries in the late eighteenth century. Jails also came to be extensively used to hold persons awaiting trial.

The prison-reform movement in England was fostered by a pamphlet written by Geoffrey Mynshal in 1618. This attack on prison conditions was followed by others, and in 1699 the Society for the Promotion of Christian Knowledge was established, in part to monitor prisons and recommend reforms. Among the abuses attacked were intermingling of first and seasoned offenders, the operation in prisons of gambling and other vices, and corrupt practices of jailers. Reform proposals included (1) separation of prisoners, by category, (2) useful prison labor, (3) regular religious services, (4) release of hardened criminals only when they showed they could obtain decent employment and posted security for their release, and (5) public campaigns to convince the people that some prisoners were capable of reformation or had reformed. In 1773, Parliament authorized chaplains to serve in the jails. In 1777, John Howard wrote *The State of Prisons in England,* which concluded that prison conditions were disgraceful and fostered crime. Within seventy-five years, a conservative backlash argued that, because of the work of Howard, other reformers, and several reform societies, prisons had become too nonpunitive. In recent times imprisonment has been less favored in Western societies and in the wealthier, more urbanized, and more industrialized American states (for the history of American prisons, see Chapter 20).

Fines and Other Property Penalties.   Fines have been imposed throughout history; they derive from the civil rather than the criminal law. Until the twelfth century in England, they were used to compensate victims. Since then, and increasingly, they have functioned to recompense the state for its trouble in prosecuting offenders. As previously noted, imprisonment started as a means of enforcing payment of fines. In western Europe, fines now constitute a major form of penalty. In the United States, fines for a time became the norm, especially for offenses of an administrative nature or for business-code violations, but in recent times they have been increasingly supplanted by imprisonment. Systems of creating and collecting fines vary; in Scandinavian countries, for example, they are generally adjusted to an individual's ability to pay. In earlier times, fines were collected by confiscation of property. The system of incarceration in lieu of payment has been criticized for its obviously discriminatory treatment of the poor. Fines are penalties that are capable of minute adjustment to exemplify society's reaction to particular crimes; they are easily and economically administered and involve less stigma than any other penalty (an argument both for increasing and decreasing their use). They bring important but not totally damaging suffering on the offender, and, of course, provide income to the state.

Restitution.   When fines became criminal penalties, civil suit for damages had to be instituted by the victim against the offender. Restitution, like fines, has certain powerful supporting arguments: (1) It permits a careful calculation of the value to the victim of the loss caused by the crime (whether that loss is a property one, where the value may be obvious, or a personal one, where money serves as a substitute value, as in civil cases). (2) It permits the offender to do something "constructive" and does not alienate him from society. (3) It permits some certainty and predictability in the penalty structure. (4) It is tailored to and emphasizes the productive capacity of offenders. Some American states in the early nineteenth century actually required that larceny offenders return twice the value of the goods received. It is probable that today restitution is still frequently and informally used by criminals who offer to return the goods to their victims in exchange for refusal to prosecute. Insurance companies may encourage this informal means of "settlement." Frequently, probation is granted upon a promise to fully recompense the victim, especially in minor cases.

NATURE AND JUSTIFICATION OF PUNISHMENT

The previous section described the range of punishments traditionally utilized by various societies. This section will discuss just why societies have resorted to punishment as the appropriate—indeed, necessary—response to crime. Knowledge of history is paramount here, as it is in so many areas of the study of crime. Punishment involves the infliction of pain upon criminals; and even after religious justifications for its imposition became less important, political philosophers attempted to explain or rationalize the need for this drastic measure.

Retribution. The oldest theory of punishment analogizes the right of the society to inflict harm to the right of the individual to obtain revenge, a principle first enunciated in the Code of Hammurabi about 1800 B.C. This form of retribution theory usually does not specify just what will be gained by infliction of harm, although retribution has sometimes been justified on the ground that without it, either individual vengeance ("lynch law") or social retreatism (withdrawal of citizen cooperation with law enforcement) would occur. Both or either would wreck the social peace.

Another justification is that retribution also serves to give the offender his "just deserts," a view of justice in moral philosophy that stresses that each is owed what he deserves because of his moral conduct. This notion, which eschews vengeance, also argues that society should mean what it says in its criminal laws and that offenders should know this in advance (in this sense, it resembles the classical justification for punishment).

General Deterrence. One tenet of the Enlightenment was the notion that punishment should be inflicted to improve the behavior of others. In this view it will simply frighten people into obedience to law. Deterrence is based on the assumption that individuals calculate their activities and rationally choose to minimize their pain. But while all criminal law is based upon deterrence theory, it is difficult to specify the forms of punishments and distinctions among punishments that will actually deter. Many classical reformers argued that deterrence is best achieved not by severity per se or by the severity for different crimes but by certainty—that is, the advance knowledge that offenders will be prosecuted.

Specific Deterrence.   One reaction to the Enlightenment was the idea that it is immoral to punish one person to deter others, since this is "using" that person against his wishes, thereby denying him his basic humanity. Rather, in this view, punishment is justified because pain will "cure" the criminal himself of his antisocial tendencies. A person who experiences pain, it is thought, will act in the future to avoid it.

Social Solidarity.   This theory argues that punishment of some will enhance respect for law and its underlying values among the population at large. Respect for law-abiding values will occur by periodic reaffirmation, a collective reaffirmation, of fundamental values.

Social Defense.   This theory has already been discussed; its positivist origins raise many moral questions (If a person is not truly guilty, should he be punished at all?), and the moral basis of the criminal law is somewhat compromised by the theory's harsh logic, realism, and scientific character.

PUNISHMENT IN PRACTICE

The theories here stated seem absolute. In many respects they are contradictory. They may be based upon certain moral or political theories or even theories of learning, but they are isolated from social reality. It is necessary to turn from the world of ideas to that of social reality to ascertain why few societies have clearly adopted one or the other of these theories. In the abstract world of theory, only the one (or perhaps combination) that reduced the most crime with least expenditure of resources would be adopted. In reality, since no theory (or combination) can be clearly demonstrated to be more efficient than any other (or combination), the social reaction to crime is mixed.

Objections to Theories.   Retribution, until recently, has been considered synonymous with revenge and was disfavored because it offered no means or hope that offenders could be reformed or rehabilitated. The theory of general deterrence has suffered from (1) its inability to measure the amount and nature of any workable deterrent or the relationship of one deterrent to others and (2) its incomplete model of man as rational. General deterrence is at base a psychological theory. It does not account for the fact that crime rates seem independent of the individual psyches of criminals. Specific deterrence is basically a theory of learning that is only partially confirmed by laboratory experiments (apparently, a mild punishment will increase learning but a severe punishment may cause panic). Also, laboratory notions may have little to do with social behavior; for instance, the prevalence of corporal punishment for schoolchildren a century ago did not seem to reduce disobedience. As previously mentioned, social-defense notions are troublesome, as are social-solidarity notions, which imply that society will always need crime to establish and maintain its values.

Social Conditions. Social conditions also drastically qualify social acceptance of theoretical ideals. If the classical emphasis upon certainty of punishment is to be realized in modern democratic society, some fundamental changes, akin to creation of a police state, have to occur. In such a state, the "legitimacy" of institutions imposing punishment will be questioned, as may well be its legal norms. Since the attitude of the offender toward both often determines his or her future criminality, crime might increase. History confirms that severe penalties are mitigated in practice (at least in societies that are democratic or on the verge of democracy).

Societies have often swung between mitigation and severity. In thirteenth-century England, for instance, a criminal could escape to a church and claim sanctuary for forty days (after that he was required to leave the country). Three centuries later, a criminal could be required to live in a specific place, and that location was branded on his thumb. In England, many offenders could claim the "right of clergy"—that is, the right to be tried by ecclesiastical rather than lay courts (the former could not impose the death penalty). The definition of those eligible to claim this right gradually expanded until it encompassed anyone who could read and even lords who could not. In part, the benefit was designed to ensure that upper classes were exempt from punishment. The right to claim clergy was gradually restricted by a reduction of (1) the types of crimes for which it could be invoked and (2) the number of times it could be used. It was finally abolished in the late eighteenth century.

Pardon. The power of pardon also mitigated the most severe effects of punishment. In England, where the power resided in the king, it reflected an interest in exempting upper classes from punishment (as it often still does today). It was extensively used in the eighteenth century to mitigate punishment against even the lower classes, perhaps as a form of propaganda to convince them that upper-class rule was benevolent and deserving of loyalty. The power, originally derived from the theory of absolute monarchy, has passed into the hands of the executive branch of government. It is possessed by the President of the United States (for federal crimes) and by state governors (or other executive officials) as one manifestation of the principle of separation of powers. Today, the pardon power is rarely used, since courts have the authority to mitigate sentences. When used, it often mitigates a se-

vere sentence meted out in opposition to a public opinion that is skeptical of
the justice of either the conviction or the sentence. That public opinion may
take hold at a later date so that some controversial criminals, especially political criminals, of a former time will be forgiven. Other powers resembling
pardon are (1) commutation (reduction) of sentence, also an executive
function, and (2) amnesty, a general forgiveness of a whole category of offender that results in mass releases. Amnesty is often a legislative act; it is
rarely used in the United States, and is most characteristic of the criminal-
justice systems of Spain and Italy.

Unofficial Mitigation. The forms of mitigation described above, of
course, are official, systemic ones. Punishment has also been mitigated by
refusal of juries to "do their duty" when public opinion strongly disfavors a
particular verdict. Both capital punishment in England in the seventeenth
and eighteenth centuries (at least for certain crimes) and torture were
eliminated or reduced to mere symbols by such public opposition. Public (or
secret) reduction of fines, during controversial eras of law enforcement, is
not unknown. "Unofficial" revolts against the system by judges, jurors, even
jailers (allowing privileges or even chances to escape to certain prisoners)
and many mob riots have often historically functioned as means of convey-
ing to a ruling class the discontentment of lower classes.

Punishments may be mitigated for reasons less noble than the ones previously mentioned. While arrests for serious crimes may not be affected by
the offender's race, age, or sex, it seems much more likely that the eventual
sentence will be so influenced. Sex is particularly important. Women are
less likely to be arrested for a crime than men in similar situations, less likely to be convicted, and less likely to receive a jail or prison term. For crimes
with mandatory death penalties, women will probably not be convicted at
all. White-collar crimes are punished less severely than blue-collar counterparts. This distinction may even apply when the same crime has been committed by different classes of people (the evidence is contradictory). Blacks
may be more likely to be apprehended, convicted, and imprisoned than
whites for the same crime, but blacks may be less likely to face the full force
of the criminal-justice system if the crime is intraracial (although this situation is changing).

THE EFFECTIVENESS OF PUNISHMENT

Since no pure theory of punishment has been fully implemented in modern
democratic society and since social reality may qualify the severity of punishment, it is difficult to ascertain effectiveness. On the other hand, the existence of theories of punishment and belief in them by the population, or by
influential segments of it, are themselves part of the social reality of modern

culture. It is probably true that if one has an ideological belief in a theory or system of punishment, he will believe that it is effective or, when faced with contradictory evidence, will argue that the system or theory has apparently failed because it was not truly implemented. Thus, those who believe in retribution will argue that the numerous exceptions to the imposition of certain penalties indicate society's inability or unwillingness to truly keep its promises; the believer in general deterrence will contend that it would work if society did catch criminals quickly and punish them certainly. Even the definition of "effectiveness" will often depend upon the observer's value system. Given these realities, it is difficult for social scientists to ascertain "effectiveness" that has no one meaning, but, of course, these difficulties have not ruled out attempts to do so.

The Death Penalty   Capital punishment has, of course, been justified, on moral grounds; thus, even if it was proven ineffective in reducing the incidence of murder, it would be defended by some. But with increasing public unease about the moral basis of the punishment, it has also been defended on utilitarian grounds. Such arguments range from its effectiveness to a simple claim of lower costs than for imprisonment of murderers. Arguments that capital punishment (1) prevents private or public revenge and (2) deters future would-be murderers often reflect both moral and practical views. Opponents of the death penalty argue that (1) death is no greater deterrent than life imprisonment; (2) its application is so uncertain that any deterrent effect is nullified; (3) uncertainty also diminishes the speed with which it is carried out; (4) it has a "backlash" effect that lowers the morale of other prisoners and custodial staff; and (5) morally, it diminishes respect for life and promotes the sacrifice of life. Finally, it also may be based on factors (such as mistaken identity) that cannot be undone once the penalty has been carried out.

Scientific attempts to determine the deterrent value of capital punishment have taken various forms. One type simply compares murder ratios in states that have abolished capital punishment with those that have retained it; abolitionist states tend to have one third to one half the homicide rate of the latter. Also, abolitionist states have a lower rate of homicides committed by prisoners than have nonabolitionist states. Critics of this analysis point out that homicide is concentrated in certain states (the southern ones, generally), so that mere state-by-state comparisons are invalid. The fact that southern states have both higher murder rates and more capital punishment may mean either that (1) capital punishment is ineffective or even counter-effective or (2) the homicide rates would be even higher in the absence of capital punishment, given the southern "subculture of violence." Some analysts have used nonsouthern and areawide comparisons to demonstrate that different sections of the United States, because of cultural uniformities, have fairly consistent homicide rates, irrespective of the existence of the death penalty. "Cultural areas" studies, which are not bounded by state boundary lines, seem to confirm this view.

Another study method is to compare the number of the homicides that occur immediately after an execution or several executions (on the theory that the deterrent effect, if any, should be greatest at that time). There appears to be no correlation between the imposition and use of the death penalty in well-publicized cases, and the local homicide rate.

It has been statistically shown that American states that have abolished the death penalty do not experience an increase in homicides (at least not a greater increase than in nonabolitionist states). Although eleven abolitionist states did restore capital punishment (usually after a notorious homicide or a string of them), the rise in homicide rates in those states paralleled developments in nonabolitionist states. The same is true of European countries. Countries that have abolished the death penalty tend to have lower homicide rates than those that have not. Thus gross statistical comparisons indicate that there is little warrant for the belief that capital punishment deters.

The death penalty is neither swift nor certain except in time of war, revolution, or other social upheaval. Juries often refuse to convict in death-penalty cases. (The long-standing practice of dismissing jurors who have scruples against the death penalty in capital cases was ended by a U.S. Supreme Court decision in 1966.) Even within a state, local jurisdictions vary considerably in the rate of conviction for capital crimes. Often, for one reason or another, even those convicted are not executed; indeed, the percentage executed in many states may be only 30 to 50 percent of those sentenced to death.

One major study by an economist* argued that gross statistical comparisons are invalid (since they do not account for the variables among states) and that a valid statistical study shows that capital punishment is a substantial deterrent (perhaps each execution deters seven or eight murders). Methodological criticisms of the study (especially those relating to the fact that much of it was calculated at a time when there were few executions in the United States and a startling increase in homicide, perhaps for reasons other than de facto abolition of the death penalty) were met by some further revisions which, the author contended, still supported the theory.

The cost benefits of capital punishment are also not clear. While the cost of imprisonment of murderers may be $10,000 per year ($200,000 for life imprisonment, assuming that 20 years is the normal span served by such prisoners), it is also true that murder trials are expensive and that the addi-

---

* Isaac Ehrlich, "The Deterrent Effect of Capital Punishment: A Question of Life and Death," *American Economic Review*, Vol. 65 (June 1975), pp. 397–417.

tion of the few murderers receiving life terms to general prison costs leads to an insignificant increase of such costs. The cost argument is rarely offered as the sole justification for the death penalty; rather it is annexed to others.

Although proponents of the death penalty deride the notion of error in its imposition, in fact, at times, perhaps as many as 10 to 12 percent of those sentenced to death (or to life imprisonment where that is the maximum penalty) have been found to be wrongfully convicted. Often, of course, the error is discovered before the death sentence is carried out.

Imprisonment. The effectiveness of imprisonment will be determined by which penological goal is selected as the basis for argument. Prisons do succeed in the goal of retribution, since they confine offenders. Imprisonment may generally deter, but it is impossible to ascertain just how much, whether longer prison terms deter more than shorter ones, and whether the entire criminal-justice process (arrest, conviction, and imprisonment) deters more than imprisonment alone. While brutalizing prison conditions may deter more effectively, this effect may be offset by jury reluctance to convict and imprison under such circumstances. Imprisonment might not incapacitate offenders, since it has been estimated that prison crime, ranging from assault to drug use, is enormous. It appears that many prisoners view prison as merely a place to commit further crime. Prison's effect on overall crime rates has been questioned, and one estimate is that incarceration of those apprehended reduces the general rate by only 8 percent. Prisons do not "reform" well, despite the specific deterrence and newer treatment arguments (to be discussed later); many of those now in prison have been there before. Recidivism patterns are high, but how high is in some dispute. The commonly accepted rate is 65 percent, but one study, admittedly only of federal prisoners, showed that after five years only 35 percent were reimprisoned for serious crimes. Some have concluded that the true success of imprisonment is reflected in the fact that many do not recidivate, given the fact that reformation is inherently impossible in a prison setting.

General Effectiveness of Punishment. Apart from the particular effectiveness of particular punishments, serious questions have been raised about the general effectiveness of the punishment response. Some view it as having certain socially negative effects. It tends to isolate individuals and to produce in them a sense of alienation from, rejection of, and hatred for society. In turn, this leads to continuing association with other criminals and an increased emotional and psychological stake in crime. This belief is held not only by labeling theorists but also by many adherents of social-process theories. Punishment may inhibit constructive change, since fear and terror alone cannot change an individual's behavior patterns. And even if long prison sentences for even minor crimes would greatly reduce crime, this solution would simply be dealing with symptoms rather than with causes of social disaffection.

The most profound criticism of punishment derives from at least one of its rationales, social solidarity. The very purpose of a criminal code is to emphasize and re-emphasize social norms that can and should be followed. The object of law—all law, not just criminal law—should be to promote social integration and a sense of shared moral values. It is difficult to reconcile this positive function of law with its negative correlate, punishment. As has been seen, operant learning theory contends that positive reinforcement is the preferred way of inducing behavioral change. However, the criminal law and its administration often provide little such reinforcement. The punitive reaction to crime may instill fear in either the criminal or the society (or both) and thereby undermine the social trust that is the ultimate basis for social interaction.

THE LATENT FUNCTIONS OF PUNISHMENT

Social scientists often find that a given social phenomenon serves both an "apparent" purpose (that which most people believe) and a "latent" one (that which is necessary to the general functioning of society but that is not perceived, or only dimly perceived, by most people). The great disparities in punishment, in both theory and practice, the fact that many forms of punishment linger for centuries though their underlying rationales have changed, and even reform movements in the history of punishment have all been analyzed in an attempt to find out why society "really" wants and needs this response.

Psychoanalytic Views of Culture. Some psychiatrists have argued that society needs criminality to provide scapegoats for general social feelings of hostility that normally are otherwise repressed. One theory argues that a given society's reaction to crime is but a function of its reaction to sexual behavior. Thus, where there are few sexual taboos, there will be little punishment; where sexual misbehavior is frequent and flagrant and some taboos exist, punishment will be frequent; where sexual behavior is repressed, punishment will be hidden.

Another theory holds that aggression is an inherent human trait, and will be expressed either by criminality, by punishment of criminals, or both, unless there are other major outlets for aggression, such as war. Thus, sublimated aggression that is socially condemned becomes channeled into socially accepted patterns of aggression. Here the analogy is to the life cycle: Expression of instinct in society leads to little punishment; repression of instinct in society leads to open and heavy punishment; additional repression then creates "secret" repression behind prison walls.

Psychoanalytic views of society are even harder to sustain than the parallel views about individuals previously discussed. Variations in societies cannot be accounted for unless we accept either the notion that everything is either repression or sublimation or some other ideas that are little more than speculative. "Innate" social aggression is as dubious as "innate" individual aggression.

The Theory of Cultural Consistency   This theory emphasizes the similarity between social views about punishment and other social attitudes. As society turned away from general notions that pain and suffering must be man's natural lot, so did it retreat from the belief that torture of criminals is necessary. The language of criminal justice (especially of retribution theory), that one has a "debt" to pay to society, in this view, reflects classical economics and its emphasis upon notions of contract and rationality. When the state punished through terror, the practice of terror in the criminal-justice system resembled its practice in other social institutions (the home, the school, the prevalent religion), and as those institutions came to rely less on terror, so did the criminal law. Also, as the social distance between the punishers and the punished diminishes, because of modern communications technology, the notion of punishment will be attenuated. Imprisonment as a general reaction to most sorts of crime also exemplifies cultural developments; the Industrial Revolution and certain social developments, such as the rise of the police, in turn created an ability and a willingness to build secure edifices that were also relatively inexpensive.

Political developments may be viewed as either reflections of cultural development or as themselves significant factors in cultural development. The notion that all men are equal derives in part from the American and French revolutions; this belief in turn has influenced criminal justice, in both theory and practice. Enlightenment beliefs about liberty also emphasized the importance of imprisonment as a sufficient deprivation of freedom for the offender. In the view of many reformers, prison itself was the punishment, and additional burdens within prison were unjustified in both political and criminological theory.

The end of slavery may have been stimulated by notions of equality, but it also occurred because of cultural and economic developments. Labor became secular and useful, and free labor is more productive than compelled labor. The utility of labor, in turn, gave rise to the notion that prison labor would aid in reformation of prisoners. When labor is in short supply, the need for prison labor increases and often is accompanied by rationalizations for it. When it is no longer socially needed, as at present, the tendency is to condemn its lack of practical value and to opt for prisoners' confinement and incapacitation rather than work. Also, changes in punishment theory and practice may reflect, at least in part, a change in the ideas and interests of dominant social and economic classes (Marxists would argue that this factor accounts for most, if not all, changes).

The Theory of Social Organization. This theory discerns less punitive reaction in homogeneous societies and more punishment in heterogeneous ones. Social disorganization, it is argued, will occur in the latter as various social groups come into conflict. In times of revolution, punishment increases as social homogeneity is threatened. Afterward, when solidarity is restored, punishment decreases in both severity and frequency.

Social-Structure Theories. These theories attempt to show that social reactions to crime mirror variations in social structure. One theory stresses the congruence of punishment with economic conditions. A punitive reaction will be strongest when there is an abundance of labor; a lack of cheap labor generally will ameliorate punishments. The nature of the labor market will also determine the type of punishment: For example, galleys replaced corporal punishment in maritime nations, and the workhouse was established because of the need for labor. Solitary confinement declined when prison labor became socially necessary. The theory is essentially an "elitist," at times a Marxist, one, which finds that upper classes will vary the punishments imposed on lower classes in accordance with upper-class needs and perceptions. Crime and property are linked, so that when there is a labor surplus, punishment becomes heavier. Thus, general economic conditions determine both the crime rate and the nature of society's (or its elitist element's) response. Part of the theory is confirmed by known data. As previously noted, economic conditions do affect prison rates.

Another theory relates variations in punishment to the presence of a middle class, a class that is particularly indignant about crime. This contention argues that middle-class people are frustrated because they are repressed, and this feeling generates the punitive response. It is a social-psychological variant of the psychoanalytic theory of punishment. Whether or not the explanation is true, the theory correlates with the known tendency of middle-class people to be more punitive than others. Indeed, recent research has demonstrated that rising urban middle-class businessmen and professionals supported the Prohibition movement, once thought to be the province of rural religious groups. It appears that the middle class, like other social classes, seeks to vindicate its perceptions and lifestyle by trying to universalize them, in part by encouraging the poor to be more upstanding, in part by compelling them to be so.

Another social-structure theory emphasizes the "division of labor" in complex societies (it ties in with at least one theory of legal development; see p. 17). As formulated by French sociologist Emile Durkheim, the argument is that, in general, conduct offensive to the collective conscience of society is more seriously punished than is conduct that offends only one person or a particular social segment. "Mechanical solidarity" is the term Durkheim used to describe the fostering of social values by a general similarity of attitudes. When, because of the division of labor, this changes to another form, "organic solidarity," society seeks to restore social balance rather than to express its collective conscience by punishment. Punishment will thereby diminish, in both theory and fact. This highly abstract theory overlooks empirical evidence that older societies also sought to redress the social balance and that severity of punishment often characterizes modern, highly labor-divided, societies.

13. Nonpunitive Responses

Either for the previously mentioned reasons or for other reasons, a significant movement away from punitive responses to crime occurred in the twentieth century. Criminologists and other experts contributed to this trend by studying the conditions which cause or correlate with crime. Many strategies have evolved, ranging from individual treatment of criminals to changing the environment, and even the definition of crime, as in the juvenile-justice movement. Whether the focus is on the individual or the society, the emphasis is upon improving conditions rather than punishing the offender. Often this emphasis precludes or limits the ability of society to designate offenders as criminals. This approach had some effect during the 1960s and early 1970s, when there was a trend away from imprisonment in the United States and western Europe. The number of prisoners in American penal institutions declined from about 225,000 to about 200,000. Probation and community treatment became the norms for disposition of all but the most incorrigible offenders. Also, since many prisoners were already in minimal-security facilities or in work-study programs that enabled them to enter the community, a number of minimum-security facilities, juvenile camps, and other institutions were closed. In Massachusetts, for instance, all juvenile institutions were closed. Since recidivism rates apparently did not rise, various public groups called for a moratorium on the construction of new prisons. In the mid-1970s a backlash set in; the prison population rapidly increased to almost 300,000, in part because of the swelling numbers of people in crime-prone ages.

It has been argued that (1) ambitious attempts to reconstruct society are unrealistic so that present social phenomena should be taken as a given and, as such, protected, and (2) it is unfair to misinform offenders that they are being rehabilitated when they are only being punished. Because many treatments failed, humanitarian notions were in disarray. Rehabilitation notions declined in popularity. The number of dangerous offenders grew; the unemployment rate rose (this, it will be remembered, correlates with imprisonment rates); and the punishment rationale (often couched in the same terms as the historical arguments previously discussed) largely replaced the treatment one.

But, as usual, society continued to have mixed reactions to crime. Criminologists studied the apparently successful treatment programs to ascertain why they seemed to work. The juvenile-court and juvenile-justice models still exist, and the "medical model" of psychological difficulty has not been displaced by punitive notions. Other movements, such as attempts to replicate the low crime rates of preliterate societies by encouraging greater social (and even economic) integration (perhaps by a redistribution of wealth), also continued.

ARGUMENTS FOR AND AGAINST PUNISHMENT

The argument that nonpunitive reactions either stimulated the crime wave of the 1960s or failed to stem it can be refuted by the counterproposition that failure to fully implement nonpunitive reactions caused the upsurge in crime. Those who would return to greater punitiveness have not proved that their policies would result in greater deterrence. Many professionals have argued that development of positive attitudes toward society is both more moral and more efficient than a system that emphasizes short-term negative sanctions. Certainly the argument that the legal system substitutes for private or public vengeance is simply not applicable to most crimes. The desire for vengeance itself is not unaffected by prevalent social notions of justice, and these notions often translate into social forms that need not be punitive. Since complaints for many crimes are instituted not by victims or relatives seeking vengeance but by law-enforcement personnel, personal feelings may be minimal. There is some evidence that the punishment ethic divides the public into "pro" and "con" attitudes toward offenders so that the punitive model does not contribute to involvement by more people to help the accused. The "social solidarity" argument does not take into account the following factors: (1) Solidarity may not be very strong, even prior to the commission of a crime; (2) not all crime upsets the social balance; and (3) infliction of punishment usually does not restore a social equilibrium (the matter is handled by agencies such as the police and courts and there are few, if any, occasions when the community feels vindicated by punishment).

Social solidarity and punishment are said to be related because disapproval of criminal acts through punishment helps to strengthen community feelings that the law and the criminal-justice system are both right and effective. However, this means that punishment is primarily symbolic. It need not be retributory or even deterrent, as conventionally understood. In addition, democratic political theory emphasizes the notion that the individual is to be accorded as much freedom as possible and that political and social arrangements must ensure that he is free to choose between obeying the law and disobeying it, and paying the consequences. Thus, theories of deterrence per se are incompatible with human liberty because they degrade humans into little more than automatons.

In democratic theory, all individuals are entitled to be treated fairly. Some have argued that this principle requires that judges in passing individual sentences assess the degree of true harm committed by the offender as well as his true culpability (in part arising from his socioeconomic position). This approach would tie together particular notions of criminal justice with broader ones of social justice. If this theory is true, then except for hardcore criminals, imprisonment should function only to demonstrate that (1) the individual has offended social norms and (2) he is being temporarily rejected from society for that reason. The old notion of restitution is also compatible with a restructuring of the punishment response. When in modern society the state was seen as the "victim" of crime, the interests of the individual harmed receded; if he could, he would obtain compensation in civil proceedings. Any new scheme of restitution should take into account the harm to society as well as the victim *and* an assessment of society's responsibility for individual criminality. Thus, crime would be viewed both from the standpoint of the harm caused by the offender and of the harm caused the offender by society.

TECHNIQUES OF TREATMENT

Since treatment has some strong justifications at least in individual cases, and since it will undoubtedly continue as a major element in criminology, its techniques should be understood.

Treatment of the Offender as a Unique Individual.   The belief that each offender is unique was stimulated by positivist reactions to a system that punished similar crimes similarly. Programs for dealing with individual offenders on the basis of their supposed personal psychiatric needs were subsequently developed.

At first, the clinical model was popular. Each criminal was thought to be sick and in need of some therapy, ranging from improvement of work habits to deeper psychoanalysis. Psychological illnesses, like medical ones, could be attributed to various causes. This view had two consequences: (1) an assumption of power by "helpers" over the offender, which often resulted in longer incarceration than would have been true in purely punitive settings, and (2) rehabilitation efforts centered on the individual offender.

Group Therapy.   Over time, a supplementary theory developed that held that the individual's interaction with a group caused criminality. In this view the individual's associational patterns had to be changed to achieve cure. The need then became one of modification of these group relations, and often haphazard correctional efforts to achieve such modification were undertaken. Group psychotherapy was designed to change the group. Among the techniques of group psychotherapy were (1) association of criminals with noncriminal peers to whom they "related," because of cultural, ethnic, and social similarities; (2) placement of the offender into a noncriminal group, in which he could retain or enhance his status (this often involved attempts to transform criminal skills into approved noncriminal counterparts); (3) a careful choice of group to capitalize upon the personal interests of the offender, often in a context where he would help other offenders and, of course, himself; and (4) bringing the criminal into contact with "high prestige" others. The most optimistic part of the theory stresses that criminals can be changed only by the help of the group, to which at some point the offender will give his loyalty. Rewards within and from the group must be based on evidence of change from criminal to anticriminal patterns.

Such intensive analysis in a group context did not guarantee either change or that society's acceptance of the "reformed" offender as truly changed. Also, this method did not deal with the underlying personal, or even cultural and social, conditions that may have caused criminality.

Recent Individual Therapies.   There has been a recent resurgence of individual treatment, in part because groups did not seem to work or were considered too expensive and time-consuming. Various forms of therapy, some adapted from outside the offender context, became popular.

Client-centered therapy (associated with the teachings of Dr. Carl Rogers) aimed at getting prisoners to understand their real problems by the analyst's clarification to them of what they were really saying. Reality therapy, developed by psychiatrist William Glasser, is based on the belief that all individuals need to give and receive love and to feel important to others. Therapy shows the patient just what obstacles he is presenting to attainment of these needs. The therapist becomes an active role model of reality and seeks to help the patient become "responsible" by stressing the need to adjust to reality and to meet others' needs as means of achieving self-growth. The analyst concentrates not upon the past but upon present concrete behavior and analyzes the offender's conduct from that perspective (often such analysis occurs in group therapy, which, when conducted solely or primarily among inmates, is a form of "reality therapy").

Behavior modification, a subject of increasing experimentation in prisons, rejects the notion of the importance of the unconscious and argues that behavior can be changed. This theory, based on learning theory, seeks to substitute acceptable for unacceptable learning. Since, according to B. F. Skinner (see p. 74), behavior can be modified by making its consequences either pleasant or unpleasant, control over such consequences will in turn lead to control over behavior. "Rewards" for good behavior are worked out in a specific program tailored to the individual offender's needs. This philosophy is not far removed from the classical model of man.

Use of Drugs. At times behavior modification goes beyond learning and seeks to cause physiological change by use of mind-altering drugs, psychosurgery, chemotherapy, and electrode implantation. Practices such as injecting drugs (for example, thorazine, apomorphine, and prolixin) that may have dangerous side effects have been severely criticized. Although many facilities use these drugs only with the "informed consent" of the patient-offender, it has been argued that such "consent" is rarely truly voluntary and often not informed.

BARRIERS TO EFFECTIVE TREATMENT

The goals of treatment may be undermined, perhaps fatally, by the dual nature of the criminal law and modern criminal justice: an insistence upon punishment combined with an occasional impulse to treat offenders as individuals. Punishment always lurks in the background of any treatment program, and to that extent tends to undermine it. While the ambivalence between punishment and treatment may occasionally contribute to innovation, the conflict more often leads to organizations and practices that function effectively to impose punishment rather than to provide treatment. Most criminal-justice organizations are designed to emphasize punitive and custodial functions, and the organizational hierarchy and mentality often constitute formidable obstacles both to change and to realization of treatment goals. Since many criminal-justice personnel are managers with a great deal of authority and discretion rather than merely employees taking orders, resistance to "change from above" may be strong. Reluctant cooperation in such change rather than the prospect of positive acceptance is the reality; that cooperation must be achieved, not by mandatory "orders" (which, in any event, cannot be carried out over resistance) but by persuasion, and persuasion often fails. Many outside (and some inside) groups influence the criminal-justice system; and these groups may be resistant to change, especially when change threatens their own values, interests, or prerogatives. Often, upper-level criminal-justice managers must respond to the power and influence of these entrenched groups. (From above, they may be responsible for budgets; from below, they may present a potential for chaos and insubordination.) Thus, for various reasons little innovation has come from within the criminal-justice system itself; there has been almost no fundamental innovation, especially in the direction of enhancing treatment objectives.

Because of prisoner perception that "treatment" and "rehabilitation" are merely punishments in other guises and because of resistance to treatment by custodial personnel, many have argued that treatment should occur only if it is truly voluntary and should not be the basis for any decision to parole or otherwise release a prisoner before his term has expired. Thus it has been argued that "rehabilitation" has not necessarily failed but rather that tying rehabilitation to expectations of early release is to blame for its ineffectiveness. For those prisoners who wish to be treated or educated, such programs should be kept available.

THE CRIMINAL-JUSTICE SYSTEM

Part IV

14. The Nature of the Criminal-Justice System

The preceding chapter emphasized the actual role of the offender and the criminal-justice system. We now turn to that system, one that interprets the law for, and applies it to, presumed offenders and that, perhaps more importantly, interprets offenders for the rest of society.

Criminologists in recent times have devoted as much, if not more, attention to the criminal-justice system than to either crime or social reaction to crime for several reasons. Police statistics, the conventional measurements of crime, cannot be understood without an understanding of the realities of the police function in modern society, especially in the United States. In a sense, the police "create" crime and the social climate about crime by their dual and often conflicting role of crime recorders and crime fighters. "Labeling" theories and other social-interactionist theories suggest that police treatment of individuals stimulate criminal-career patterns for some, perhaps many. Also, the activities of criminal-justice agencies may well lead to the creation of new laws and hence to new crime, new criminality, and new groups of people who habitually engage in once legal but now outlawed conduct subject to the law. For these and other reasons, the subjects of crime and of the criminal-justice system are not separate; they constantly interweave with each other.

A CASE STUDY: MARIJUANA

A brief history of the criminalization process for possession and sale of marijuana will vividly demonstrate that law-enforcement agencies may play a significant role not only in the creation of law but also in influencing public opinion to accept the legitimacy of the law and even to enact more law on the subject. This situation has been demonstrated in relation to banning of opiates, but most Americans (perhaps because of inertia or successful propaganda) have come to accept the precepts of modern legal reactions against opiates. Marijuana is, of course, a much more debated topic, and its criminalization provides an excellent case study of the role of law enforcement when public opinion may be indifferent, ambivalent, or hostile.

Throughout history, *Cannabis sativa,* an Indian hemp plant, has had a multiplicity of uses, including the making of rope and cloth, oil, and bird-food. It can grow easily and wildly almost anywhere in the world. A chemical resin of the female plant flowers, THC (tetrahydrocannabinols) is a mild hallucinogen. In highly concentrated form, the substance is called hashish; its milder, less concentrated form is called marijuana. Although marijuana is commonly thought to slow work performance and physical reactions, some research has indicated that it may actually increase the pace of work. Hallucinogenic effects vary according to the receptivity and perceptions of the smoker and his group, and there are no withdrawal symptoms. Although some claims have been made that long-term deterioration occurs from heavy use of hashish, these claims have not been verified and, even if true, cannot shed light on the American experience with much milder and usually less heavily used marijuana.

Marijuana use in the United States in the early twentieth century was largely confined to poor slum blacks and Mexican Americans. Jazz musicians and some artists also adopted it to enable them to relax. In the 1920s, some southern states banned it, probably because local elites perceived it as a stimulant to disorderly behavior among the poor. At first, the federal Bureau of Narcotics viewed it as a minor problem worthy of state but not federal regulation. By 1937, the Bureau was engaged in a major crusade to (1) equate marijuana with opiates; (2) characterize marijuana use as leading to murder and suicide (later this changed to the argument that marijuana was the forerunner of opiate use); and (3) persuade state legislatures to criminalize possession and use of the hallucinogen. In 1937, the Bureau persuaded Congress to pass the Marijuana Tax Act and to provide stringent penalties for violations, thus bringing the subject within the Bureau's law-enforcement jurisdiction on the theory that the federal power to tax could be used to outlaw the substance. Some scholars have maintained that Harry J. Anslinger, head of the Bureau of Narcotics (like J. Edgar Hoover of the FBI), was a "moral entrepreneur" who used his bureaucratic position, prestige, and authority to wage a crusade, while others have seen the antimarijuana drive as inspired by the internal needs of the Bureau of Narcotics, especially the need to maintain its financial position. (Congress had cut the Bureau's budget prior to 1937 because Anslinger maintained that the agency had virtually abolished opiate addiction in the United States.) The 1951 Boggs Act, the 1956 Narcotics Control Act, and most state laws continued to analogize marijuana to opiates, and penalties for possession and sale of marijuana were increased. Even the 1970 Controlled Substances Act equated the two. However, the Drug Enforcement Administration (formerly called the Bureau of Narcotics and Dangerous Drugs) has abandoned that characterization. Evidence mounted rapidly that (1) most marijuana smokers do not progress to heavier drugs (just as most juvenile delinquents do not become adult criminals); (2) marijuana is not addicting; (3) whatever progression that occurs is attributable to the fact that the same slum dealers sell both items (in the case of heroin, often to people who have already committed crime); and (4) progression greatly depends upon the social circles within which the marijuana user circulates. Any progression argument lost all validity in the 1970s when marijuana use spread far more rapidly than did use of opiates and when many white middle-class youths adopted the hallucinogen as the relaxant of choice. Progression is then not the inevitable result of continuing drug use but only of the fact that the social milieu fostering use of one substance may foster use of another.

However, while previous "progression" theories have been discredited, there is some evidence that habitual use of marijuana, especially by the very young, by pregnant women, and by persons with heart and respiratory ailments may have both short- and long-term deleterious health consequences. This is especially true of newer varieties of the hallucinogen, which are more powerful than earlier ones. The evidence for short-term effects, especially on motor skills (such as driving), is fairly conclusive, while the evidence of effect upon genetic normality, as a potential cause of cancer, and other long-term health problems is not yet well established.

Although many affluent youths also tried LSD, this product was quickly abandoned because of publicity about its harmful effects and because marijuana was milder, less frightening, more readily available, and cheaper. As more high-school and college students smoked marijuana and as older people began to share youth's concerns about the values in American society, penalties for marijuana possession began to decline. In 1973, Oregon became the first state to decriminalize (not legalize) the possession of small amounts for obviously personal use. At least ten states followed Oregon's practice of imposing a small "civil" fine for possession for personal use. The reform movement grew after "harassment" arrests by the police of youngsters led to increasing cynicism about the law, and after outrageous police practices (often involving violations of constitutional rights or entrapment) had inflamed the situation. States that have decriminalized marijuana possession have experienced no great increase in use, and it is conceivable that partial legalization (perhaps in the form of licensing sales, as occurred with alcohol after Prohibition ended) will soon occur.

The history of marijuana laws thus indicates that criminal-justice-agency needs may create crimes and that their practices may lead to reform movements. These are but two of the many ways in which crime and the criminal-justice system are related.

THE WORKINGS OF THE SYSTEM

In addition to previously mentioned reasons, social scientists study the criminal-justice system in order to understand how criminal-justice agencies actually function, both as bureaucratic structures and as "political" groups that must interact with each other and with the public at large.

In essence, there is no criminal-justice "system," but rather a series of fragmented agencies established for different purposes, having different philosophies, and responsible to different branches of government. There is no central control agency that can give directions to the "system." Indeed, such an agency would violate the United States Constitution and state constitutions. The social scientist, who is interested in the informal as well as the formal functioning of organizations, is delighted to study various relatively independent organizations, each of which is characterized by (or beset with) internal struggles to capture the organization and to shape its goals. Quite often, as will be seen, the formal duties of each organization become subordinated to bureaucratic and political needs of the organization or of dominant members of the organization.

Legally (though not necessarily in terms of actual functioning), the criminal-justice system can be divided into (1) the police, an agency of the executive branch of government whose duty is to enforce the law; (2) the prosecutor, another executive official whose duty is to ensure justice by prosecuting those believed to be guilty of crime and also by not prosecuting those against whom there is insufficient evidence of crime; (3) the judiciary, members of the judicial branch of government whose duty it is to determine whether or not the evidence presented in court is sufficient to warrant conviction (often this power is given to a jury, which, in essence, becomes a part of the judicial branch of government); and (4) the correctional authorities who administer jails, prisons, and other facilities to hold those convicted or awaiting trial; these correctional authorities are also members of the executive branch of government. In addition, there are numerous functionaries who provide support services (for example, court clerks, probation officers, and bail bondsmen) and whose decisions have a major impact on the processing of criminal suspects. Indeed, there are even personnel such as defense lawyers who are theoretically assigned to play an adversary role in the system. All these officials have broad authority and discretionary power. All play roles within the system, though often not the roles to which the system theoretically assigns them. Such role-playing is studied by social scientists.

Finally, the social scientist has come to know that the criminal-justice system is a vast funnel through which many people enter, but few emerge. At various points the funnel narrows and more and more cases are shuffled out of the system (or simply lost) as the consequences for those charged with crime become more significant. The social scientist wishes to study and to try to ascertain the policies, practices, and "social laws" of conduct that operate within the criminal-justice system.

While the criminal-justice system operates directly on adults (and on some juveniles who are treated as adults), much activity that is significant for the lives of juveniles and their potential criminal or delinquent careers occurs in the juvenile-justice system. A great deal of crime is treated as delinquency; criminal careers often commence with delinquency; and treatment of the juvenile by agents of the state may be a significant factor in the child's later life. A fuller understanding of crime can be achieved only by paying sufficient attention to this system, which is truly part of the criminal-justice system, though often not designated as such.

15. The Police

An individual's first contact with the criminal-justice system usually occurs through the police. Police have the strategic discretion to define acts that they see or that are reported to them as criminal or probably criminal. They may overlook some criminal conduct or interpret a given technically criminal activity as noncriminal and thereby eliminate a particular person from further contact with the system. A decision to take someone into custody may well commence the labeling process by which society (and the individual himself) begin to define and categorize a person as a criminal. In contrast, contact with the police may well stimulate an individual's strengthened resolve to lead a law-abiding life. The police are also significant because it is their activities and reputation that define, for many people, the "meaning" of the law. The police are quite simply the law's most visible representatives, and it has been said that the future of society depends in large part upon the honesty and efficiency with which they carry out their functions. In many societies the growth of the police has paralleled (or perhaps caused) a reduction in the severity of punishment, and the police have proved to be more effective in fighting crime than a former system of severe penalties without an organized police.

AMERICAN POLICE HISTORY

In early America, the first law-enforcement official was the constable, a derivation from English practice. Serving in the constabulary was considered an obligation of citizenship, and constables were unpaid. Much of their time was spent providing services to people—a continuing attribute of modern police forces—rather than merely enforcing the laws. Indeed, their early function consisted not so much in law enforcement as in order maintenance (prevention of breaches of the peace or, more often, calling attention to disorder). In both England and the United States, the early police became figures of ridicule, since they often avoided altercations with the rebellious elements, including youths, in the society. In theory, the police were to function as (1) general reporters of unusual activities and (2) upholders of the general welfare and public order. Their reputation was not high in either capacity. Resistance to constabulary service, however, became so widespread that as early as 1695 fines were imposed for refusal to serve.

By 1800, the constabulary had become quasiprofessionalized, at least in large cities, and constables were paid. Commencing with New York City in 1845 (inspired by the formation of the Metropolitan Police in London sixteen years earlier), the constabulary system was transformed into a modern police force with twenty-four-hour responsibilities. During the 1845–70 period, cities were growing rapidly; immigrants were pouring in; living accommodations became overcrowded; prosperity, and a concern for protection of property, were spreading. But most critically, the city was rapidly becoming divided into different and often hostile social and economic classes. In the United States, the major response to social tensions and clashes caused by these events took the form of creation of the police. Also in the United States, unlike England (where lower-class distrust of the police led to a conscious decision to present this authority as impartial, unaffiliated with any class, and somewhat militaristic), the police were regarded with suspicion by the lower and working classes. In most large cities, in response, they reacted by becoming affiliated with local political machines. The early police function in both England and large American cities consisted in immediate apprehension of criminals and upholding public order.

In the 1850s, a separate police force of detectives whose duties were not to enforce laws but to recover stolen property developed in American cities. They often worked for fees or a portion of the property recovered, or they corruptly agreed with criminals to return only a part of the stolen goods and to share in the remainder. Gradually, detectives were merged with regular police forces.

The police acquired jurisdiction in fragments; various police forces were created whenever new laws were passed to regulate new industries and trades serving the public. There were special police forces supervising butchers, bakers, hack drivers, elections, and liquor distribution. Eventually these police became absorbed either into regular police forces or into other municipal regulatory agencies. Still, the police were called upon to perform numerous regulatory and service functions (including provision of shelter to the homeless), a characteristic of many police forces today.

American policing became unique because of its extreme localism and close ties to political machines. Selection, assignment, and promotion were political prizes to be contested for. Usually large cities controlled by the Democratic Party attempted to continue local policing while Republican-dominated state legislatures tried to create large metropolitan forces with state-appointed commissioners. At the end of the nineteenth century, both police managers and patrolmen sought in various ways to take the police out of politics, and this effort was abetted by the virtually unanimous adoption of civil-service selection procedures at the beginning of the twentieth century.

Early American police antipathy toward uniforms (considered "badges of servitude") vanished after the Civil War. Wartime and postwartime riots resulted in transformation of the police into a trained, semimilitary, disciplined force (especially the newly established state police units in Pennsylvania and New Jersey) for combating riots. Thus the police came to act as a buffer between mobs and elites, and much social animus was directed away from elites to the police. Police enforcement of morals laws (for example, regarding alcohol distribution, gambling, and brothel keeping), especially when directed by political elites who feared lower-class vices and depravity, led to more public animosity. This feeling in turn increased the internal police drive to become free of political alliances. In the early twentieth century, the movement took the form of police claims to "professionalism"— that is, that they were highly skilled workers with complex social tasks to perform. At times, these claims coincided with objectives of reform groups, so that the police did largely succeed in achieving real freedom from political oversight and influence (except that reform proposals for tenure for chiefs rarely succeeded, and their appointments and dismissals continued to be politically influenced).

CONTEMPORARY POLICE FORCES

The police today, as in the past, are employees of the state (any legal unit of government) who are responsible for maintenance of law and public order and enforcement of the criminal law. Both the federal government and the state governments maintain police forces; also, subunits of government, counties, cities, towns, and villages are empowered to maintain such forces. There are approximately 40,000 police forces employing perhaps 400,000 to 450,000 sworn police officials and more than 100,000 support ("civilian") personnel. Approximately 75 percent of these agencies have 5 or fewer employees; but in cities and large towns, there are on average 2.5 policemen for each 1,000 residents. About 40,000 policemen work for a state government directly, and almost that number are employed by the federal government (many with less than full law-enforcement powers).

Private security police personnel, including private detectives, number perhaps more than 300,000, and such forces are growing much more rapidly than public agencies. (Many private firms are not licensed by the states.)

Private firms provide security guards for large companies and local businesses under contract. The guards are often (1) untrained or ill-trained, (2) either very young or quite old (often retired policemen), and (3) armed, though often ill-trained or untrained in the use of firearms.

The functions of private and public police are not always clearly separated, since public police frequently protect private property (on patrol or on assignment to civic or sports arenas during public events). The two types of agencies work with each other, both legally and illegally, in matters such as furnishing records, cooperating on investigations, and control over and response to burglar-alarm systems and operations. At times, such cooperation may seriously impair constitutional rights protected against public police activity: For instance, private "illegal" searches do not violate the Constitution, so there is temptation to use private guards to obtain evidence not otherwise legally available to the police.

Quasipolice agencies have some police power but not the general authority possessed by what most of us think of as the "average" policeman. Factory inspectors, building inspectors, and food and health inspectors are among the vast regulatory apparatus of modern government with such power. Excluding employees of firms that manufacture police and security equipment, there are more than one million people in the United States in the "police, inspection, and security" business. The growth of public and private police personnel has exceeded that of the population at large, and at least eight billion dollars each year is spent on the public police alone. It may well be that 1 percent of our gross national product is spent on domestic police service.

THE POLICE FUNCTION

In theory, the police are required to function solely within the boundaries set by their legal authority, and they are often blamed for exceeding that authority. Historically, as we have seen, their authority has included maintenance of public order (and legal definitions of public order tend to be hazy), so that the general boundaries of their function—even under law—are vague. Their mandate is to enforce the law, but the police have the authority to determine (1) whether a given law has been (or probably has been) violated and (2) whether to deal with the offender by means short of arrest. There are few formal guidelines to determine whether and when a disposition other than arrest (warning, for instance) is appropriate. This discretion has bothered many, especially when, as is often true, it is exercised against minority groups. (The police contend that minority groups commit more crimes so that it is not bias, but experience, that is the basis for arrest decisions in these cases.) Although some have argued that discretion could be controlled more closely by policy and practice directions from the central police authority, much discretion is and will continue to be unavoidable. However, the dangers of discretion are real: arbitrariness, corruption, and the always present possible injustice of selective enforcement of the law.

Although U.S. Supreme Court decisions have limited, if not completely eliminated, the "third degree" and other coerced confession methods, police may use "excessive force" during the arrest and subsequent processes (the major consequence will be the possibility of a lawsuit by the victim). Brutality is commonly justified by the police when (1) they feel they have been the victims of disrespect and (2) information may be obtained, not for the purposes of prosecuting the individual who is compelled to furnish the information.

Many encounters with the police fall short of physical brutality and involve instead what might be called "psychological brutality." Practices such as (1) police abuse (especially verbal abuse), (2) threatening displays of firearms or other weapons, (3) orders to move on, and (4) threats of force fall when unwarranted into the broad category of police abuse. In one study, it was found that police abuse of whites was greater than that directed against blacks, and that the most abuse was committed against lower-class people. While police abuse may alienate the public (or at least some segments of it), it is often encouraged by the crime-fearing citizenry (or, again, some segments of it).

As previously noted, lower-level personnel in the criminal-justice system, especially in the police part of it, are not really controlled by superiors. Rather, the lower the level of function, generally the greater the discretion available to the functionary. Often, directions from above conflict with other mandates also insisted upon by superiors. While certain relatively unimportant matters, such as dress and appearance, can be readily controlled from above, there is little that can be done about the manner in which officers perform their duties. Although the police are admonished to enforce the law and catch criminals, most policemen will display considerable discretion in even defining conduct they observe as criminal. Even attempts to "structure" discretion by announcements, either public or in internal departmental directives, about selective enforcement of the law may be fruitless. Such announcements may (1) reflect superior officers' lack of knowledge about street conditions (at least those conditions that policemen believe are important) and (2) result in little more than more frequent punishment. Further restriction of police discretion may result in greater injustice toward economic or racial or politically weak minorities. Perhaps it would mean even more arrests of the poor (especially for vague "public order" crimes) in middle-class communities or in communities with middle-class mores. Middle-class people often view the poor as disorganized and unstable, even dangerous, and there is some evidence that present police practices may mitigate the consequences of these attitudes as well as often reinforce them.

The police deal not only with crime but also with public order. Traffic control, licensing of taxis, such public activities as parades and demonstrations, and emergency functions all impinge upon the law-enforcement role. As licensing and inspection of many activities increase, so police inefficiency and discretion grow. Serious proposals to create other agencies to perform these public-order functions (as noted earlier, supported by past precedent) have been made.

The police function is also overwhelmed by the nature of modern urban life and modern crime, along with technological developments that require large staffs and expensive equipment. This situation results in establishment of "specialized units," the withdrawal of men on street patrol, the creation within police departments of "fiefdoms" (loyal not to department goals but to subgoals of these new units), and diminution of control by the police commissioner. Often, the difficulties of orderly police work are increased by public crusades (perhaps media-inspired) to catch particular criminals or perpetrators of heinous or dangerous crimes. Mayors and other public officials may put pressure (politically oriented or reflections of public or media concern) upon vulnerable police chiefs who, as noted, are not, in the United States, regarded as independent professionals.

POLICE ARREST

The law of arrest reflects the difficulties of the police function. Arrest warrants, signed by judges after the police have sworn to facts sufficient to indicate "probable cause" to believe that the named individual has committed a crime, is the preferred legal method, but such warrants are rare. More often, police are empowered to arrest without warrants (1) in felony cases, when there is probable cause to believe that the individual has committed a crime, and (2) in misdemeanor cases, when the violation is committed in the presence of the officer. Some states have broadened the latitude of police in the latter situation. Private persons may arrest without a warrant (citizen's arrest), though they have less latitude than that possessed by a police officer. Private persons cannot generally arrest for misdemeanors, although some states now permit such arrests for misdemeanors that (1) involve breach of the peace and (2) occur in the presence of the arresting party. Arrests on suspicion, either by private persons or the police, are illegal, though not infrequent. Taking a person "downtown" for questioning without his consent cannot be a "cover" for an otherwise illegal arrest; and all confessions or other admissions by the person (even if he has been properly cautioned) are not admissible as evidence. Dragnet and other sweeping arrest procedures serve several functions, including gathering evidence of more serious crime and public-relations considerations. The police are criticized (and often sued) for making illegal arrests, but they are also publicly condemned for not making arrests that are probably illegal.

LIMITATIONS ON POLICE PRACTICES

There is a basic dichotomy in public and in police attitudes toward the role of the police. Many regard the police as being bound by the Constitution and the "rule of law"; others see them as vigorous enforcers of the law. This apparent contradiction has been interpreted as stemming from two models of the criminal-justice system: (1) the "crime control" model, which stresses efficiency and "factual guilt"; and (2) the "due process" model, which stresses scrupulous adherence to constitutional rights, fairness rather than efficiency, and "legal guilt" rather than "factual guilt." The U.S. Supreme Court has stressed in several landmark cases that (1) police in federal cases who obtain confessions during a period of illegal detention (when a suspect could have been taken before a magistrate) cannot use that confession; (2) "Miranda" (so-called from the famous case) warnings are necessary before any police can properly interrogate suspects, and statements given in the absence of such warnings cannot be used in evidence; and (3) illegally obtained physical evidence cannot be used in any trial court.

Another impediment to law enforcement stems from the varying jurisdictional boundaries within which the police must operate. American traditions have stressed the division of the police function among many forces, and a crossing of geographical boundaries may result in illegal arrests.

The police function is also affected, as it has been since its beginnings, by political pressure. Politicians and those they represent may not wish full law enforcement, and these politicians may control appointment to the upper levels of the police force. While political control or influence upon the police always presents problems, the difficulties are exacerbated by corruption—either external corruption involving police and the public, or internal corruption involving the relationship of policemen to the police force. External corruption may include (1) payoffs by noncriminals (at least nonprofessional ones), such as traffic violators, members of licensed occupations, and even businessmen seeking favors; (2) payoffs by criminals; and (3) "clean graft," involving small amounts of money paid to police for minor services rendered. Internal corruption involves matters such as (1) payoffs to superiors for such benefits as desirable shift assignments or promotions and (2) payoffs for assignments that involve access to opportunities for external corruption. A spate of investigative reports in many cities have revealed that corruption, even to the extent of police participation in organized-crime activities, is not unusual. Gambling and drugs have provided the major sources of much contemporary corruption. In general (though there are some dramatic exceptions), a pattern of police corruption indicates a pattern of prevailing political corruption. Corrupt departments also tend to be inefficient and to hire underqualified, or even unqualified personnel.

The police function, or what the public believes to be that function, is limited by the fact that it is not solely, or even primarily, concerned with crime. The police most often provide social services that no other agency is equipped to, or wishes to, provide. Also, the very nature of American society—its commitment to individual freedom and fear of governmental and police power—creates nearly insuperable obstacles to police success. The very existence of the professional police (and the often self-inflated claims about their ability) often ensures that the public at large will withdraw from participation in the criminal-justice system on the assumption that "we're paying the police to do that."

POLICE AND PUNISHMENT

The police have no formal authority to "punish" in the American legal system; that is a function of the courts. Legal exceptions occur where particular states may allow (1) "police courts" to deal with minor traffic offenses, (2) police to destroy contraband (property such as drugs and gambling devices), possession of which is illegal; (3) police to hold property (such as an illegally parked car that has been towed) until the owner reclaims it; and (4) police to act as jailers in county jails administered by sheriff's departments. Many police use extralegal force to inflict punishment because (1) they believe that the victim deserves it and (2) they perceive the system as too lenient. (Discourtesy, often directed at the powerless, is a form of punishment, albeit a minor one.) In general, police are working-class people who are expected to be tough with other working-class (or lower-class) people but to be deferential to the middle class. Sometimes police force is necessary, though often not by the "book," because those they deal with may be violent or potentially violent.

The police have followed society in paying at least some attention to treatment rather than punishment; most often, this activity occurs unofficially. Occasionally, the police regard arrested offenders as candidates for "rehabilitation" rather than strict punishment, and they may refer juveniles to counseling or youth agencies if they appear to need help. Sometimes, informal police practices such as placing juveniles on "police probation" (requiring them to wash cars or to do work around the stationhouse) abet the treatment reaction. Some groups, including police organizations, have argued that the operation of treatment programs is an improper role for the police to undertake, since there are other agencies designed and better equipped to perform these tasks.

TRENDS IN POLICING

The police, partly because of newer social demands and partly because of increasing organizational identity and cohesion (as well as stresses), have undergone—and continue to undergo—certain changes.

Politics. As noted previously, the police have steadily fought to reduce the influence of politics, corrupt or otherwise, upon hiring, promotions, and policy decisions. Civil-service reform has reduced patronage problems for the police as well as for municipal government generally. Even in cities characterized by corrupt politics, police chiefs may no longer be hired and fired capriciously. Because of civil-service protection, they have an assured term and are removable only for cause. (Often, however, despite tenure or definite-term legal provisions, mayors use a variety of pressures to remove police chiefs.) Police participation in direct political activities has been reduced by federal, state, and local laws prohibiting such involvement. Graft, once the backbone of many police departments' illegal activities, has gravitated toward the upper levels, so that the average officer has little opportunity to become involved; this trend has reinforced the notion that graft is criminal. Although many departments still defer to prestigious individuals and perhaps leading politicians, the growth of independence and power of police administrators has generally resulted in relative immunity from both politics and general citizen influence. Indeed, by seeking to influence legislators, police administrators have become increasingly involved in policy-making, and they have exercised substantial influence in obtaining greater budgets and other resources from a society frightened by crime. The balance has thus shifted from undue deference to particular political interests to undue freedom from the democratic electoral process and responsibility and accountability.

Organization. The traditional separateness of the forty thousand police departments in the United States has been reduced by greater coordination required or encouraged by law. For example, the rise of county police, who are centrally directed within the county, and amalgamation of all county constables and marshals under the county sheriff's office have led to greater cohesiveness. There have been some trends toward amalgamation of metro-politanwide police departments or greater cooperation among them and toward contracting for police services by smaller jurisdictions. "Strike forces" combining federal, state, and local agents in a particular activity, usually involving organized or white-collar crime, has also increased. Growth of state police agencies and the granting to them of greater law-enforcement powers, along with the expansion of federal police jurisdiction, have further accelerated the trend. Impediments to further and more rapid development of this trend are (1) the fear of a national police and (2) labor-union memories of state police as strikebreakers during the 1930s. However, there is little evidence that centralized police forces are any greater danger to individual liberty than are locally organized ones.

Personnel.   In at least 75 percent of U.S. cities civil-service recruitment of police has tended to upgrade personnel. However, police departments are often understaffed because of the stringency of the tests. Tests may emphasize certain aspects of police work (such as crime control) but be insufficiently sensitive to other aspects (such as social work). Police training programs have proliferated and been extended from recruit training to in-service maintenance and upgrading of skills. Many training programs emphasize the formal (record-keeping) and militaristic nature of police function as well as such controversial issues as police discretionary powers.

Criminal-justice higher education may consist of little more than training conducted by retired police officers and district attorneys. The curriculum, especially at the junior- or community-college level, often runs to the mundane, emphasizing administration, the patrol function, and basic techniques of identification and investigation. Recently, there has been a movement to upgrade the material and to add large doses of liberal arts and social science in an effort to broaden the prospective officer's horizons. A few departments require some college training, and some require completion of a two- or four-year degree program. In-service officers have been paid for such training by federal monies disbursed by the Law Enforcement Assistance Administration. There is little proof that college education makes for better police officers. However, there is some evidence that college graduates are the objects of fewer citizen complaints (which may mean that they are less aggressive); and, of course, they score better on promotional examinations and thus are promoted out of the often boring patrol function more quickly. Minority and the women's groups tend to benefit from educational requirements, since members of these groups may be educationally qualified (or even overqualified) but unable to secure other jobs commensurate with their education and skills.

The assumption that better-educated and better-qualified police will improve police practices may mean little unless particular departments specify just what practices should be changed and how. Do the "new" requirements really attract recruits who are as much social workers as law enforcers, or do they merely attract additional well-qualified law enforcers? "Reformers" often have different goals in mind. Some may wish to continue what the police now do but would like to find better individuals to do traditional police work; some may want to impress the public (in order to obtain higher salaries from public funding agencies); others may see newer recruits as the instruments of fundamental change in the nature of police work. These conflicting goals reflect other differences, such as that between the patrolman's actual function as a street-level social worker and his (and his superior's) image of himself as a crime fighter. Good social work does not earn promotions; good (even if occasional) crime fighting does. Training and higher education, therefore, may seem "unrealistic" to recruits who are primarily interested in "hard data" about their jobs and the system within which they function.

The police, either in a sincere attempt to "professionalize" themselves or to convince others that they deserve more money and prestige, have steadily increased recruitment standards. There are an imposing battery of physical and mental tests, psychological screening, background checks, and in-depth personal interviews, at least in large and middle-sized cities, and many applicants fail to surmount these hurdles. Recently, the federal government has sued many police departments, contending that these tests have the effect (occasionally, the intention) of unduly impeding the ability of women and minority groups to gain entrance to police forces. Courts have struck down a number of tests, including minimum height and some other physical requirements, and automatic disqualification for a minor criminal record. As new types of recruits enter the force, the "professional" image of the big, muscular, and aggressive policeman may change.

Assignments. The traditional notion of the "patrolman" walking a beat (derived from the English model) to (1) forestall crime ("high visibility") and (2) be on the scene to apprehend offenders has given way to such technological developments as the patrol car, the telephone, and improved communications equipment (for example, the car radio and the walkie- or handi-talkie). These devices have enabled police departments to "deploy" their forces in statistically demonstrable high-crime areas. Under the "responsive" patrol-car systems, cars do not patrol randomly but wait for calls. The greatest specialization of all is to be found in the traffic division; as much as 25 percent of a given police force may be assigned to this operation. Vice, narcotics, robbery, and other specialized squads have largely replaced the neighborhood-patrol concept. Experiments such as neighborhood-team policing (wherein a police unit is permanently assigned to a geographic area and given complete responsibility for policing it) and "decoy" police (who, disguised, lure criminals into attacking them) have been used to stimulate detection of criminals. While some spectacular results from these methods have been reported, there is a question about whether crime is really reduced or only displaced to other criminal activities. Indeed, while more criminals may be apprehended by these techniques, the general crime rate within the experimental area may not change (or change inconsistently); thus vigorous police activity may do little more than dip into the "dark figure" of unknown crime. Also, the experiments have been marred by (1) unscientific measurement methods and (2) organizational jealousy, which may lead to premature termination of the techniques.

These new activities have tended to make police work much more "proactive" (police initiated) than merely "reactive" (response to citizen complaints). Such practices have frequently become the focus of (1) public resentment, especially when they involve the enforcement of "victimless" crime and (2) some departmental disorganization, since they overlap traditional intradepartmental boundaries and foster new loyalties.

Despite these changes, much police work still consists of patrolling of "neighborhood beats" (generally with patrol cars replacing foot police). The assumption that a strong and visible police presence deters crime may not be true in modern urban life (especially if such presence takes the form of motorized patroling). A famous Kansas City, Missouri, study indicates that there may be little connection between crime rates (and citizen perception of crime) and the vigor and presence of police activity. The fact is that most "police work" does not involve crime fighting at all, but rather the provision of social services, which occupy 80 to 85 percent of actual police activity time. The police argue (with some justification) that many "social work" situations are potentially criminal ones (husband-wife disputes, for instance, may escalate into crime) and that, even if crime fighting is a small portion of police work, it is still a crucial one.

Scientific Detection. Since only 25 percent of all crimes solved are solved by immediate apprehension of the suspect at or near the scene, investigative work is usually performed by scientifically trained detectives (on occasion, also by patrolmen). Large police departments have modern elaborate scientific laboratories. Identification of human or nonhuman evidence is the primary work of the laboratory. Also, there may be scientific apparatus relating to testimonial validity, such as lie detectors. But the crime laboratory is actually useful in only a few cases. Often, bad, shoddy, and simply incorrect analysis is produced there. Since most crimes are not "solved" and many that are solved are solved either on the scene or by questioning of witnesses, there is little value to either "pure" detective work or the crime lab itself, and many have argued that enhancement of the patrolman's authority to investigate crime would largely do away with the need for detectives. The truth is that a few patrolmen account for a majority of arrests within a particular force, and the same is true of detectives.

The most effective and most frequently utilized identification procedure is police use of the fingerprint file maintained by the FBI. The Bureau re-

ceives approximately six million sets of fingerprints each year, half from police agencies dealing with criminals and suspects, the remainder from civil-
service and military agencies. Computerized interconnections between the
Bureau and state and local police agencies efficiently manage to identify offenders in cases where (1) fingerprints are found and (2) they belong to
people previously arrested or otherwise previously fingerprinted.

Another quasiscientific development has been the attempt to identify offenders by their characteristic criminal habit patterns *(modus operandi)*.
Examples of this means of identification range from informal files to computerized descriptions used in large city forces; these files may contain, or
be cross-referenced with, mug shots and known-offender lists. Registration
of all city residents and visitors is a characteristic of many European police
systems, but some police attempts to institute this system have been rejected
in the United States. Some departments and municipalities do require registration of ex-convicts. Fingerprinting and registration requirements for different purposes (noncriminal ones, include voting, receipt of some municipal services, driver's licenses, etc.) do provide a rudimentary form of
identification check.

New Concepts of Police Work. In recent years, there has been some
emphasis upon "preventive" police work, a term that covers a multitude of
programs ranging from harassment of known criminals to frequent patrolling to public programs to convince the citizenry to take safety measures
such as registration of property. Some attempts have been made to counter-
act the supposed "causes" of crime by enlisting the police in recreational
and athletic programs for juveniles and in frequent police visits to schools.
In part, such programs function to employ policewomen, and are regarded
by most police as not "true" police activities.

Police-Community relations. In response to (1) occasional public criticism and (2) general public indifference to daily police activities, many departments have established public or "police-community relations" divisions
both to educate the public and to receive feedback from the public about
controversial police activities. Training of policemen for this work is quite
limited, despite many public-relations claims. Police cooperation with the
mass media may be stressed by some departments, while others may have
an active program of police participation in school or community groups.
Often, a detective's true role is not to investigate crime but to improve public relations. Probably the most effective form of public relations is to actually improve police behavior along the lines, for example, of greater respect
for minority groups or more temperate dealing with demonstrators and traffic offenders. It may be expected that better behavior will result in (1) more
efficient police work because of increased public cooperation and (2) improved police morale.

CONTROLLING THE POLICE

Because the police represent the "law" and have great discretion in carrying out their activities, many have claimed that greater legal and/or public control of the police is necessary. In the past, when the police were part of a political machine, a certain (usually partisan political) control was exercised. As the police freed themselves from politics, they increasingly freed themselves from oversight. However, many departments, especially in large cities, have established internal investigative units to monitor police conduct, particularly in relation to corruption. ("Shoo flies," as members of these units are called, are extremely unpopular with the remainder of the force.) Internal review of civilian complaints, with the final authority to act on them reserved to the chief (or to a high-level officer), have become formalized in many departments. The police have strongly resisted "outside" review, in the form of either (1) subordination to other criminal-justice agencies (district attorney's offices, for instance) or (2) "civilian" participation on complaint review boards. In New York City, in 1966, the police led a campaign to abolish the civilian-dominated complaint review board and succeeded; a few years later, the Philadelphia police won a lawsuit contending that the city's civilian review board was illegal. In the 1960s there was a movement to exert "community control" over police recruitment and policies in particular areas. It failed because (1) such control would have undermined standard recruitment policies; (2) it would have led to differential law enforcement in different areas of the city; and (3) to many it meant the return of "politics" in the form of undue influence by politically powerful though not representative community groups. While an occasional prosecutor will crusade against police abuses that involve illegalities, most district attorneys feel that already difficult problems of police cooperation in prosecution would be increased by any persistent or permanent hostility between the two agencies.

In part, the lack of control agencies and the difficulty of using the civil courts for lawsuits against errant policemen, their departments, and their employer-municipalities have led to increasing involvement of the criminal courts in such matters, but the major judicial decisions about illegally obtained evidence and coerced confessions, do not reach many of the control problems created by modern police power. When those few decisions impinge upon important police activities, they are likely to be regarded by the police as "illegitimate," so that evasion may become the normal response. The courts, in any event, cannot—and cannot be expected to—monitor police activities on anything like a consistent basis.

POLICE PERSONALITY AND POLICE PROBLEMS

Social scientists have spent much time analyzing and attempting to explain the "police personality" and its receptivity to many of the reforms and new techniques discussed in this chapter. In general, it has been found that there are no particular personality quirks among recruits (who seem to be no more authoritarian than others from the working class, although within that class, pro-authoritarian attitudes may tend to run high). Policemen, especially in large and middle-sized cities, do tend to become cynical and mistrustful as part of the "socialization" process. This process may consist in either or both of (1) contact with older officers and learning from them and (2) patrol duties in high crime areas. Even neutral racial and ethnic attitudes may change after such experiences, although these attitudes may not be followed by biased behavior. As a result, after a few years, the most idealistic rookies tend to become "streetwise" cops who regard the public as corrupt and mendacious and come to distrust even other police. Habits of secrecy and not "ratting" on brother officers develop in many respects like those in the "prison culture" (see pp. 212–13). Thus adverse criticism by anyone outside (or even within) the force is regarded as self-seeking and self-serving, and bitterness (often amounting to paranoia) toward "do-gooders" develops.

Although the police generally enjoy much public confidence (except occasionally when crises arise), they perceive the public as a suspicious enemy who give society's "dirty work" to the police and then handcuff the police by unrealistic rules. Hypocrisy is a charge often leveled by the police both at the public and the upper echelons of the department who, they think, are "selling out" to public demands. Strangely, as power within the police department drifts down toward the lower ranks (because of discretionary authority and increasing labor-union involvement in the police function), police cynicism and sense of being entrapped grows. This makes it difficult to change police policies or practices or to secure acquiescence to the idea that meaningful control mechanisms over police activities are necessary. "Professional" police forces (those having high educational recruitment standards and expensive scientific paraphernalia) may be less cynical and paranoid, but they tend to be more arrogant toward the public, especially minority groups and the poor. Such forces also often demand freedom from review or oversight because of their very claim to "professionalism." There is some evidence, however, that "professional" departments with many minority-group employees may be more sensitive toward public attitudes.

16. Between Arrest and Trial

Most persons who are arrested are not tried. In the criminal-justice process many events can occur before trial that may either prevent trial or influence the outcome of the trial. As with much other police decisionmaking, the activities of various members of the criminal-justice system involve vital but "low visibility" decisions. The police may release offenders (or those thought to be offenders); the prosecutor may drop charges or may plea bargain a case out of the trial system; and the question of bail may be significant for both the system and the individual defendant.

PRETRIAL RELEASE PRACTICES

The police may release arrestees prior to any appearance before a magistrate, although the law technically does not permit this. In turn, magistrates may dismiss cases at the defendant's first appearance when they feel that the crimes involved are minor or that the victim will not testify against the defendant (perhaps because of their personal relationship). The magistrate may "divert" many of those brought before him to community and social-agency programs designed to deal with particular problems (such as drugs or alcohol) and order that the cases be dismissed after such treatment. This factor is of particular importance in the juvenile-justice system. "Diversion" results from the belief that many of those accused should not be subjected to the formal processes of the criminal-justice system. It may be institutionalized in the form of "adjournments contemplating dismissal" or may be discretionary with little, if any, legislative guidelines. Perhaps 50 percent or more accused (higher for minor crimes) will be "diverted," usually on condition (or threat) of further proceedings if they fail to participate in the program ordered by the magistrate.

Many of those charged will plead guilty to a minor crime (often as the result of police or prosecutorial willingness to reduce charges, a form of informal plea bargaining. Magistrates have the authority to take such pleas, though pleas of guilty to major crimes are not within their jurisdiction. In such instances the accused, of course, waives his rights to counsel (unless, though this is unlikely, he is represented by counsel at the initial hearing), as well as other rights, including that of trial by jury.

In serious cases, the magistrate will (1) inform the defendant of the charges against him and of his rights to remain silent and to obtain a lawyer; (2) order the defendant to be held over for further proceedings—usually a preliminary hearing; and (3) set bail or release the defendant on personal recognizance (a promise to return for future proceedings).

This procedure will be followed within forty-eight to seventy-two hours, by a preliminary hearing by the magistrate to ascertain if there is a *prima facie* (apparent) case against the defendant. Often, defendants waive their rights to preliminary hearings, and they may even at this time, as the result of a plea bargain, plead guilty or be released. In states that still have grand juries, the defendant may be indicted before the preliminary hearing, so that this proceeding is unnecessary, since indictment itself means that a *prima facie* case exists. Preliminary hearings are designed to quickly test the validity of the case against a suspect, and to dismiss charges for which no, or little, evidence is present. Often defense attorneys use preliminary hearings to cross-examine the police or other witnesses either to discredit them or, more important, to "nail down" their stories early in the case (before they have been prepared by prosecutors for their trial testimony). The accused may testify or present witnesses at this hearing, but rarely does, since to do so would mean disclosing his defense in advance of trial.

States that do not use grand juries are required under the United States Constitution to rapidly hold preliminary hearings. If the hearing produces sufficient evidence to give the magistrate "probable cause" to believe that the accused will be found guilty at later trial, the magistrate must decide again whether to set bail, to increase or reduce previously set bail, or to release on personal recognizance. Unless dismissed (this is rare), the case will then proceed to a different court for trial, at least if it involves a serious crime.

Pretrial release may take several forms. Police will release a person whom they have illegally arrested, often a harassment arrest of a known criminal when there is no real evidence. Minor offenders such as some juvenile delinquents, disorderly persons, and public drunkards (where public drunkenness is still a crime) may similarly be released in the interests of justice. The circumstances of, and the reasons for, such release vary. For example, (1) a petition of habeas corpus (calling for the police to give reasons to a judge why they are holding someone) may be filed with a court where an illegal arrest has occurred; (2) the drunk may have sobered up; (3) the juvenile may be sufficiently frightened by the arrest to "go straight" (or the police may so believe); (4) the vagrant may promise to leave the jurisdiction. Often, especially with drunks, arrests are made to benefit the individual. Many departments are now required by either law or departmental policy to take apprehended drunks to detoxification centers that are not part of the criminal-justice system. Release may be conditioned upon a promise to enter a treatment program (drug or alcohol) or to repay stolen money or the value of stolen goods, and the threat of future prosecution is used to encourage compliance. Sometimes a magistrate or a local probation program will specifically impose these conditions. Whether legally justified or not, such informal dispositions serve to mitigate the rigidities of the law.

BAIL

Bail involves the promise that a defendant will return for later proceedings and the giving of financial security to ensure such return. While most offenses are "bailable" (some by law even at the police station where the defendant is booked), and the United States Constitution requires that "excessive bail" shall not be set, magistrates have great discretion in determining whether to impose bail and in assessing the amount of bail. Of course, the amount of bail ordered can be paid in cash by a (usually wealthy) defendant; this means that his cash will be returned if he makes required future appearances.

The Bail Bondsman.   Most defendants, of course, cannot provide cash bail, but they can employ professional licensed bail bondsmen who will provide a "bond" or pledge of money to the court. The usual fee to the bondsman for his service is 10 percent of the face amount of the bail. The bondsman may want additional security and may demand that the defendant or his friends or relatives give mortgages on property or turn over personal stocks and corporate bonds to him. Professional bondsmen have replaced the older system whereby friends and relatives of the accused acted as sureties and provided the pledged property directly to the court as the bond. England has no professional bail bondsmen; as once was true in the United States, bail can be provided only by the accused, a relative, or a friend (indeed, it is a crime in England to provide bail for profit).

Bail in America is often a collusive system whereby fee splitting between the bail bondsman and another (a lawyer, a police officer, or a jail employee), and other forms of cooperation occur. A bondsman may refuse to write bail for someone disliked by a judge and, in return, the judge may not demand collection of a forfeited bond when another person who has been released has "skipped." In many big cities, the bail bondsman, though not a public official, is part of a system that pressures defendants to enter guilty

162

THE CRIMINAL-JUSTICE SYSTEM

pleas. The bondsman might suggest that the defendant obtain a courthouse "local" defense lawyer (a hack) or the bond will not be written. The local lawyer may then pressure the defendant into a guilty plea, since he earns his small fees from many defendants by quickly processing them through the system by such pleas.

Bondsmen also serve other functions in and for the criminal-justice system; they (1) ensure that defendants show up in court; (2) actively pressure guilty pleas, since their responsibilities end (and their profits are assured) when the case has terminated; and (3) have great power, much more than law-enforcement officers, to capture errant defendants (bondsmen can go into any state and abduct their "clients," without legal liability for kidnaping).

Criticism of Bail.   Because of heavy criticism of the bail process, some states now provide that the defendant will be freed if he (or friends or relatives) provides 10 percent of the bail amount to the court; if he appears, he receives a refund of 90 percent of this deposit. Many states enforce traffic codes by requiring a deposit of a sum equal to the usual fine for that offense. If the defendant fails to appear to answer the charge the "cash bail" is often forfeited and the case is considered closed. This is not the general rule with bail; nonappearance can result in both a forfeiture of the bail or bond and a warrant for the defendant's arrest to compel his appearance for trial.

Because many courts do not have the proper information about the defendant, decisions about bail are not made on the legal basis of whether the amount set will be sufficient to assure his return but on theoretically improper grounds such as the nature of the offense charged. Since often even small amounts of bail cannot be raised, it may be used to "teach" the alleged offender a lesson or, in essence, to punish him before he is found guilty. Defendants who fail to raise bail are more likely than bailed defendants either to plead guilty or eventually to be convicted. Reformers argue that this is a consequence of their inability to find witnesses readily or to work with their attorneys while in jail. The police believe that those who receive high bail are more likely to be guilty than those released on low bail. Certainly, confinement in jail is a significant factor in forcing the defendant to plea bargain, and to do so from a disadvantageous position. Also, the claim that only the true guilty receive high bail can be questioned when the figures are analyzed: Even at low bail sums, many accused are still remanded to jail. For the poor, almost any bail is excessive. While most of them may have committed a crime (not necessarily the one charged), some have not, and for a significant number there may not be sufficient evidence to prove them guilty at the trial. (The general acquittal rate for all those standing trial is 20 to 25 percent in most jurisdictions, and most acquittals occur because the evidence is insufficient.) It is likely that a substantial number of defendants jailed for failure to make small amounts of bail will plead guilty in situations where trials would have resulted in acquittals. In England, it should be noted bail is usually set at an extremely low rate so that only 1 percent of those charged are imprisoned for failure to raise bail (in contrast to the United States, where the percentages can range between 50 and 90 percent). In England, however, an accused person may be remanded (returned to custody) without *any* bail for a short period while an investigation continues, a practice generally illegal in the United States.

Studies have indicated that many more defendants can be released without bail on personal recognizance than most judges and other members of the criminal-justice system believe to be true. Of course, speedier hearings and trials would also obviate some of the problems.

JAIL

In theory, pretrial (or preplea-bargained admission of guilt) detention exists only for the purpose of assuring the accused's presence at trial. Jails are not supposed to be punitive institutions, and those awaiting trial should be separated from those serving short-term sentences after conviction. Also in theory the "presumption of innocence" that attaches to every accused should mandate that jail conditions be as consistent as possible with individual freedom. However, the U.S. Supreme Court held in 1979 that the presumption applies only to trial procedures; this ruling sanctioned the vast number of jail restrictions (on visitation, communication, etc.) imposed upon those not yet convicted.

Types of Jails. Police stations have cells to hold arrestees until preliminary proceedings against them can be scheduled. In small towns, local jails run by police or marshals may hold arrestees, those serving short sentences, or both. County jails, controlled by sheriffs, hold (1) persons arrested by the sheriff's department, (2) persons committed to them by courts without jurisdiction to finally dispose of a matter, and (3) offenders serving short sentences for misdemeanors. Segregation of the different types of persons involved rarely occurs. In some jurisdictions, juveniles charged with serious offenses are detained in special facilities. Although many state laws require at least segregation of juveniles, where no separate facilities exist, this rarely occurs.

Detention. In general, only 40 percent of the 150,000 people confined in U.S. jails in any given day are in jail to serve sentences. Despite this, most custodial personnel are law-enforcement officers; very few perform any rehabilitative function. Physical conditions of jails are deplorable (and have always been so), and often are even worse than those in state prisons. Most jails have no recreational or educational facilities, and a bare majority have medical facilities. There is little or no segregation of inmates from detainees. County jails, 75 percent of whose inmates have been convicted, also exercise a dangerous influence on the defendant awaiting trial. English prison reform of the late eighteenth and early nineteenth centuries was, in reality, jail reform, since prisons served as detention centers. Many of the foregoing criticisms were voiced by reformers at that time.

At present, the "system" works to defeat reform. Jailers are granted certain sums per prisoner for his maintenance; this encourages jailers to maintain low costs and to pocket the difference. Other factors, such as threats to their power and influence, also engender resistance by jailers to reform. Public attitudes tend to defeat reform, since they often assume that one jailed must be guilty. Public attitudes toward the poor generally are reflected in corresponding feelings about jails.

Alternatives and Reforms.　　Among the proposals to alter the present deplorable state of detention are (1) increased use of bail and release on personal recognizance; (2) reduction in number of arrests, since more than one half of those arrested will never be prosecuted, and almost one half of those prosecuted will be released without conviction; (3) greater use of citation and summonses in misdemeanor arrest situations (the federal government's experience with this reform has been favorable); (4) faster court disposition of cases, including use of speedy trial legal provisions and liberal grant of credit for "time served" in jail toward the eventual sentence (if any); (5) improvement of physical conditions and state supervision of local jails to foster uniform and high standards in this realm; (6) establishment of larger centralized jails, since there are now too many jails in too many counties (this would also allow specialization and segregation of different types of prisoners); (7) segregation of convicts from detainees, as some states have already done, with work-release programs for both; (8) state support services for dependents of detainees; and (9) indemnification (payment of money) to those acquitted, as provided in many European countries; this last proposal would also, it is thought, lead to greater caution in making needless arrests and a speed-up of court proceedings.

17. The Criminal Courts

Criminal courts are designed to adjudicate individual cases and to sentence the convicted to terms decided upon by the legislature. As with other agencies of the criminal-justice system, criminal courts exercise great discretion—in dismissing cases, in awarding probation instead of sentencing to prison, etc. They are also bureaucracies that often serve their own interests. This chapter will discuss the "apparent" and "latent" functions of the criminal court and its personnel from both a "legalistic" and a "functional" viewpoint.

ORGANIZATION

The lower courts, called justice of the peace or police or magistrate's courts, adjudicate minor cases (usually misdemeanors), hold preliminary hearings in felony cases, and initially determine questions of bail. Trial courts for serious crimes may be called county or district or superior or circuit courts. These courts (1) hear appeals from the lower courts and (2) perform the judicial (trial and sentencing) function in felony cases. In addition, there are some specialized courts such as traffic courts, which deal with only one subject, and appeals courts (also given various names), which review convictions to determine whether or not the accused received a fair trial. These courts have traditionally functioned separately (often within a state there are different systems in different counties in a state). But numerous court reforms have operated to weld courts into one statewide system or have integrated the lower courts on countywide basis.

The lower courts, and most of the others, are administered by chief magistrates who are not involved in, for instance, ensuring uniformity of substantive judgments, primarily sentencing. Since many judges are simply not talented executives, court-management reforms that place day-to-day supervision of the courts in the hands of professional administrators have been enacted in many states and in the federal court system. State judicial councils, composed of judges of various courts, generally collect statistics and recommend new legislation to simplify and speed up court procedures.

Courts are often criticized for not "contributing" to the supposed general mission of the criminal-justice system: the prompt apprehension and conviction of offenders. Many proposals to more closely integrate the courts into the divided "criminal-justice system" have been suggested. But it must be remembered that courts are not really members of that system, as so defined, but part of the judicial branch of government, which, under the American system of constitutional law, is designed to be separate from executive and legislative agencies. Of course, many judges (often former district attorneys) do perceive themselves to be members of the criminal-justice system and behave accordingly, tending to be hostile toward the defense and impatient with defense conduct of trials or pretrial proceedings. These judges may also intentionally or unintentionally pressure the defense into plea bargaining by indicating such hostility. Such judges thereby undermine their theoretical function.

PROSECUTION

For misdemeanors, prosecution occurs when a victim, a witness, or a police officer files a complaint. For felonies, professional prosecutors receive the evidence and then either "accuse" a specific person by filing an "information" in court (which must be followed quickly by a preliminary hearing) or by presenting a case to the grand jury.

The Grand Jury. The grand jury (usually consisting of twenty-three members, though in some states the number may be lower) then hears the evidence and decides whether or not to present an indictment. In English history the purpose of the grand jury was to "check" the ability of a private person to maliciously accuse another and, later, the authority of a government prosecutor to carry a case forward. In most jurisdictions where grand juries continue to exist, they are regarded as tools of the prosecutor, and grand-jury acquiescence to prosecutors is notorious (except in a few well-publicized instances where "runaway" grand juries have compelled prosecutors against their will to call witnesses). England and most American states have abolished general grand juries for this and other reasons (primarily because of the expense involved), but federal grand juries to indict for "infamous" crimes (felonies) are required under the United States Constitution. The "investigative grand jury" still exists in many states for crimes involving white-collar and corruption issues where district attorneys may have to compel information. The grand jury usually hears people who are victims of crimes or police officers who volunteer testimony. Fairness in the selection of grand jurors, as well as trial jurors, is required by the United States Constitution. However, often, for one reason or another, grand juries are not representative, especially of minority social, racial, and economic groups within the community.

After the charge has been made, the defendant is arraigned. The charge or charges are read in open court, and the defendant may plead guilty or not guilty. Or he may request an adjournment to obtain an attorney or to attack the charges on legal grounds. A plea of guilty will result in one further proceeding: sentencing; a not guilty plea will lead first to pretrial hearings involving the legality of searches or interrogations if such issues are present, and then to the trial itself.

The Prosecutor.   The prosecutor is the most powerful figure in the criminal-justice system, at least after a suspect has been arrested. The prosecutor decides (1) whether to charge (or whether, where the grand jury still exists, to present a case to it) and (2) what to charge or to recommend to the grand jury as a proper charge. Many accused may have committed (or probably committed) several crimes in one incident, and the power of the prosecutor to charge with all or only some is awesome. The charges automatically include others, called by the law "lesser included offenses," so that a defendant can be convicted, for instance, of trespass or illegal breaking and entering when the higher charge of burglary is not provable. The prosecutor's power in this situation is as great as his power to charge different substantive offenses (each with its own subcategory of "lesser included offenses"). Both powers give prosecuters strong weapons in the plea-bargaining process that often follows.

If the case is not plea-bargained, the prosecutor amasses the evidence against a defendant and presents it in court. The prosecutor may also make recommendations for sentencing once a conviction has occurred, although in some jurisdictions there may be specific prosecutorial policies that limit, or negate, this authority.

Most prosecutors in the United States are elected, usually on a countywide basis. They are thus politicians who must perform as other politicians do, by "balancing" constituency interests. Perhaps to get re-elected (or to keep the position in the hands of his political party), a prosecutor must show favorable conviction statistics. He may prosecute cases because other criminal-justice agencies (especially the police) or the public insist upon this. The political nature of his office ensures the existence of several conflicts: (1) often punitive public attitudes toward crime versus equally vociferous demands that he be fair; (2) charges that prosecutions, especially those of members of the other political party, are "politically motivated" versus the need to prosecute when the evidence is present; and (3) demands of the mayor or the public for prosecution of many public-order offenses versus judicial skepticism about the use of criminal-justice resources to attack minor crimes. There may be conflicts of interest caused by the fact that in small cities and counties, prosecutors work only part-time in this function and are also practicing lawyers. In large counties, there are assistant prosecutors, generally recent law-school graduates, who do not remain on the job very long either because they are there "to learn" or because political administrations change. While state laws, of course, apply uniformly, local prosecutorial practices may be divergent, with the possible exceptions of the three states (Alaska, Delaware, and Rhode Island) where the state attorney general's office handles all prosecutions. Of course, politics affects prosecution, whether the system is local or statewide; it is just that the nature of those politics may be different. In general, prosecutors may be analogized to law-enforcement "franchises" where, within a general framework (state law), local variations are tolerated.

Prosecutors often treat the police as their real constituents and think of themselves as front-line commanders in various "wars against crime." But this tendency may be diminished somewhat in large cities where prosecutors have little control over the activities of their assistants, paralleling the problem of control exercised by higher police authority over the entire agency.

THE DEFENSE

The United States pioneered in requiring that all accused persons have the right to be represented by legal counsel. The Sixth Amendment to the United States Constitution, binding upon both federal and state government, has been interpreted to require appointment of defense lawyers for the indigent in any case involving a threat of imprisonment. Thus America has pioneered both in allowing lawyers to defend the criminally accused and in requiring the lawyers' presence (unless waived by the defendant).

Representation for the Poor. Because of these constitutional requirements, the private criminal bar, which is very small, has been supplemented by various schemes for appointment of counsel for the poor. (1) In some jurisdictions (usually smaller ones), judges may assign private attorneys. There may be an office of public defenders (with historical antecedents in ancient Roman and modern European law) who are state employees assigned to represent the poor. (3) There may be privately funded legal-aid offices; this service is often supplemented by assignment of private counsel, especially when there are two poor defendants whose interests clash and who cannot be represented by the same attorney or office. There have been charges that the second and third systems have led to the virtual "integration" of the defense attorney into the criminal-justice system. Many defendants believe (rightly or wrongly) that large legal-aid agencies or public-defender offices are in collusion with "the system" to speed cases through more rapidly and to induce pleas of guilty.

Private Attorneys.   Criticism has also been leveled at the private criminal bar in general (with the exceptions of a few well-known lawyers usually affordable by only the wealthy). Defendants who are not "indigent" may not be eligible to qualify for public assistance and may have to rely on "retained" (compensated) legal representation. These attorneys are (1) usually cooperative with law-enforcement agencies (indeed, those agencies may have been the source of recommendation of the attorney); (2) often actively involved in local politics; (3) of rather low social standing within the bar; and (4) tend to be adept at "bargaining" rather than courtroom performance. They earn less than their civil counterparts, are graduates of less prestigious law schools, and often do not particularly like the work they are doing. They may provide as poor legal representation as do the staffs of public-defender offices and legal-aid societies (usually, in fact, their representation is worse).

Public-defender offices tend to be inadequately budgeted and staffed, and many of their trial lawyers may be young and inexperienced. There may be an undercurrent of competition or perhaps collusion between these defense lawyers and prosecutorial staffs. Also, such agencies are bureaucracies, and bureaucracies are often concerned with speed and efficiency rather than with justice for clients. Some bar associations have proposed a system called "judicare" whereby lawyers would volunteer to defend the poor and be paid by state funds through bar associations.

Plea Bargaining.   An important function of the defense attorney (and arguably that of the prosecution) is to plea bargain. Since most of those obviously innocent or against whom the evidence is weak have probably left the system long before trial (often because prosecutors will not even bring cases to the grand jury unless they are sure they can obtain a conviction), the remainder are probably guilty of something. The defense attorney's job is to use his personal, at time political, and informational resources to induce the prosecutor to drop or reduce charges, all with the goal of ensuring the most minimal sentence possible in the circumstances. In establishing his strategy the defense attorney must weigh the resources of the state (considerable compared to his own) and assess the other demands on the time and interest of the prosecutor.

This function of the defense lawyer is highly controversial, for it negates the right of the defendant to ensure that guilt will be determined by jury trial. It often perverts the course of justice, because defendants who are not guilty may be persuaded or perhaps coerced into bargaining away their rights while dangerous criminals may receive light (or no) sentences.

Plea bargaining may consist either in "crime bargaining" (reduction of the charge) or "sentence bargaining" (agreement on a specific sentence, whatever the charge). Often, serious felonies become transformed into minor misdemeanors that do not at all resemble the original charge. But despite much resentment about the process, studies have shown that it often operates to "humanize" some of the severe penalties of the criminal law. The defendant's background and his commitment to criminality are studied as are the circumstances of the crime itself. Plea bargaining occurs most often in courts where volume of cases is high (surprisingly, second most often where volume is low). Reduction of charges may be justified when the evidence indicates that the crime was not so serious as first believed, or where fact situations are so vague and ambiguous that prosecutors can legitimately decide that a less severe interpretation of the "facts" is warranted. Often, prosecutors may file the most severe conceivable charges and then, as the evidence develops, reduce them, even without bargaining.

The bargain must be kept. If a judge, with or without knowledge of the bargain, imposes a heavier sentence than that arranged, the defendant is ordinarily allowed to withdraw the guilty plea and demand trial. The same is of course true when the prosecutor, a party to the bargain, reneges. There is some evidence that in such cases judges tend to treat defendants who are found guilty after trial more harshly than if they had initially pleaded guilty.

At times, it is difficult to ascertain whether critics of plea bargaining are attacking the practice itself or the secrecy and hypocrisy surrounding it. Many feel that the defendant is overwhelmed by the pressures to plead guilty and becomes cynical when the judge in open court requests statements that no promises were made to induce the plea. Among the reforms suggested is a confrontation in open court between or among all the relevant parties and an open acknowledgment that the "bargain" is one fair to all.

Some jurisdictions claim to have abolished plea bargaining without slowing up court calenders; the vast majority of defendants still plead guilty, but to the original charges, partly because prosecutors in these places feel no need to overcharge in the first place. These innovations are too recent to be adequately evaluated. In any event, they may not be applicable to the culture and politics of many places that continue the practice of plea bargaining.

The Role of the Criminal Lawyer.   Since plea bargaining will no doubt continue, it is obvious that the defense lawyer is both less than the ardent champion of the defendant as envisioned by the law and more than a passive tool of the prosecution as often occurs in totalitarian countries. He does not generally identify with or advise his poor, perhaps dangerous, client and he will rarely win a case—though occasionally he will manage to exclude an illegal confession or physical evidence illegally obtained. He will seek approval from judges and prosecutors as a "moderate" who does not make waves; he will not seek approval from his client as a "fighter."

THE JUDGE

The judge has two formal functions: (1) to "try" the case and (2) if the defendant is convicted, to impose sentence. The first role is essentially passive. The judge "rules on" various objections made to the introduction of evidence and "instructs" the jury as to the applicable law. He will sum up all the evidence for the jury, but will remind the jury that his summation is only a guide so that if jurors remember the evidence differently it is their memory that rules. The jury decides the question of guilt (and what degree of guilt) or innocence. In England and some American states judges are permitted to give their opinions about the truth of the evidence and witnesses, but must make it clear that the jury is required to form its own, independent opinion. When the judge tries the case without a jury ("bench trial"), he makes the legal decisions and the *factual* ones (Did the defendant in fact commit the act? Was it the act charged?). Some have argued that judges should have a greater responsibility to investigate the evidence and prepare accusations, as is true in Europe, but not to try the particular case (in Europe he would do both).

Sentencing. In classical theory, judges have no sentencing discretion. And in some states the sentences for certain crimes (usually death or life imprisonment for first-degree murder) are still set by law, though an invariable death penalty for a particular crime has been held unconstitutional. Neoclassical and positivist influence led to the provision for wide discretion in sentencing on the theory that the individual, not the crime, was the proper focus of the sentencing process. To aid the judge in passing sentence, most states have imposed a requirement that a presentence report be furnished in certain types of cases. This report is compiled by a probation officer who is supposed to gather materials from numerous sources to apprise the judge of the defendant's background. However, reports may (1) not be required in many jurisdictions, especially for misdemeanors, (2) be incomplete, or (3) be vague. In any event, the judge is not bound to follow the report's recommendations.

Judges have been widely criticized for either too great disparity in sentencing or too little. The latter occurs when one judge may always sentence to prison for the same crime; the problem is accentuated when another judge sitting in the same jurisdiction habitually releases convictees on probation. Many have claimed that judges' personal beliefs or biases have caused this variation. Since few judges habitually are lenient or punitive, varying practices by the same judge often result in similar criticism.

For various reasons, sentencing disparities between judges or even by one judge have engendered a sense of unfairness. Proposals for reform include: (1) a return to definite sentences for particular crimes with no judicial discretion; (2) "presumptive" sentencing whereby a generally accepted standard is the norm, and variations from it must be justified by the judge in writing; and (3) removal of the sentencing function from the judiciary and the creation of an executive agency with "professional" standing and standards to exercise it. To an extent the third alternative already exists in the form of the parole board (itself a source of great controversy), which "expertly" determines if or when an offender is to be released prior to the end of his sentence. Other arrangements, such as "sentencing councils" of a panel of judges to discuss and *recommend* appropriate sentences, have been tried, usually in the interests of uniformity and fairness. Model sentencing guidelines have recently been enacted in various jurisdictions. Denver, Colorado, was the first jurisdiction to use the system wherein deviations must be explained in writing.

Legislative imposition of sentences often follows a crazy-quilt pattern. At one time, Colorado determined that someone convicted for first-degree murder could not be eligible for parole for ten years, but that someone convicted of a lesser degree of the crime could be eligible only after fifteen years. In California, car theft carried a maximum ten-year sentence, but theft of objects from a car was punishable by a fifteen-year maximum. In Iowa, check forgery was punished by a ten-year maximum, but manslaughter only carried an eight-year maximum. The disparities are especially glaring in penalties for drug crimes. A federal court overturned a ten-year-minimum sentence for narcotics possession as a "cruel and unusual punishment" in a jurisdiction where it exceeded the maximum sentence specified for extortion, blackmail, and assault with a dangerous weapon.

Sentencing problems are caused by the ambiguity between opposing principles of "fairness": One stresses fairness as uniformity (a principle accepted by most offenders); the other defines fairness as "justifiable disparity." The former overlooks the nature of the individual criminal, while the latter may tend to become arbitrary or subject to racial or other prejudices. Interestingly, recent studies have concluded that judges tend not to base sentences on factors such as age, race, sex, and socioeconomic status (as critics allege) but on such legally significant grounds as nature of the offense, defendant's prior record, use of violence or carrying of a weapon, and other related data. Thus at least one major argument for limiting or abolishing judicial discretion seems to have been undercut. In fact, public attitudes veer between discretion and uniformity about as much as they veer between other classical and positivist notions about crime and punishment.

Even if obvious bias is largely eliminated as a major sentencing factor, judges are naturally influenced in imposing sentence by their backgrounds and associations as well as their conceptions of the role of the judiciary. Surveys have shown that a judge's general attitudes about society (liberal, moderate, or conservative) will be reflected in his attitudes toward sentencing. However, the matter is complex; one study found that "liberal" juvenile-court judges often sentenced more juveniles to institutions than did their "conservative" counterparts because liberals ran their courtrooms more informally, and because of their greater sophistication, believed that juvenile facilities were benign, while conservatives believed they were punitive. Judges may well be more punitive toward males, the poor, and blacks because they have reason to think that these groups produce the most violent criminals rather than because of prejudice.

Selection of Judges.   The argument about judicial discretion often reflects a more fundamental problem, that of selection of judges. Most judges in the United States are elected, either with a political party affiliation or in nonpartisan fashion. Generally, the worst judges are produced by a partisan electoral system, but the average judge appears to be as well qualified and competent as his appointed counterpart. A "pure" appointment system may produce judges as politically minded as those elected, but the nature of their politics may be different (control or influence by state rather than local politicians, or by statewide interest groups). The "Missouri Plan," which has been adopted by several states, combines election and appointment: a "citizen's commission," including some lawyers (but not numerically dominated by them) recommends three candidates for each open judicial position to the governor, who is required to choose one. After one year of service, voters decide whether the judge should continue. This system seems to be effective.

OTHER COURTROOM PERSONNEL

Clerks, bailiffs, and other courtroom personnel play a significant, though rarely publicized, role in the criminal-justice process. They may give advice to judges, split fees with lawyers to whom they steer defendants, manipulate trial dates for the convenience of either the prosecution or the defense, or ensure that certain defendants will be tried before certain judges (usually to abet the prosecution). Court clerks may even issue search and arrest warrants. These people administer an ancient and inefficient court system and tend to resist professional management reforms.

THE CRIMINAL TRIAL

Though few cases are disposed of by trial and even fewer by jury trial, it has been claimed that the existence of a jury system and the community values it embodies have an effect upon pretrial or nontrial events such as plea bargaining.

A trial commences after a jury has been selected. In theory, each side should desire an impartial jury; in practice, each side strives to select a jury that it feels would be sympathetic to its case. In the United States, jury selection has become a sophisticated process (in England, in theory, the first twelve jurors are seated with very little inquiry and with limited rights to challenge them). In celebrated cases, usually involving political crimes, defense lawyers have used social scientists to aid in the selection process. Most lawyers, defense or prosecution, have their own theories (often hunches) about what type of person would make the best juror for their case. Different states have different rules about the type of questions that can be asked by lawyers of prospective jurors, but all states allow for unlimited challenges "for cause" (wherein reasons must be presented) as well as a limited number of arbitrary challenges to jurors simply disliked for no easily describable reasons. Since trial by jury is slow, expensive, and cumbersome, about three quarters of the states provide for the alternative of trial by judge alone. This alternative is often chosen by the defendant, perhaps because a judge is regarded as more free of prejudice resulting from notorious publicity about the case or because he can understand a technical defense better than a layman. Some defense lawyers argue that juries are always "better bets" than judges. This feeling is borne out to some extent by a major study that showed that, although juries and judges agreed in about 75 to 80 percent of the cases on which both sat, juries tended to be more liberal when they disagreed. Jury decisions are usually required to be unanimous, although a recent U.S. Supreme Court decision found that a requirement of less than unanimity was constitutional in state courts, and some states have adopted a 10–2 or 9–3 system. Since a 12-member jury is not constitutionally required, some states have permitted lower numbers. Important studies have shown that (1) juries do tend to follow judges' instructions; (2) jurors of higher-level socioeconomic status tend to lead juries in their deliberations; and (3) as noted, juries tend to be more liberal than judges.

A trial consists of witnesses furnishing evidence; they are subject to cross-examination that attempts to question their honesty or their ability. Witnesses are often reluctant to participate because of (1) their relationship to the defendant or other persons in the case; (2) repeated delays not only of trials but also of all pretrial proceedings (often delays are instigated by defense attorneys for this very purpose); (3) manipulation of their testimony and insults leveled against them during cross-examination; and (4) fear, which is often a factor in organized-crime prosecutions. Of course, witnesses may be honestly mistaken or may even lie.

After the evidence has been presented, the attorneys for both sides will deliver summations to the jury; this will be followed by the judge's "marshaling" of all the evidence presented and instructions to the jury about the law relating to the case. The jury will then adjourn and return either with a verdict (which usually, but not invariably, must be unanimous) or to inform the judge that they are "hung," or deadlocked. If a defendant is acquitted, he cannot be retried for the same crime because of the "double jeopardy" provision of the United States Constitution. If the jury is hung, retrial can occur despite that provision.

A criminal trial is supposed to be public, and the U.S. Supreme Court has held that it can rarely be closed to the public (and the press) even when all parties agree. It is often to the defendant's advantage to close the trial.

In summary, the legal purpose of a trial is to determine the truth. However, there are often other purposes that may negate the professed one. The trial must be fair, and fairness may result in the exclusion of evidence relevant to the truth. Trials have traditionally been a form of community entertainment, perhaps forums for community prejudices, and to some extent still are. Trials also involve a form of combat between attorneys, who are encouraged to use every strategy to delay, manipulate, and attack. This adversarial ideal—which stresses the duty of the state to amass enough evidence to convict, not the duty of the defendant to disprove the charges—is reserved for those few cases that actually go to trial, although, as mentioned, it may be important even for cases not going to trial.

THE SPEEDINESS OF JUSTICE

Justice, in moral and penological theory, must be swift, and, indeed, the United States Constitution mandates the right to a speedy trial. Often, in crowded urban courtrooms, trial is either too slow or too fast. In felony cases defendants may be jailed in lieu of bail and wait for months to obtain their trials. The federal government and many states have passed laws to ensure that certain types of trials occur within specified time periods after indictment or charge, but they are riddled with exceptions and often manipulated by defense lawyers who believe that speedy trials may not necessarily be in the best interests of their clients (especially those released on bail). Justice may be too speedy in misdemeanor, traffic, and petty-offense cases, which, in urban courts, are so frequent that "assembly line justice" is virtually assured. This dehumanizing process of course affects the poor most heavily. The fault is often inherent in the system, and some decentralization of large urban courthouses may be necessary to remedy it.

18. The Juvenile-Court System

At one time, juveniles over a certain age were considered to be as fully responsible for their crimes as adults and triable as such. The first formal breach of this assumption came with the founding of the New York House of Refuge for children in 1824, an institution designed to confine juveniles separately from adult criminals. In 1831, some Illinois laws were changed so that lesser penalties for the same crime were imposed upon minors than upon adults, and thirty years later probation of juveniles (until they reached the age of seventeen) was made possible by a Chicago law. Separate parts of courts to deal with juveniles were established first in Boston and then throughout Massachusetts in 1870 and 1872. These and other reforms preceded the establishment of the first juvenile court in Chicago in 1899. Youngsters under sixteen were to be labeled delinquents instead of criminals, and the new court was not a conventional criminal one. Between 1899 and 1945, all states adopted separate juvenile-court systems, and the idea spread rapidly through the Western world.

Evidence indicates that juvenile-court reformers were not solely altruistic; they were members of the rising middle classes who sought to "Americanize" newly arrived urban immigrant groups by such innovations as public school, Sunday school, and other civic movements. The values they wished to inculcate were those of the dominant Anglo-Saxon middle class; it was thought that "reaching" immigrant children and trying to break their ties to immigrant culture were necessary. The juvenile court was seen as one means of destroying immigrant deviance and reducing the hold of immigrant families over their children. This factor may partially account for the broad definition of delinquency used by the juvenile-justice system.

CHARACTERISTICS OF THE JUVENILE COURT

Although juvenile courts vary, they are generally characterized by (1) a supposed absence of adversarial combat; (2) proceedings in the form of a "hearing" rather than a "trial" designed to fix guilt; (3) a serious investigation into the character of the juvenile; (4) a disposition of the matter in accordance with such character; (5) the goal of protection of the juvenile, instead of punishment, and (6) tailoring of correctional methods to the needs of the individual juvenile.

Definition of Delinquency. The definition of delinquency is broader than the definitions of crime. Delinquency includes (1) acts that would be criminal if performed by an adult; (2) generally offensive conduct such as "incorrigibility," bad associations, and presence at places that may morally degrade the juvenile; and (3) judging the status of the juvenile as a dependent person or one in need of supervision. The purpose of these broad, even catch-all definitions is to ascertain when intervention by the state, allegedly for the youth's own good, is justifiable. In practice, many juveniles are brought into contact with the court for specific acts that would be criminal if committed by adults. However, perhaps as many as half the complaints, often made by parents who believe their children are unmanageable, involve the second and third categories, and many juveniles are placed into juvenile facilities under these rubrics. There has been a movement to remove dependent noncriminal offenders ("persons in need of supervision" or PINS) from juvenile-court jurisdiction. Law enforcement has resisted this reform on the ground that today's neglected juvenile is tomorrow's criminal.

There is a certain amount of sexual discrimination in juvenile-court proceedings. That may work both for and against female juvenile delinquents. Many states permit incarceration of girls who have committed only "status" offenses (more accurately, been the victims of those offenses), while only males who have violated adult criminal laws can be sent to training schools. Although many young females commit petty crimes, they are rarely arrested for them; in contrast, concern for their sexual morality results in frequent status-offense cases. Detention may be meted out more often to girls than to boys for the same conduct. Many girls who commit less serious offenses than boys may receive longer "sentences."

Procedures. Since juvenile courts were not, in theory, criminal courts but rather courts of "equity," informal procedures developed early in their history and continue into the present. If a juvenile has not been first arrested, a complaint can be filed against him and he is summoned to appear in court with his parents. An informal "initial hearing" or "intake interview" is the substitute for the criminal process of arraignment, and a probation officer informs the juvenile of the "charge." A social worker-intake officer then discusses the matter with the juvenile and dismisses the charge, counsels the juvenile, or, in many states, places him on informal probation. Approximately half of all cases against juveniles result in these dispositions.

In more serious cases, the intake officer files a "petition" calling for a future judicial hearing. The petition is, again, filed allegedly on behalf of the juvenile. Usually, prior to the hearing, a probation officer investigates the case to ascertain (1) whether or not the alleged offense actually occurred and (2) the juvenile's general social, economic, and environmental conditions. In many places judges rely heavily on the recommendations made by probation officers after this investigation. Prior to the hearing, juveniles may be held in detention or "paroled" in their own recognizance. A trial (called a "hearing" or an "adjudication") is then held. If the juvenile is found "guilty" the sentencing (called a "disposition") will follow.

The hearing may occur either in the judge's chambers or in open court. Its records are regarded as confidential. Standards for admission of evidence are looser than those in criminal courts. There is no constitutional right to trial by jury (although some ten states grant that right). However, the U.S. Supreme Court in a landmark decision, *In re Gault,* has held that there is a right to counsel. Final disposition may be (1) a dismissal (comparatively rare); (2) a continuance, wherein the court makes no definitive ruling but retains jurisdiction to see how the juvenile acts in the future; (3) probation, similar to a continuance, except that the juvenile is under the supervision of a probation officer; or (4) commitment, in some states, to an adult institution. All states but one provide for appeals to a criminal court.

DELINQUENCY AND CRIME

The aforementioned terms and procedures mask the reality that many judges treat juvenile delinquency as crime. Juveniles view commitment to an institution as punishment. To most people, including the police, the process is criminal, especially since most juvenile complaints are brought by the police. This fact has led the U.S. Supreme Court to apply certain, though not all, protections offered to criminal defendants by the Bill of Rights to juvenile proceedings. Thus constitutional requirements such as notification of charges, specificity of charges, right to counsel (appointed counsel for indigents), the right against self-incrimination, and the right to confront hostile witnesses are now applicable to the juvenile-hearing process. However, since most juvenile-court personnel believe that these requirements unduly "criminalize" a treatment process, they rarely observe them.

THE JUVENILE COURT IN PRACTICE

About half the states have created totally independent juvenile courts. In some of these states, the separate courts exist only in some counties. In the other states, the juvenile court is part of some other noncriminal court. In all systems, the judges are likely to be ordinary judges of other courts. Only four states have juvenile courts funded and operated by the state itself rather than by the county or municipality. In the vast majority of states, the juvenile court has exclusive jurisdiction over juveniles; in the remainder, there is concurrent jurisdiction in the juvenile and criminal courts. In most states, juveniles over a certain age may be transferred to criminal courts if the charge is serious. Increasingly, in the wake of much juvenile crime in the late 1960s and early 1970s, the number of crimes for which transfer can occur has grown and the age of potential transferees has dropped, in some jurisdictions to thirteen for murder. In some states, juvenile courts have no jurisdiction in capital cases. Before transfer is accomplished, the United States Constitution requires a hearing and the right to counsel. Of course, a state may simply change its substantive laws to require that juveniles over a certain age always be tried in criminal courts, and recently many states have done so, at least for certain crimes.

Most states define juveniles to include those seventeen or under; some set the age at sixteen, and a few at fifteen (the age, as noted, may be lower for certain crimes). In some states, a person brought before juvenile court can remain under its jurisdiction until he is twenty-one. Thus, in theory, a juvenile "sentenced" to incarceration may find that the length of incarceration is greater than the maximum prescribed for an adult offender committing the same act. Of course, the opposite may be true: An older juvenile may be committed for only a few years until he is twenty-one for an offense for which the adult minimum may be longer. Jurisdiction over adults who contribute to the delinquency and/or dependency of juveniles may also lie, exclusively or concurrently, with the criminal courts and/or with juvenile courts.

JUVENILE-COURT JUDGES

Juvenile-court judges are elected in a few states and appointed in others; most are simply elected judges who are assigned to the court (or the juvenile part of another court). Judges frequently rotate into and out of the juvenile court and serve short periods in it. Some juvenile-court judges are not qualified; they may not even be lawyers. They may have other duties. It is estimated that two thirds of juvenile-court judges spend not more than one fourth of their time on juvenile cases. Their attitudes may reflect other judicial backgrounds and experiences although, as noted, one study found that liberal judges more often sentenced to juvenile facilities (which they viewed as rehabilitative) than did conservative judges. As is true of courts generally, particular dispositions may not be in the juvenile's interests but may reflect the demands of other constituencies both within and without the criminal-justice system. This situation may well result in punitive dispositions, even in minor-crime cases or mere status-offense cases. Juvenile-court judges thus play the roles of judge interpreting the law, social worker applying child-welfare principles, and elected official aware of constituency needs. Many states permit appointment of referees to preside at hearings; their decisions are subject to the approval of the juvenile-court judge. This system is used in rural areas at times when the juvenile court is not in formal session.

JUSTICE AND THE JUVENILE COURT

Since (1) the definitions of juvenile delinquency vary from state to state; (2) there are few statistics about the juvenile delinquency in a state before a juvenile court was established; and (3) there is a general lack of statistics, comparison of juvenile-delinquency ratios in states with and without such courts is difficult. In general, juvenile recidivists constitute a large portion of offenders treated in the juvenile courts, and many repeaters are third and fourth offenders. At least 25 percent of adult offenders have juvenile records, but this is a crude measurement. It is not even certain that "advanced" juvenile courts with modern treatment methods and low caseloads for probation officers are in fact superior to courts having fewer facilities. Measure of success and failure are often based upon inadequate criteria such as (1) whether *any* recidivism has occurred and (2) whether the deprivation of due-process rights in the name of "treatment" is justified.

It has been argued that juvenile courts should be merged with family courts, since juvenile difficulties often reflect other, deeper family problems such as neglect, nonsupport, and desertion. Two states and parts of other states do operate such courts. Another suggestion has been that juvenile courts handle *only* cases of true delinquency (conduct that would be criminal if committed by adults) and refer all other matters involving juvenile welfare to social-work agencies. Both these reforms would limit the "labeling" of a particular juvenile as delinquent, labeling that is believed to be harmful to the child. In this view, juveniles should be helped toward social adjustment; their social, but not criminal, problems would thus be removed from the courts altogether. Believers hope that these radical changes would change general public perceptions about the nature of juvenile delinquency, since for every juvenile who has committed a serious crime there may be ten who have committed no crime whatsoever but are still incarcerated.

There are numerous formal diversion programs that encourage police to do something other than refer to juvenile court. But informal police diversion will be followed by reference to a court if the conditions of diversion are violated. Indeed, the existence of formal diversion programs may actually encourage their use by police who would have, in earlier days, simply released the juvenile; court intake officers may also be tempted to use these programs rather than release. Sometimes such programs may be little more than "labeling" agencies, and they may bring harmless juveniles into contact with dangerous ones. Youth-Service Bureaus, not connected either to the juvenile court or to the criminal-justice system, often receive runaways and other "predelinquent" juveniles. The programs of these bureaus (and similar agencies) may be successful because they (1) avoid the labeling of juveniles as delinquents and (2) are not thought of as state agencies. Unfortunately, other diversion programs operate only after someone has defined juveniles as "predelinquents" (or even delinquents) and are thus perceived as part of the coercive juvenile-court apparatus. The programs may involve greater intervention by the state into the lives of juveniles than was true of past informal practices.

Since juveniles are often deprived of rights that they should have or that adults in their positions do have, there have been proposals for merging of the juvenile court and the criminal court. Many believe that distinctions between adults and juveniles are arbitrary, especially in modern society. Why a person at one moment is free of criminal responsibility while at the next is considered to be fully capable of it, is not clear. Since juvenile courts operate as adult courts do, to determine "guilt" and "innocence," and since criminal courts often attempt to "help" offenders, the distinction between those two courts has become blurred. Thus liberal reformers may join conservative reformers in advocating the same policy, though for different ends. In a system still dedicated to the notion of punishment, it is clear that abolition of the juvenile court (or reduction of its jurisdiction) would result in even greater punitiveness than presently exists. This, of course, may well accord with the general social mood.

19. Probation

Probation occurs when a judge suspends the sentence of, grants liberty to, and sets conditions upon the conduct of particular offenders. The concept dramatically clashes with the classical theory of punishment. Probation involves more than mere suspension of sentence, for it envisions a program of aid and guidance. Indeed, some states now permit a suspended sentence *only* if probation is attached. At times, a judge may order probation without even announcing the term of the sentence he would have otherwise imposed, so that the defendant literally does not know the sentence to be received for violation of probation. Probation is the alternative to either imprisonment or release without conditions; but at times it may be attached to a definite jail or prison sentence.

HISTORY

Probation arose from the "inherent" right of the English judiciary to suspend sentences at first for short periods, and then for increasingly longer periods. Initially, offenders had to guarantee good behavior by posting financial bonds. In the United States, perhaps because of a national optimism about human nature, probation, with volunteers acting as sureties for the good behavior of convicts, became increasingly popular. Augustus Johns, a Boston shoemaker, performed this function for some 1,990 people between 1841 and 1858. In 1869, Massachusetts established what was in effect a probation agency for juvenile offenders; nine years later, the state enacted the first known law to provide for public probation officers in Boston. At first, mayors were given the authority to appoint probation officers, but after 1891, judges in Massachusetts gained that power. Most American states quickly followed. Europe to this day does not have a system of public probation officers.

Only fifteen states provide for the possibility of probation for all crimes;

many states exempt crimes of violence and certain other specified crimes from eligibility. Where probation is extensively used—in cities, not in rural areas—it often constitutes the normal disposition of a case.

ORGANIZATION

Since probation originated in the authority of courts to suspend sentence, most probation departments are part of the judicial system. Court appointment of probation officers has been criticized on the grounds that (1) probation is an administrative, not a judicial, function and (2) judges are too busy to administer probation, so that probation departments tend to become independent anyway. Also, patronage considerations heavily affect judicial appointments of probation officers. As a result, most states have chosen to centralize probation in state agencies independent of the judiciary, at least in adult criminal cases (only sixteen have done so for juvenile cases). Available evidence indicates that probation is most effective when administered by a state rather than a county or municipal agency. In thirty states, probation and adult parole are administered by the same agency.

ELIGIBILITY FOR PROBATION

Although probation is usually imposed after conviction, at least five states permit it for those charged but released into diversion programs (this resembles juvenile-court authority to make similar dispositions). Procedures for imposing diversion under these circumstances raise significant questions of due process of law, since no prior determination of guilt has occurred. After conviction, judges are required to demand either probation or presentence reports (in about half the states, at least for certain types of crimes), or have the discretion to request such reports and to make probation decisions with or without them. Although judges may follow their impressionistic hunches about awarding probation, they often agree with report recommendations favoring probation and usually follow recommendations against probation.

The presentence report is diagnostic in nature. It attempts to ascertain the causes of criminal conduct and to formulate a program to rehabilitate the individual. Thus background factors, including the defendant's attitude toward crime, his previous criminal record, family and socioeconomic conditions, education, and work history are taken into account. Often the data are unsystematically collected, especially in smaller probation agencies. Funding for most probation departments is usually inadequate, and probation officers are viewed by defendants as law enforcers rather than helpers. (This is most often true when the same probation officer both investigates the defendant's background and supervises his program of rehabilitation.) The lack of centralization of records in most communities, the legal inability to check juvenile-court files, and the heavy caseloads carried by many probation officers are among the reasons why data collection is difficult. The problems are reduced in statewide probation systems with centralized record-keeping procedures.

CONDITIONS OF PROBATION

State laws, court decisions, and probation department practices determine the conditions of probation. Such conditions may include (1) obeying all laws, (2) regular work or school attendance, (3) living at home or in some other designated place, (4) avoidance of undesirable friendships and associations, and (5) nonuse of alcohol and/or drugs. Payment of fines or restoration of stolen property may also be made conditions of probation. Objections to the latter include arguments that (1) restitution simply may be impossible for most defendants; and (2) probation departments may tend to become little more than collection agencies, a practice that undermines the agency's social-service role. Probation periods are usually the same as those of the suspended sentences. The probation officer's role in probation revocation hearings most clearly demonstrates the contradictions between their "helping" and "punitive" functions, for officers in effect charge defendants with violating the terms of probation. The U.S. Supreme Court has recently required that such revocation proceedings require counsel for the probationer. In many jurisdictions, probation ends automatically when the period of the suspended sentence ends. It may be ended earlier by judicial order or even at times by order of the probation department.

SUPERVISION

Supervision takes various forms. Ideally, probation officers should visit the homes of their clients, but in practice, visits are few and the time spent in the home is minimal. More frequently observed is the requirement that the probationer report to the probation officer, perhaps as often as once a week. This may involve a short interview about the probationer's work and leisure or even the submission of written reports from employers or teachers. Probation officers may try to find employment for probationers (some agencies have an employment unit) and to provide necessary financial assistance. However, since the latter function often creates conflicts with other agencies, most probation officers simply refer their clients to appropriate welfare agencies.

Probation officers attempt to treat their clients by methods as diverse as gaining friendship, stimulating ambition, and personal and financial counseling. Psychiatrically oriented probation officers attempt to encourage self-analysis and to become "role models" while encouraging probationers to become "independent." Probation officers who believe that criminality is caused by group associations and learning processes attempt to change the client's personal interactions rather than to change him by individual therapy. This method necessitates (1) selection of probation officers from the communities in which probationers live and (2) development of community programs to reduce crime.

Usually one officer is assigned to oversee all probationers living in a given geographic area. Some departments assign officers who match the probationer's sex or ethnic or religious background. Some of the larger departments divide the caseload on the basis of the individual officer's "expertise," assigning him to probationers with particular problems or programs. In practice, supervision—the rationale for probation—is almost impossible with any ratio exceeding fifty to one, but many departments have caseloads of several hundred per officer. Probation officers are now regarded as skilled professional social workers, and volunteer officers have been largely dispensed with. Recently, however, the use of volunteers, either civilians or ex-convicts, has been reinstated to supplement the work of professionals. There are now more than two hundred thousand such volunteers, many of them skilled. Although it is difficult to evaluate the success of volunteer programs, it should be noted that European countries rely exclusively on such persons for probation supervision.

HALFWAY HOUSES

Placement of probationers in residential centers or in nonfamily homes is termed "community corrections." England maintains hostels for juvenile probationers who live at the home and either work or attend school. Work in the community has been an option for a long time in England and New Zealand. The United States has tended to use this system or "work release" for parolees rather than for adult probationers. The very existence of halfway-house programs apparently tends to increase the numbers of juveniles who are adjudicated as delinquents and then remanded to available programs.

RESULTS OF PROBATION

Although probation departments regularly claim that 75 percent of probationers "succeed," probation officers may not know enough about the lives of their clients to make accurate judgments. The probation officers may also have a vested interest in "success" that prevents acknowledgment of high failure rates. As police department record-keeping procedures improve and are computerized, probation failure rates may well rise; indeed, "good" probation agencies that maintain complete records have more known failures than the reputed norm. Although probation departments do not report relapses into crime after probation has ended, follow-up studies indicate that there is no startling increase in the failure rate. Many probationers or ex-probationers are rearrested, though they may not be convicted. Since probationers by definition are regarded as likely to reform, few comparisons with those incarcerated or those released without probation have been made. Certainly, recidivism is great among those incarcerated, but it is impossible to ascertain whether the rate would be lower had ex-prisoners been placed on probation instead of sent to prison. Studies on the number of probationers who are subsequently imprisoned are of little value, since they do not compare that number with the total number of probationers.

Probationers who most frequently violate probation are likely to be those with (1) previous criminal records, (2) irregular work habits, (3) low economic status, (4) family members who are criminals, and (5) criminal friends and associates. In one study, it was found that 44.8 percent of probationers who lived in high-delinquency areas violated probation, while only 30.7 percent of those living in low-delinquency areas did so.

Probationers, of course, can support their families and even make restitution to those they have wronged. Probation is cheaper than incarceration; while adult probation may cost $140 per year per probationer, imprisonment costs are at least fifteen times as high. Ironically, well-run probation programs may cost more than imprisonment programs, but the success of well-run probation programs will probably reduce total correctional costs for the system as a whole since recidivism rates will be lowered. There is no statistical likelihood that jurisdictions that grant more probation experience more crime or that jurisdictions with many probationers (irrespective of the proportion of convicts allowed probation) have a high crime rate or a large number of probation failures. California has claimed success for its program wherein the state pays counties for probation services. There is no proof that victims of crime will be less likely to prosecute where probation is widespread or promises to become widespread. Indeed, the ability of the criminal court to demand restitution from probationers may well aid victims (at least of property crimes) who, it may be presumed, are interested in restitution rather than retribution. Insofar as existing probation failure can be attributed to a "bad" environment, the answer would appear to involve an improvement of the environment rather than curtailment of probation.

In essence, probation performs much the same role as plea bargaining: the mitigation of harsh laws in cases where "deserving" defendants should not be subject to broad, legislatively mandated sentences. Probation differs from plea bargaining in that probation is an open process. It may be more effective than plea bargaining because defendants are less cynical about the process and because they have been exposed to the shocks of trial and conviction. While sentencing discretion, plea bargaining, and even parole are highly controversial subjects, it may be surprising to find much less debate about probation, a subject that involves many of the same issues. Such public acceptance may reflect the success of probation or more fundamentally the general recognition that somewhere within the system there must be at least one agency flexible enough to deal with offenders rather than with offenses only.

IMPRISONMENT AND POSTIMPRISONMENT

Part V

20. The Development of the Prison System

While imprisonment is not the fate of the average criminal (assuming such a person exists), the idea of prison looms behind the activities of criminal-justice agencies and even public sentiments about crime and punishment. Imprisonment is an awesome experience for any convict; it cannot fail to make significant changes, perhaps permanent ones, in his character. The presence of prisons brings into dramatic focus virtually all theories of punishment and most of those relating to social reaction to crime. The fundamental decisions in the criminal-justice system, by all its agencies, is whether this defendant deserves to be imprisoned. Thus prison is not just another criminal-justice institution; it is the most dramatic demonstration of the power of the state over the lives of its citizens. Whether or not the prison—with its physical awesomeness, its dedication to total control over every facet of inmate life, and its function as a powerful learning experience—has shaped the design and meaning of other institutions (for example, the factory, the school, the welfare office), as some contend, is irrelevant. It is enough to know that virtually every problem of the criminal-justice system and every value of democratic society and its relation to individual liberty are embodied in and powerfully affected by the prison system. Also, the greatest controversies in the realm of crime and punishment in society revolve about prison "reform" (a subject of endless debate for the past two centuries). Thus the prison as institution and symbol stands alone.

While the study of history may be useful in general analysis of crime and criminal justice, it is imperative when we consider imprisonment. Since imprisonment is a historically novel reaction to crime, its history is not "dead" but vitally important to an understanding of why it came to be conceived as a better social reaction to crime than previous institutions and practices and why it persists as a major (symbolically, *the* major) reaction in the face of waves of criticisms and reform proposals. (These proposals are almost invariably repetitive and come in cycles.) Attacks upon this or that system of imprisonment or even upon the idea of prison wax and wane, while prison, largely unchanged, goes on. The fate of prison reform highlights the fundamental difficulties of changing criminal-justice institutions, especially when those institutions embody deeply held, almost mystically religious beliefs. So what is said about prison, especially its history, can be said to a lesser (perhaps, though rarely, a greater) degree about the criminal-justice system as a whole.

EARLY HISTORY IN THE UNITED STATES

Jails, initially for those detained and then for those punished, were established early in American history. In the United States as in England, they came into being because of increasing revulsion against capital and corporal punishment. Houses of correction, at first used to incarcerate vagrants, gradually became places where sentences were served (in 1788, New York allowed this). By present standards, conditions were intolerable: There was no labor; much idleness, drunkenness, and vice; no separation of those accused from those convicted; no separation of debtors from other prisoners; no beds; and liquor and other contraband were sold by prison officials. Prisoners were detained to pay jail fees even after acquittal.

Philadelphia Quakers instituted the first major reforms. In 1776 Richard Wister provided soup to prisoners who would otherwise have starved in the county jail. Later, the Philadelphia Society for Alleviating Distressed Persons (later called the Philadelphia Society for Alleviating the Miseries of Public Prisons) was formed. The society broadened its activities to encompass a movement to abolish capital punishment and to substitute for it imprisonment in solitary confinement.

In 1773, Connecticut established the first state prison; prisoners were fastened at night by heavy chains attached to beams, and iron bars were placed on their feet. Massachusetts in 1785 provided for imprisonment with solitary confinement and hard labor at an island in Boston Harbor, and, in 1803 authorized the building of a new state prison. Labor, silence, and presumed penitence were the goals of the new prison system, which spread rapidly throughout the East. Concern for prisoner welfare was subordinated to a need to demonstrate the power of the state and to place long-term prisoners in secure settings. Opposition to capital punishment also played a major role. After the American Revolution, Pennsylvania quickly abolished capital punishment except for murder, as well as corporal punishment. Street gang labor, resembling later road gangs, was tried; but after Philadelphians became outraged at this system, it was replaced by sending prisoners to county jails. Prison labor was introduced because (1) institutional expenses could be paid from it and (2) imprisonment per se was not regarded as sufficient punishment.

THE PENITENTIARY

Some historians have viewed the rise of the penitentiary as the great symbol of capitalist society's determination to change the offender by constant surveillance of his activities in the context of a "total institution" for the purpose of first "breaking" and then "remaking" him into a docile worker. The evidence for this motive is thin and requires an imaginative re-evaluation of the role of Quaker reformers to stress their business conduct and interests rather than their humanitarian motives. This theory also overlooks the fact that surveillance and "treatment" were positivist-inspired notions that did not gain currency until later in history. Certainly, as noted, the penitentiary and imprisonment generally have played some critical roles in periods of depression (when labor is in oversupply), but the question of whether early reformers meant the new system to be adapted to such ends remains open.

In 1778, England passed a law (never implemented) authorizing the creation of penitentiaries to impart habits of sobriety and Christianity to inmates. Pennsylvania Quakers were the first to develop a system of prison discipline for the purpose of reformation. Since criminal association was considered so dangerous, segregation of prisoners in the form of solitary confinement became a part of Quaker theory; it was thought that such confinement would also enable the prisoner to meditate on his sins. The Philadelphia Walnut Street Jail, which housed state prisoners, was the first experimental ground for this policy. Labor was required, at least during the latter stages of imprisonment, but labor was always subordinate to meditation. Some official visitors (governors, state legislators, judges, sheriffs, and public-spirited bodies) came to break the tedium of solitary confinement. Religious exhortation by the Philadelphia Society for Alleviating the Miseries of Public Prisons was a characteristic of the visitor system.

The Walnut Street Jail featured (1) solitary confinement; (2) prisoner classification (on the basis of sex, age, separation of those convicted from those awaiting trial, and separation of those imprisoned for debt from those imprisoned for crime); (3) workshops for most inmates; (4) prohibition of irons or chains; (5) silence during work; (6) limited hours of work and payment for it; and (7) generally humane treatment. However, within a few years, overcrowding increased (the system of solitary confinement was expensive), and a decline in work facilities, politics, and increasingly lax discipline led to a closing of the jail.

The Walnut Street Jail was supplemented in 1826 by the Western State Penitentiary in Pittsburgh, which eventually permitted work in solitary confinement. The "Pennsylvania System" was most fully developed in 1829 by the Eastern State Penitentiary (located in Philadelphia), where prisoners engaged in spinning, weaving, and shoemaking in their cells, and left the cells in blindfolds to perform prison maintenance work.

In New York, the "Auburn System" was instituted in 1821; after capital punishment had been essentially abolished, the new prison system treated three types of offenders: (1) the most depraved, who were kept in continuous solitary confinement; (2) a less dangerous group, who were kept in solitary for three days a week; and (3) the least dangerous, who were confined in a cell for one day a week. There was no provision for work in the cell. Eventually, New York (under the Auburn System) permitted work in association with other prisoners (though under complete silence) during the day and solitary confinement at night.

Between 1820 and 1860, a great controversy raged between the Philadelphia Quakers and the Boston Society for the Improvement of Prison Discipline and for the Reformation of Juvenile Offenders, the latter defending the Auburn System. Most states adopted the Auburn System because it was cheaper than its counterpart and was thought to have the same advantages. Most European visitors (including commissions from England and several other countries) preferred a modified Pennsylvania System.

The "Irish system" (actually introduced in Australia), characterized by (1) indeterminate sentences, (2) a credit or "mark" system whereby good behavior reduced length of sentence, and (3) a resultant form of parole, was introduced in the Elmira, New York, reformatory in 1876. Reformation by means of education and meaningful labor were to abet these liberalized procedures. The setting, as has generally been true in this system, was that of a maximum-security prison that featured corporal punishment. Elmira left the ambiguous reform-versus-punishment legacy for later American prisons and reformatories.

JUVENILE INSTITUTIONS

The New York Association for the Prevention of Pauperism, a private group financed by the state, opened the first institution devoted to juvenile reformation in 1825. The first state institution was established in Massachusetts in 1847; the number rapidly burgeoned until it reached approximately three hundred. These institutions stressed education and reformation rather than mere punishment. They incorporated religious teaching, academic instruction, indeterminate sentences, good-behavior release, and even inmate self-government. But despite the professed intentions of early reformation efforts, the New York House of Refuge resembled a prison, and educational and work programs were exploitative in nature and subordinate to punishment goals. The major innovation was simply to separate juvenile from adult offender. The cottage system (imported from Europe) was established in 1858 in Lancaster, Massachusetts; the replacement of cell blocks with individual cottages was favored because cottages were (1) cheaper to build and maintain, (2) more homelike, and (3) tied to classification of juveniles. These institutions also reflected conflict between punishment and treatment approaches.

PRISON SPECIALIZATION

At first, jails were the only form of penal institution. Vagrants were later incarcerated in houses of correction, but this system soon died. State prisons were then established for juveniles, the insane, women, different races, and for other types of criminals. The trend toward specialization concentrated upon (1) the nature and seriousness of the crime and (2) the nature of the offender. The rationale involved prevention of undesirable contact between different types of offenders and use of special facilities for various categories of offenders.

21. Prisons Today

Today, the most serious form of differentiation involves the nature of the crime; felons serve time in state prisons, misdemeanants in county and municipal facilities. But this has little to do with the characteristics of particular offenders. Some states have created state farms for long-term misdemeanants, but these institutions are rarely specialized. The system is different elsewhere; in England, for instance, the national government runs local prisons and they are conceded to be both more efficient and less expensive than the dual American system.

The major forms of specialization today are by sex, age, and in large states, personal characteristics. In practice, the dividing line is not always clear, since young offenders are often sentenced to prison, and recidivists often are incarcerated in juvenile institutions. In those states with large prison populations and in the federal prison system, gradations of institutions from "minimum"- through "medium"- to "maximum"-security prisons have been established. Also, some states have sought to treat particular categories of prisoners (for example, alcoholics, drug addicts, and defective delinquents) in special institutions and to create special programs for them.

PERSPECTIVES ON IMPRISONMENT

Today, solitary confinement has been eliminated (except as temporary punishment), as have other early features such as silence, bad diet, and intolerable living conditions. They have been replaced by increased community contacts and more meaningful educational and vocational programs. Imprisonment per se came to be viewed *as* punishment rather than as a locale for further punishment. However, treatment of the criminal, not by early methods of religious exhortation and ritualistic labor but by newer forms of therapy, was haphazardly tacked onto the punitive nature of imprisonment. Deliberate infliction of suffering for its own sake—that is, imprisonment itself—has distinguished prison from other restricted environments such as mental hospitals.

PURPOSES OF PRISONS

Since (1) most prisoners return to the outside and (2) punishment alone does not reform, Americans came to assume that a diagnosis of the reason or reasons why convicts committed crimes, and treatment of the individual to overcome those conditions, were the purposes of incarceration. Punishment was theoretically subordinated to establishment of positive therapeutical relationships between prison personnel and prisoners, but the reality of institutional needs for security and discipline and the lack of trained and well-paid therapeutic personnel insured that the goal would not be met. Today, rehabilitation, even in theory, has been increasingly discredited.

A vast array of nonpunitive programs, ranging from therapy and group counseling to educational, work, and recreational programs have been instituted, although not all of these may be truly related to the needs of particular prisoners. Participation in one or more of these programs has often become the basis of the judgment of a parole board that a prisoner has become rehabilitated. Again, as noted, even "liberal" reformers have questioned this connection. Failure of rehabilitation—at least in a punitive environment— has had the recent backlash effect of calls for restoration of "pure" notions of punishment or at least segregation of the dangerous criminals from society and "voluntary" rather than compelled use of prison treatment programs. Yet classification and diagnosis of individual inmates and specialized programs of treatment still exist, although the latter are generally no longer mandatory.

Prisons continue to serve a variety of purposes; they are supposed to hurt criminals by the fact of incarceration, deter them from further crime, deter others, protect society by isolating the most dangerous people, and reform criminals by treatment. Some of these goals require high degrees of prison discipline and great restriction of free movement within the prison, while others do not necessarily involve such methods.

There is no necessary contradiction between imprisonment as a means of changing the offender and as punishment. In early American prisons, even vocational and educational programs were viewed as punitive; labor was meant to be "retribution" for the crime. The nature of the labor—its repetitiveness, its infliction of physical pain and exhaustion (often, its pointlessness)—helped keep prisoners out of trouble and helped to develop attitudes of industry and obedience.

Early reformers attacked many prison "punishments" as ineffective and morally unwarranted since imprisonment was deprivation of liberty, in itself sufficient punishment. Thus whipping, forced standing at attention, and other "tortures," whether mild or severe, no longer became routine. Prison administrators feared that relaxation of these methods would produce rebelliousness and even further criminality among prisoners. They therefore substituted psychological punishment for physical torture. Thus, while the idea of prison reformation through terror was replaced by the idea of rehabilitation through treatment, prisons remained punitive and newer treatment programs were set up alongside (perhaps in competition with) older punitive ones.

The contradiction has not been resolved; prisons have never become transformed into treatment centers, nor have they remained unalloyed models of repression. Compromise, achieving the results of neither orientation, became the answer—until the 1970s, when rehabilitation itself became increasingly questioned. The contradiction remains, although it is being increasingly resolved in favor of punishment.

CLASSIFICATION

"Classification" of prisoners serves two purposes: It (1) segregates prisoners on the basis of age, sex, and dangerousness for the sake of prisoner welfare and (2) proves the opportunity for administrative control and discipline of prisoners. Classification later expanded to the introduction of certain vocational and educational programs to selected groups. With the onset of the treatment rationale, classification became diagnostic, an attempt to understand the character and personality of inmates. Classification also involved programming to meet particularized needs of individuals and of groups into which they fell according to psychological insights. Thus, now (1) psychologists and social workers determine the prisoner's case history; (2) a "classification committee," including prison officials, decides on an individualized program for the offender and (through the warden) assigns the inmate to a particular form of custody and program; (3) the "classification committee" then monitors the inmate's performance in the program; (4) "reclassification" based upon the inmate's experiences is periodically undertaken by the classification committee. Thus, in theory, the inmate's stay in prison is accompanied by a continuing surveillance of his (perhaps changing) needs.

But the theory is undermined by the facts. There are very few diagnosticians available. The ratio of diagnostic personnel to inmates may run as high as one to two thousand in some states. The diagnostic process is also flawed, since it is difficult to prove that the "medical" analogy of cause and effect is valid. The inmate is given very little time to participate in his diagnoses and to acquaint the social worker or psychiatrist with the complexity of his life and psychological condition. Classification committees may rarely meet (so that one person makes the decisions), or when they meet may classify on the basis of institutional needs rather than individual needs of the inmate. Security and punishment considerations may readily prevail. Thus, someone who is both high-risk and in need of specialized treatment may be denied access to the latter because it is reserved for minimum-security prisoners. Other institutional needs may predominate. The availability of treatment facilities and programs or even of jobs may determine the number assigned to those programs. Or, conversely, the need to fill certain jobs may result in "forced recruitment" of prisoners into them, irrespective of individual needs. Often a compromise is made, so that an inmate may do something for which he is unsuited part of the day and something relevant to his needs for the remainder. Actual assignment and monitoring of the assignment may simply not fit the needs of the institution, and custodial personnel may not even know of the classification reports on particular inmates; this is especially true where no custodial personnel are members of the classification committee.

Prisoners are often shifted into and out of special programs as rewards and punishments for prison behavior rather than as responses to their particular needs. Also, some programs, especially counseling and group-therapy ones, may be regarded by custodial personnel as occasions for malingering. Inefficient administration of prison therapeutic programs is the norm, often because professional staff members are too busy writing reports and attending meetings. The term "reclassification" is also often meaningless because of (1) time constraints on the classification committee and (2) preoccupation with the inmate's good or bad behavior. In some institutions, inmates can request reclassification, but it may be denied for reasons of administrative inconvenience, poor work record, violation of prison rules, or simply a judgment that the inmate doesn't need the program he wants.

The general reception center, which decides where an inmate is sent, is a recent innovation. Federal judges may commit a convict to the Bureau of Prisons before final sentencing in order to obtain recommendations about the institution in which he should serve that sentence. In California, diagnostic agencies may refer cases back to the sentencing judge with a recommendation that probation be instituted; also, that state has begun an admission-orientation program, a counseling program, and a group-therapy program. This system formulates a later institutional treatment program prior to assignment to a prison. But none of these measures changes the fact that society sends people to prison to be punished, and none addresses the issue whether or not it is correct to treat the criminal as a "sick" individual. It appears that where imprisonment rates are high and sentences are long, there will be a concomitant need to ameliorate harsh prison conditions by at least the appearance of treatment programs and processes.

PRISON CONDITIONS

The primary function of a prison is to compel obedience to custodial rules. To achieve this aim, and to keep the prison running as a functioning institution, rigid controls appear necessary. Specific scheduling of work, meals, education, even haircuts become institutional necessities. Prison employees are as divided as the rest of us on issues such as the degree of freedom and creativity that is healthy for inmates, and these views affect theories of prison organization. Thus one theory may stress that programs are therapeutic; another that they are wastes of time; and a third that they enable inmates to adjust to prison repression of liberty.

Views about the nature and degree of prison discipline also mirror more general social notions. While all may agree that discipline is necessary, some may define it as the minimum necessary to run an orderly institution; others may see it as requiring detailed rules covering most aspects of inmate life and strict punishments for violation of those rules. What is the role of punishment in effecting good order? Is a person merely the product of social relationships? Does he gain his sense of identity from the rules and procedures (formal and informal) in those relationships? Or is the individual autonomous? Does one's personality submit to organization? Do all institutions—but prisons especially—operate to stifle the natural and spontaneous outburst of individual personality? The answers, both to society and to prison administrators, are confused and contradictory.

Rules.   Whatever the answers, infraction of prison rules, if detected, leads to a report to a senior custodial official. The inmate is offered a hearing and the right to present a defense and perhaps to call witnesses; the reporting guard also submits a statement. If the inmate is guilty, he most often loses certain privileges (movies, television, sports, educational training opportunities, etc.); he may also lose credit ("good time") toward early release or, in serious cases, will be kept for a time in solitary confinement. A prisoner must obey not only the law but also all rules of the institution. Some of these rules aid in the prison's punitive function, while others are solely directed toward order in a closed, close society where many people live and work together. Some rules are very general; others deal with petty behavior that would be totally innocent outside the prison context (for example, oversleeping, horseplay).

At hearings, many procedural protections, including the right to counsel, normally considered essential to due process of law, are ignored or limited. Also, the prison world differs from the outside world in that all violations are punished; none is overlooked (although a punishment may take the form of nothing more than a reprimand). Prison discipline has historically been shaped by four attitudes: (1) belief in reformation, which occurs after the instilling of new habits by compulsion; (2) the view that the presence of authority must be demonstrated to prevent criminality in prison; (3) the desire to inflict pain, pain within the prison added to that inflicted by incarceration itself; and (4) fear of escapes, to which all else is subordinated. The backlash to the rigidity characteristic of the punitive response in some prisons, has resulted in abandonment of discipline to the extent that prisoners regularly commit crimes against other inmates or bribe guards to obtain contraband.

Personnel.   Prison wardens (and ultimately their staffs) may well be political appointees, thus often ensuring that (1) they will not be competent and knowledgeable; and (2) they will have short tenures of office. At present only a minority of states put wardens within their civil-service or merit systems; in contrast, a substantial majority of states include professionals (teachers, psychologists) and even custodial guards in their merit systems. Civil service, as presently administered, may be circumvented by (1) "temporary" appointments (which may become *de facto* permanent); and (2) "tailoring" higher-level examinations to fit the qualifications of one person. Often, civil service only eliminates the most obviously unqualified and does little to assure appointment of the most qualified. Performance on civil-service examinations may not correlate with later outstanding, or even satisfactory, job performance.

Any qualitative deficiencies in custodial guards are especially harmful because they have the most contact with and impact upon the inmates. Personality types of prison guards, it has been shown, strongly resemble those of inmates. Guards tend to be cynical, emotionally shallow, temperamental, egotistical, and alienated from society. Of course, these traits may be functional for their roles, but they may also lead to exploitation of inmates. However, it is not necessarily true that guards will act on these impulses. Since guard roles have become increasingly ambiguous (where treatment goals conflict with punishment ones), guards have tended to develop the characteristics of a subculture. Despite the frequency (and intensity) of contact with guards, most inmates report that they have been most helped by noncustodial counselors.

In response to reform pressures, in the 1950s and 1960s, prisons became "correctional facilities" and guards became "correctional officers." Guards thus were regarded as front-line therapists who, in some manner, were supposed to assist other professionals at their therapeutic jobs. Pre- and in-service training were designed to "sensitize" guards to their new roles. In some states, able, high-ranking correctional supervisors hired higher-quality correctional personnel, but the rehabilitative results were no better in these places than elsewhere, since in practice custody and punishment functions were still paramount. Guards are, or should be, supervisory management personnel, but they cannot play this role because they (1) cannot legally offer incentives and (2) are themselves subject to administrative rules that hamper any initiative. Guards continually teeter between "law enforcement" and less punitive responses to rule violations, just as police officers do. Guards cannot exact the most severe punishments or keep all malefactors in solitary confinement. Yet guards must both ensure smoothly running systems ("order") and demand compliance with rules ("law"). And as in society, these functions often become contradictory. If they are too authoritarian, guards may be labeled as neurotic and as causes of inmate discontent; if guards administer the rules flexibly, they may be labeled "softheaded," dangerous (because they create danger for other guards), or even corrupt.

OBSTACLES TO NONPUNITIVE TREATMENT

The normal obstacles to innovation within the criminal-justice system—the failure to restructure agencies and agency thinking, the social conflicts about punishment versus rehabilitation throughout the criminal-justice system, and bureaucratic lag—are compounded in the prison. Little specific direction is given custodial personnel about the meaning of "treatment." Treatment may be thought of as anything that does not inflict pain, even if particular "treatments" are either unproven or ill suited to particular prisoners. Rarely is treatment defined as the necessity to do something positive rather than merely refraining from punishment. The mere assumption that abstinence from punishment is treatment may often characterize attitudes of prison personnel.

Treatment, as administered, may only be basic humanitarianism or merely a sophisticated version of punishment. Prison personnel, the men and women in the "treatment" trenches, are subject to political review. Since politicians often decry "coddling of criminals," it may be prudent for prison personnel not to advocate or publicize treatment programs. Also, the bureaucratic organization of prisons ensures that routine, conservative routine, will be the norm. Innovation threatens organizational routines—and, perhaps, jobs.

Professional Groups. Paradoxically, the very "professionalization" of groups such as social workers has contributed to lack of innovation. Professionalism is a cultural concept that implies (1) the existence of specialized knowledge, (2) stable definition of the knowledge, (3) training and entrance examination for future practitioners of the profession, (4) peer judgment about proper use of the knowledge, and (5) exclusion of unqualified persons. Professionalism also involves status, with "grubby" work relegated to others. Thus professionalism breeds both elitism and conservatism. Professional prison administrators are not mere practitioners of social work or psychology; they are status-minded heads of organizations that provide high-status jobs, and the need to maintain status often becomes as important to them as the need to do the job. This tendency of professionals to see themselves as prestigious and successful has often contributed to unwarranted claims of "cure" of prisoners.

Prisoner Reaction to Treatment. Treatment programs also meet with significant prisoner resistance. Prisoners may believe (often correctly) that treatment personnel are primarily custodial personnel and only secondarily interested in inmate welfare. Treatment personnel (1) are usually under the authority of custodial administrators and (2) tend to believe that the function of treatment is to "adjust" the inmate to the conditions of captivity. Treatment and its concomitant necessity to collect intimate information may lead many inmates to feel that such information will be used against them or will be used by middle-class people to make judgments about them. Prisoners cooperate with treatment programs because they believe that such cooperation will help them to achieve either early release or at least a lessening of the pain inflicted by the prison.

Many prisoners regard their identity as precious and deride attempts to take it from them by criminal-justice labeling processes. To them, treatment involves just such another label (a worse one because it is deceptive). Since many treatment programs seek to change personality rather than only actions, they become particularly threatening. Also, inmate group norms are threatened by the presence of competing treatment norms. In addition, individualized treatment programs are regarded by many inmates as examples of special favors and therefore unfair. Prisoners not released view the process as continued punishment, not for the crime they committed, but for their prison conduct or simply because prison administrators have set their own standards for appropriate conduct.

JUDGING IMPRISONMENT

If the penological goal is retribution, then all prisons are successful, for imprisonment causes pain. If the goal is general deterrence, then imprisonment may be considered moderately successful, for the public knows of the painful nature of prison treatment (but this might imply that *any* incarceration for any period of time would be as effective as long-term incarceration). If incapacitation of the dangerous is the penological goal, then imprisonment has been of only dubious success. One study indicated that long-term incarceration of the present prison population would reduce crime only by a total of 8 percent. Prison crime is very high, especially for assaults and homicides, theft, and drug use. Unless we revert to the old Pennsylvania System of complete separation of prisoner by category of crime, this situation is not likely to abate. If reformation (or, in modern terminology, rehabilitation) is the goal, then incarceration may not be successful. Recidivism appears to be high and may range from 55 to 75 percent (see pp. 235–37). Federal prisoners show a lesser recidivism rate; in one major study, only 35 percent of released offenders committed serious crimes within four years after release, while 52 percent had no further contact with the criminal-justice system and 13 percent had only a minor record.

Whatever the statistics on recidivism, it should not be surprising that prisons have failed to rehabilitate; they cannot. Rather, the prison system should be designed to minimize the inmate's chances of forming any deeper commitment to criminality.

Since 1973 the number of prisoners has risen dramatically, from 200,000 to 230,000 (1974) to perhaps 300,000 today. This trend may be attributable to (1) revival of the punishment response because of the perceived failure of treatment; (2) increasing criminality among a crime-prone youth population that itself dramatically increased in proportion to the total population and that strained the resources of community treatment programs; (3) the availability of diversion and treatment, which probably increased the numbers of offenders actually processed by the criminal-justice system, thus creating a greater pool of potential recidivists; (4) the presence of more truly dangerous hard-core criminals among the total criminal population; and (5) an increase in general unemployment (always correlatable with the prison rate, though not the crime rate). Since rehabilitation in prison has failed, rehabilitation itself came into disrepute.

22. Prison Programs

The three major programs in prisons are labor, education, and group discussions. They exist as much to control inmates as to rehabilitate them. Until the 1930s, prison labor was thought of as rehabilitative. After prison factories were closed by law (often because of labor-union objections to competition), educational programs were regarded as rehabilitative. Group discussions later became the vehicle for inmate achievement of maturity, also in the name of rehabilitation. Perhaps each program had its heyday in accordance with social demands: at first for productive labor, then for workers with basic skills (education), and then for well-adjusted people in our "service" society.

PRISON LABOR

Although early Quaker reformers believed that work interfered with meditation, most Americans have taken the position that prison idleness is a great vice. Labor was initially conceived of as both punishment and potential source of income, if not profit, for the prison system. Labor was hard and totally useless for the prisoner, and even, by law was designed to disgrace him. Although the rhetoric of "useful" labor has largely replaced that of punitive, monotonous labor, the idea that the latter fosters habits of industriousness and obedience has not died out. Today, prison labor is largely regarded as time-filling. Although production for profit has largely been abandoned, prisoners today are considered morally required to work at least to pay for their upkeep.

Prison Labor Systems. There are six prison labor systems. (1) Under the *convict-lease system,* private contractors control employment, discipline of the prisoners, and the sale of products made by prisoners. (2) Under the *contract system,* while the state controls discipline of the prisoner, the type of employment and product made are controlled by private contractors. (3) Under the *piece-price system*, the state employs and disciplines the prisoner, while private contractors sell the products. (4) Under the *public-account system*, the state is the employer in all respects, and can sell the products made by prisoners anywhere (in competition with private enterprise). (5) Under the *state-use system*, state public agencies are the only permissible purchasers of prison-made products. (6) Under the *public-works system*, the state is the only buyer, and what it buys are public works (roads, buildings) services by prisoners. The last system, in the form of road building, was the earliest use of convict labor—even before the advent of the prison system. For a time it was abandoned, but then revived with the advent of the automobile. "Road gangs" are still used in the South, and forestry camps and various forms of park, public hospital, and nonprofit private-agency work (often by juvenile offenders) are modern versions of the system. The public-account system flourished from 1800 to 1825, but prison-made goods failed in competition with new capital-intensive, machine-made, private-sector goods. There are, however, a few surviving prison industries that still compete with the private sector. The contract system became popular in the 1820s as capitalists found that prison labor was cheap and could be harnessed to new production and marketing organizations. Auburn Prison's adoption of this system was a major reason why this rather than the Pennsylvania type became a model for future prisons. Work was performed within the prison under slavelike conditions. The rise of the American labor movement in the 1880s led to the system's gradual disappearance, and by 1940 it was no longer in existence. The piece-price system, wherein products made by prison labor was sold (by the piece) to a private contractor, was used by both Pennsylvania and New Jersey in the early nineteenth century; it followed the contract system in the 1880s. But since it was but a variant of the contract system, it too went into rapid decline. The convict-lease system was popular in the South after the Civil War (often as a substitute for payment of fines). The state-use system was another replacement for the contract system in the 1880s. Even today, many states are required to buy certain products only from prisons. This requirement is evaded in practice, since employers and labor unions oppose it and the prison-made products are usually inferior. Ninety percent of prison labor is now engaged in the state-use or public-works areas. In 1934, a federal law permitted states to regulate goods manufactured by prisoners in other states, and every state now prohibits sales of such goods. Federal laws also bar most of these goods from shipment in interstate commerce. These restrictions have contributed to the decline of prison labor and account for the fact that very few prisoners now work except to maintain the prison itself. Idleness has not been ameliorated by either educational or counseling programs, which have become substitutes for prison labor.

Payment for Prison Labor.   Prison labor originally involved payment of wages, but this system disappeared from 1780 until about 1853. Most states now have a modest wage system (many pay less than sixteen cents per day). Only twenty states pay wages even when the prisoner is not working; the remainder pay only if the work results in prison income (often there is none because the institution is unable to sell the products made). The United Nations has taken the position that (1) prison labor is a right and (2) it should be compensated at normal pay rates.

Conditions of Prison Labor.   Assignment to prison labor (either internal institutional maintenance or labor to produce products to be sold externally) ideally would be made on the basis of individual preferences and abilities. However, usually institutional needs for convenience and safety predominate here as elsewhere. Since inmates have few skills and generally bad work habits, they cannot readily produce efficiently, especially with the antiquated machinery provided in most prisons. Vocational training in reading, use of simple machinery, and other basic skills are necessary—but still may not be sufficient to operate the complex machinery of modern automated industrial enterprises. In addition, prison labor cannot be efficiently used at the workplace. Prisoners often leave their work assignments for other prison-related activities; and administrative practices such as head counts and commitment of inmates to cells in the early afternoon when guard shifts are changed also impair efficiency. The increasing emphasis upon treatment and the perception that "true" therapy is unrelated to work have tended to undermine ideas of the prison as a place to learn work skills. However, prison officials still regard work as the most important priority, generally because it may show a profit.

Prison Labor and Rehabilitation.   Prison officials have always equated labor with rehabilitation. They believe that labor skills will best prepare inmates for productive lives in society. They hope that inmates with newly acquired skills will be encouraged to forego their former criminal associations and to change both personal companions and attitudes toward the law. Since work improves morale, and since in practice lack of work means idleness (rather than participation in often nonexistent therapy programs), work has at least an indirect role in rehabilitation. In some countries, prisoners are granted an actual legal right to work. In practice though, most prison skills are not transferable to the outside, since (1) they may have been only inadequately acquired and (2) ex-inmates are reluctant to tell employers where they learned them. Only a few can use their prison experience creatively in the job market, but some have benefited from being able to maintain, or even sharpen, job skills acquired prior to incarceration.

PRISON EDUCATION

The narrow meaning of prison education is formal schooling. The broad meaning involves the creation of any learning experience that will change attitudes and behavior. Some classroom educational experiences can meet both definitions. But something more than classroom work, including contacts with law-abiding outsiders, is usually necessary to achieve the second. It is difficult to correlate postprison success with prison education programs.

History. From the beginnings of imprisonment, church groups have been intensely interested in education, and ministers have regularly visited with individual prisoners or groups. Some early houses of correction had resident chaplains who also functioned as academic instructors, but before the midnineteenth century there were few such resident clergymen. Early resistance to teaching prisoners how to read and write (through Bible study) centered on the fear that education would only make criminals more dangerous.

In the New York House of Refuge, in the nineteenth century, juveniles were required to attend classes for two, then four, hours a day. They studied the Bible for one hour and learned the basics of reading, writing, arithmetic, geography, and bookkeeping thereafter. In 1847 New York provided for the appointment of two teachers for each state prison and for an instructional program in English for an hour and a half per day. This program, later adopted by other states, provided only for evening instruction, and there was no group participation. After the Civil War, the educational mission came to full bloom, with better citizenship as the goal. Prison education was spurred by creation of the first reformatory, at Elmira, New York, in 1876. Warden A. F. Brockway, in an effort to give convicts a moral as well as an academic education, hired college professors trained in several disciplines. He also instituted a major industrial program at the Detroit House of Correction in 1861. The definition of education broadened to include lectures, group discussion, and the teaching of ethics as well as traditional classroom courses.

Present Practices. Today, grade-school education for five to ten hours per week in the classroom is the norm. Since half of all inmates are illiterate, the teaching of the three R's is stressed. Practical courses like bookkeeping and stenography and inspirational ones such as civics are also prominent in the curriculum. Several commissions have recommended increased emphasis upon social studies such as sociology, economics, and political science to enable the inmate to learn about the world he will re-enter. Some states, notably California and New York, have integrated prison schools into the general school system of the community. Community teachers and programs of education are provided by the local school district under the broad supervision of the state's Board of Education. Diplomas are granted by the school district, and a vast array of elective subjects are also offered. In states with advanced education systems, juvenile institutions provide the most adequate education, while little schooling occurs in local jails. Inmates in one federal institution, a juvenile facility in West Virginia, receive "points" for scholastic and other accomplishments and can convert those points into "rentals" for individual cells and special purchases; these incentives have resulted in superior academic performance. College education, either by correspondence courses or by visiting college instructors (and, at some point, "education release" into regular college classes), has also been popular. Inmate teachers are deemed too amenable to inmate pressures (for good grades, allowance of cheating, and lax supervision of classes) to be effective.

Vocational Training. While "vocational training" generally is equated with work to which inmates are assigned, a few prisons offer skills training abetted by related academic studies. Some vocational education programs lead to apprenticeships in particular fields, such as cooking, baking, meatcutting, etc. Often inmates are assigned to work programs because they already have certain skills, not because they could learn such skills. The most middle-class-oriented inmates are often chosen for vocational training even where they lack specific skills for it. Jails and workhouses, because of the fluidity of their populations, give little vocational training. Vocational training per se may not involve changes in attitudes, and this is the real problem for all educational programs.

Obstacles to Education. The greatest obstacle to educational training is the nature of the prison itself as a place for punishment. Punitive attitudes, of course, predominate among prison personnel and affect prisoners negatively. Many inmates who participate in educational activities are viewed suspiciously by their peers. Decent facilities are lacking: Libraries may be small and located in the visiting room; little money is available for instructors and equipment; there are few rooms in which true education can take place; textbooks may be the same as those used in the public schools for children. In addition, prison routine disrupts the educational process, as do work activities. Wardens do not want school to interfere with work.

PRISON THERAPY

Treatment of individual inmates has gradually evolved into experiments in group relations. The assumption is that individual attitudes are often shaped by groups and can be modified by new group associations. The groups may mix prisoners with the law-abiding or be confined to prisoners themselves. To an extent, this work is undermined by the isolated nature of prison life itself.

Visit and Furlough Programs. To remedy this impediment, visitation and correspondence rights, though restricted, have grown substantially. Conjugal prison-visit programs have developed rapidly in a number of countries. In Sweden, wives are permitted to visit prisoners in their cells for an entire Sunday in so-called "open prisons" (in "closed prisons," visits are limited to one half hour, one Sunday per month). For jail detainees serving a six-month or longer sentence, conjugal visits for up to one forty-eight-hour period once a month are allowed. Jails have special comfortable rooms for such visits. Several Mexican prisons provide similar privileges. In Mexico and some Far Eastern countries, isolated penal colonies even permit family living. The Philippines also has a system of penal colonies, where prisoners are given some land, a small house, clothing, and farming tools by the government.

The Mississippi State Prison at Parchman established the earliest, and still one of the very few, conjugal programs in the United States. About one fourth of the prison population are permitted to participate. A limited experimental program at the California State Correctional Institute at Tehachapi permits conjugal visits only to prisoners nearing the end of their term. Since such programs are expensive, may lead to conflicts among inmates about favoritism, may result in pregnancy or venereal disease, and run counter to the idea of rehabilitation within the community rather than the prison, American correctional administrators are virtually unanimously opposed to them. Instead, many states have adopted inmate furlough programs to permit prisoners either in minimal-security institutions or at the end of their terms to regularly visit and stay with spouses at home. The convict can also begin to seek employment on the furloughs.

Home-visit systems, jail (and some prison) work-release programs, and weekend imprisonment with community work for first offenders have also been adopted in places. Success has been mixed.

Self-Government. Inmates in some prisons participate in self-government, both to perpare them for life on the outside and to simplify administrative problems of the institution. Inmate self-government dates back to the Walnut Street Jail, but some early self-government organizations were directed from the administrative hierarchy. Prison administrators are generally not in favor of the concept and there are very few inmate councils in American prisons. Fears of manipulation by long-termers, especially in meting out reward and punishment, have sometimes proved justified. Indeed, prisoners themselves have often rejected the concept for that reason. Power-

ful prisoners may manipulate the system much as powerful politicians dominate local governments that are ostensibly democratic. In some institutions,
administrative control over the councils (exemplified by the warden's veto
power over council decisions) and the choice of docile leaders have undermined the program. In these institutions, council decisions tend to deal with
trival rather than fundamental questions of prison governance.

A variant of self-governance is the honor system, whereby selected prisoners are rewarded for past obedience on condition that they continue such
conduct in the future. These programs have been most successful in honor
camps and minimum-security prisons, a result perhaps attributable to the
fact that the best prisoners, the ones most likely to become law-abiding, are
chosen for these programs.

Group Therapy.   After World War II, group-therapy programs, consisting of small groups of prisoners guided by a trained or untrained therapist,
became popular, although many inmates were (or felt they were) compelled
to join. The major purpose was stimulation and reinforcement of positive attitudes toward the law. Therapy has often been justified on the narrower
ground that it allows inmates to "bitch" and "gripe" against "the system"
without danger. It may also contribute somewhat to overcoming feelings of
isolation fostered by prison.

California group-therapy programs assumed that (1) inmates would be
compelled to be realistic by hard peer questioning of their rationalizations
for criminality; (2) sessions would enable inmates to see their own hostile or
guilty attitudes more clearly and such insight would lead to reform; (3) inmates' acceptance of criticism would acclimate them to the notion of social
restrictions upon their conduct, and such attitude modification would foster
altruism rather than egotism; and (4) law-abiding attitudes formed in the
group would be transferable to society. Evaluation of the California treatment program, involving one thousand offenders (many in a control group
that received no treatment), showed that treated offenders (1) were not less
hostile to treatment staff; (2) did not commit fewer or less serious violations
of prison rules; (3) did not violate parole less frequently; (4) did not remain
out of prison longer before violating parole; and (5) did not commit less serious offenses on parole than the ones for which they were originally sentenced. Recidivism did not depend upon (1) size of caseload of parole officers, (2) type of treatment, *or* (3) commitment of narcotics addicts to
halfway-house treatment. Thus California, with the most frequent and most
sophisticated treatment programs, did not demonstrate any greater success
than did other states in curbing recidivism.

23. Prison Life

Prison is more than just an institution; it is a living situation that creates new forms of social relationships (1) between inmates and other inmates and (2) between inmates and guards, administrators, psychologists, and others. Some inmates may be "rehabilitated" as a result of their contact with the system, while others may become "hardened," and still others may be totally unaffected. Prison, like other organizations, has a culture consisting of certain values and norms, and different inmates may play different roles in that culture.

PRISON CULTURE

All organizations have an "official" component, a structured hierarchy of authority that theoretically governs, and an "unofficial" hierarchy that determines when, how, and why things really happen. Inmates are influenced by both structures, though the latter is probably more significant, for it deals with the daily questions of life within the institution. Attitudes of guards and social workers may be important only in their official roles; attitudes of other prisoners create ties of friendship, obligation, loyalty, and status that are more important than even administrative attitudes and commands. Since there is no geographic mobility in prison, inmate conformity is essential, and nonconformity may be punishable subtly (ridicule) or dramatically (punishment). The question is: "Conformity to what?"

The Prison Code. Most prisons are informally governed by the "inmate code," which stresses (1) inmate reciprocal loyalty (let other inmates "do their things" without interference); (2) avoidance of arguments and emphasis on nonconfrontation; (3) reciprocal fairness and not taking advantage of other inmates by force, theft, fraud, or exploitation (honesty is a tenet); (4) maintenance of individual identity by emphasis upon strength, toughness, and manliness; and (5) disrespect for administrative officials, especially guards. Many of these "rules" are disobeyed in prison and afterward and many are redefined to apply only to members of specific peer groups (often based upon color or even membership in a particular clique). Some of the tenets are implacable: Informants are ostracized and often their lives are endangered. The appearance of guilt is often taken for actual guilt (for example, conversing with a guard, certainly more than once, violates the code). All outsiders are to be treated the same (shunned), and this suspicion is readily extended to other inmates who may break the code.

The Function of the Code.   The code is maintained by inmate refusal to accept the formal governance of the prison (to which they have not consented) and by the ability of inmates to provide their own goods and services (material goods, including contraband, and even "governmental" services in terms of a self-regulatory "law-enforcement" system). In some respects, however, the code represents a contract between the administration and prisoners. It reflects the necessity to adjust social life to a system of total control. It stresses cooperation, thus minimizing the pains of imprisonment, restoration of a lost self-respect and even "manliness," the ability to "take it." The code and the social system therefore act as agents of social control, and peer pressure enables the individual to adjust and retain some status and reputation. By stressing individuality, the code keeps prisoners unorganized; by stressing avoidance of arguments, it encourages administrators to reward well-behaved convicts. Code-encouraged psychological separation of prisoners has been effective. When inmates are either (1) isolated or (2) organized loosely into groups that fight each other, the ability to govern large numbers of people with a relatively small staff is enhanced. Inmate leaders interpret the code to benefit themselves often by exploiting fellow inmates and then relying on the code to prevent defense or retaliation. Administrators frequently use inmate leaders to control other inmates by rewarding these leaders with the few privileges available in a prison setting. Inmate leaders often violate the code by reporting on inmate rule infractions when those infractions threaten to jeopardize either the status quo or the leader's power. Admonitions to guards not to talk to inmates and vice versa strengthen inmate leaders' control over information and communication, vital assets in a prison.

Socialization in Prisons.   Prisons, like other social institutions, are composed of a variety of individuals with different skills, backgrounds, emotions, and values. As with other social institutions, the differences are subordinated by the culture to enable the institution to function. Just as the child becomes "socialized" to the norms of the adult world, so new prisoners become "prisonized" to those of the institution. Unlike children, prisoners must unlearn inappropriate behavior patterns and must overcome an initial resistance to prison itself. Prisoners learn anonymity (similarity of haircuts, uniforms, and reduction of names to numbers) and inferiority. They also learn the "code" and its particular variations in particular institutions. Socialization, of course, affects different prisoners differently; some will become more "socialized" than others and will actively participate in "code" use and manipulation. The willingness of prisoners to accept the code and prison culture may depend upon expectations of postrelease life "on the outside"; those with positive expectations will be less attracted to the prison culture. In general, new inmates whose preprison experience most closely resembles inmate cultures, who are lower-class, or who have little contact with the outside world, are most likely to join the inmate subculture. All prisoners find that even minimal adherence to the code will reinforce procriminal norms, thus making rehabilitation more difficult. The maximum influence of prison culture occurs during the middle of imprisonment; at the beginning and end, other outside influences are or become important. Also, those serving short periods of incarceration are likely to be least affected by prison culture.

Forcible homosexual rape, in both prisons and jails, has apparently dramatically increased in the past decade, although its extent is unknown. This increase may be attributable to (1) prison overcrowding due to more frequent incarceration; (2) longer sentences, which may diminish sexual self-control; (3) presence of gangs in maximum-security facilities and the use of rape to gain and maintain power over unaffiliated prisoners; and (4) the emergence of newer prisoner types who do not adhere to the "thieves' code." It is clear that power and desire to humiliate rather than sexual gratification are the primary motivators, and prisoner-rapists are usually not homosexually oriented either prior to, or after, incarceration. There have been no scientific studies about the incidence and character of prison rape or of the effects of such rape upon its victims.

SUBCULTURES

Prison culture cannot be viewed solely as the product of peculiar conditions of imprisonment. For one thing, the "code" is a part of the general criminal code, and (contrary to traditional theories of socialization) many prisoners have served time before and bring to a new prison some older attitudes, which are reinforced in the new setting. Thus prison culture is in varying degrees (1) a convict subculture, (2) a criminal subculture, and (3) a straight subculture.

New subcultures, taking racial and ethnic forms, developed in the late 1960s and early 1970s, as new divisions in the outside world—racial, reli-

gious (or, as with the Black Muslims, both), and even by gang affiliation—
were imported into prisons. Outside radical political ideologies have also
been imported, and these make it difficult to "rehabilitate" prisoners into a
culture they believe to be evil. These recent divisions are variations of older
ones; Irish and Italian inmates were as hostile to each other as are racial
groups now. Religious divisions have also been traditionally strong. Imprisoned political radicals of the past resemble their contemporary counterparts.

The *criminal or thief subculture* is exemplified by the conduct of professional thieves in prisons, conduct that mirrors their street code. A thief can
be trusted; he is a "right guy" or "real man" who will not exploit other inmates. He is respected for his personal qualities as much as, or even more
than, for his professional skill. This subculture stresses loyalty and toughness, but eschews troublemaking for its own sake. It closely resembles other
street cultures, including those of lower-class delinquents. Indeed, the subculture's values resemble loyalty patterns in straight counterparts. Thieves
know they will be imprisoned on occasion and prepare themselves for the
experience in advance.

In contrast to the "criminal" or "thief" subculture, the *convict subculture*
does not derive from prestige outside the prison. Participants do favors for
each other and provide goods and services (often those to which inmates are
entitled as matters of right) at a price. This subculture seeks to manipulate
the prison environment and to provide useful goods and services. Most participants do not use violence and are simply businessmen, but there may be
nonmanipulative inmates who rise to power within this group; they are likely to be either diagnosed or potential psychopaths who tend to use violence
and to run prison rackets.

The *convict subculture* is not solely a product of prison conditions. Despite much bravado, many lower-class urban males are not independent and
actually seek authoritarian living structures with detailed rules of behavior.
Many members of this subculture have extensive juvenile or reformatory
prison records and have mastered exploitative techniques in those institutions. Such inmates, despite their extensive records, are not part of the thief
subculture; they do not have the prestige of thieves, in part because the institutions in which they served (juvenile institutions and short-term jails, for
instance) may not have had a thieves' subculture.

Another subculture is simply that of unaffiliated prisoners who accept legitimate values and isolate themselves from dominant prison subcultures.
These "straights" simply wish to serve their time without incident.

Inmate Typologies. While subcultures can be identified and their values described, who is likely to join these groups? As with criminal typology

generally, an analysis of social attitudes of inmates involves the selection of one trait or set of traits and may not account for all possible types; also, the "fit" between type and subculture may not always be apparent.

Prosocial inmates have often been convicted of violent crimes against persons, or naïve property crimes; they have strong ties to the community and family, feel guilt for their crimes, and are the inmates most capable of rehabilitation (indeed, most have been "rehabilitated" even before entry into prison). They have been unable to deal with personal or social problems and view the prison as a place to receive help and support; they are conservatives who are "straight."

Antisocial inmates are recidivists who have committed relatively sophisticated crimes such as robbery, burglary, and even assault. They are rebellious both before and after imprisonment, and readily rationalize their conduct to avoid guilt. Although they reject most social norms, they are often close to their families. They probably grew up in subcultures of delinquency or illegality and are members of the thieves' subculture. They know prison argot and are highly antagonistic to rehabilitation.

Pseudosocial inmates have usually committed offenses such as fraud; they tend to be occupationally and educationally superior to antisocial offenders and to play "political" roles that mediate between staff and inmates when conflict arises. Pseudosocial inmates are often the products of inconsistent discipline. They will at times accept legitimate values and at other times deviant ones, all for the purpose of enhancing their personal status. They do not know much about prison when they enter, but they learn rapidly and adjust well. They are innovators who readily accept prison treatment programs, though often without real commitment. They may be marginal members of the inmate subculture but probably are not committed to it; they may manipulate it as well as other prisoners for limited, practical purposes of comfort rather than as an expression of deep hostilities or power drives.

Asocial inmates are often behaviorally disordered and commit a variety of crimes. They are egocentric and have a high recidivism rate. They have usually been rejected by their families; in prison, they are impulsive and nihilistic and often become leaders during escapes. They are, of course, members, often leaders, of the inmate subculture.

Subcultural Behavior Patterns.   While straights and thieves are oriented to outside status, members of the inmate or convict subculture seek power and influence within the prison itself. This may take the form of either (1) access to information, a valuable commodity in prison or (2) a job that provides opportunities for participation in a prison racket (for example, stealing of food or cigarettes). "Straights" tend to seek prison positions that are valued in the outside world or by prison administrators rather than by prisoners. Thieves seek to maximize both leisure and consumer privileges (for example, a radio, recreation) and often take "low status" jobs to make life easier, in contrast to convicts, who may work at the same job but for the purpose of facilitating stealing. Thieves and convicts rarely steal from or attempt to exploit each other.

The thief subculture is more influential than the convict subculture, because thief values and attitudes tend to be clear and consistent. But the convict subculture is more open and visible and actively attempts to recruit newcomers, particularly men who wish to "make it" in prison. Thieves measure newcomers by their outside reputations and often exclude newcomers when they have no such reputations. Since some newcomers will not adopt either the thief subculture or the convict subculture, "inmate culture" is really a combination of the three. Because many minimum-security institutions, women's prisons, and federal prisons have a high percentage of straights, the balance tends to favor straight culture. Because there are few representatives of thieves' culture in reformatories and (increasingly) in maximum-security prisons, convict culture (especially its coercive "goon" form) tends to predominate there. Increasingly, straights are being diverted from prison by probation and release programs, so that convict subcultural values tend to predominate.

Subcultural Attitudes. The ability of prison culture to negatively change an inmate's behavior is not solely a function of association with particular fellow prisoners but rather a result of extended contact with a whole lawless culture. Many prisoners come to redefine themselves as an elite at odds with an often repressive administration and therefore the law generally. In part, inmates are influenced by the attitudes and values inherent in the particular subcultures they experience, often as a result of their particular prison-job associations. Many inmates compromise by partially participating in both the thief subculture and the convict subculture, while members of one of these subcultures may drift toward the other.

Recidivism and Subculture. As might be expected, those who remain "straight" while in prison have the lowest recidivism rates, while members of the convict subculture, trained in either manipulation or violence and fearful of life outside, have the highest rates. Thieves sometimes have high recidivism rates but also occasionally reform and retain status by claiming that new work is not "sucker" (or ordinary) labor. Although no meaningful study of the recidivism rates of these groups has been made, it has been found that "straights" have a low recidivism rate, which is not affected by the amount of time spent in prison. Thieves who have been imprisoned for lengthy terms tend to (1) lose their thief identification and (2) have recidivism rates resembling those of convicts. Convicts have the highest rates of all. Thus, except for thieves who "become" convicts, there is little correlation between amount of time served and recidivism. The type of prison also has little correlation with recidivism.

Changing Prisoner Attitudes.   There is little hope for improvement by individual therapy or prisoner self-government, since antisocial attitudes cannot be modified within prisons as we know them. Attempts to change prisoner attitudes have been most successful in minimum-security prisons such as Norfolk Prison Colony in Massachusetts, where officers did not wear uniforms, were located outside the prisoners' communal areas, and had a friendly attitude toward the twenty-five inmates each one personally supervised. The operating principles resembled those of large-scale group therapy and Alcoholics Anonymous. The Norfolk program was derided by the public, and a more traditional program was substituted for it before any measurement of its success could be made.

Some attempts to reduce the influence of convict subcultures have been made by lessening the deprivations of imprisonment. These efforts have been criticized because the tendency has been to select "straight" prisoners, the "best bets," and to ignore the group whose exploitative and violent attitudes may have been formed prior to imprisonment itself. In some prisons, changing the patterns by which information is distributed and held has had some positive effect. The technique emphasizes control over communications by staff, not selected (or self-selected) inmate leaders. Yet the difficulties are substantial, since most people still regard prisons as meant to induce pain rather than change inmates.

PRISON RIOTS

Prison riots bring into sharp focus the peculiar conditions of confinement. The nature of the prison, the interests that are satisfied with present prison characteristics and wish to maintain them, and inmate loyalty patterns are vividly demonstrated. Riots have come in short, periodic waves, commencing in the early 1950s.

Causes of Riots.   Although many prison riots can be ascribed to brutal conditions, some appear to occur where (1) a reform movement has just begun and (2) inmate leaders, the stabilizing element in traditional prisons, lose power. The result is a stirring up of disgruntlement and then the occurrence of an incident that triggers a riot. Any change in the system of authority, or decentralization of authority, and the ending of traditional informal means of airing grievances may be precipitating factors.

Patterns of Riots.   Riots followed, and continue to follow, certain patterns. (1) No mass escapes were attempted. (2) Many riots occurred after disturbances and clashes among *staff* members. (3) Planning was rudimentary. (4) The purpose was to gain public attention. (5) Hostages were taken. (6) Inmates barricaded themselves in and began to bargain for such things as better food, better medical treatment, improved recreational facilities, and improved parole practices. Riots tend to commence with general violence, and continue with the emergence of inmate leaders. Riots are followed by a period of negotiation with either prison or political authority, and finally inmate surrender occurs. During riots, at first the most violent inmates take charge. Destruction of property, drinking and other licentiousness, abuse of hostages, and inmate settling of grievances against other inmates occur. The ability of prison guards to protect inmates from each other is lost. Thieves and "con men" then take power, sometimes after hurting or killing the original leaders. These thieves and "con men" become the negotiators and squelch any escape plans. In the third stage, the actual negotiations are taken over by members of the convict culture. Most demands of prisoners are for material improvement rather than significant social or structural changes.

Effects of Riots. A riot is usually followed by some change in administrative policy of either a cosmetic or a substantive nature. The riot usually reveals the fragile nature of the staff-inmate system of informal cooperation. Riots often serve to reinforce punitive attitudes of staff members who are revolted by crime, hate many criminals, and stress the ethic of hard work. Reform prison wardens and corrections commissioners may be fired or demoted after a riot. (Sometimes antireform staff personnel may wittingly or unwittingly undermine reform efforts and stimulate riots). Riot commissions reviewing the incidents often blame reform wardens for "permissiveness" in dealing with inmates. Participants in the convict subculture who fear that reform may end their prerogatives may gain from riots, and the system of mutual benefit between certain guards and certain inmates may be restored after the riot has ended. Proposed reforms usually threaten the thief and inmate subcultures, and these groups may encourage more violent prisoners to initiate spontaneous riots.

The recent authority and power of thieves has meant that violent prisoners (also prisoners who have become "politicized") retain power beyond the first stage. Political militancy has changed the nature of prisoner power and disrupted the pattern of privileges accorded to thieves. Imprisonment itself rather than its conditions has now become the focus of prison rebellion.

24. Release from Prison

Prisoners may be released after serving out their full terms, or obtaining early parole, or release without conditions, or pardon.

RELEASE BY EXECUTIVE DECREE

A *pardon* may be granted by a high executive official (the governor of a state or the President of the United States) and may be either absolute or conditional. It is rarely used today in the United States. An absolute pardon imposes no conditions and has the effect of eliminating the finding of criminal guilt. A conditional pardon requires that the inmate perform certain tasks to keep the pardon; if he does not, the pardon becomes null and void. Pardon also restores civil rights. In a large minority of states the power to pardon is shared by the governor and an executive board; in most, it belongs to the governor alone. In some, an advisory board has been established to aid the governor.

A *commutation of sentence* may be issued by an executive official to reduce a sentence. It is less than a pardon and does not restore civil rights.

Amnesty is the exercise of the power to pardon large groups of prisoners. It has been used on occasion in the United States but is more characteristic of European countries.

GOOD-CONDUCT REDUCTION OF SENTENCE

Generally, state laws provide for a reduction in sentence for inmates who have shown good conduct. While the specific amount of reduction time is set by law (one month for the first year, two for the second year, etc., is the norm), a prison board determines whether or not particular inmates are eligible for such reductions. Despite a slow start in the United States, most of the states adopted a "good time" system after the Civil War. Today, all but

California use the concept. Many states also provide "merit" or "industrial" good time for inmates who behave very well or who work in certain occupations. These programs do not involve a reduction in the sentence but merely accelerate the date for parole eligibility. Objections to good-time provisions stress the fact that superficial inmate conformity rather than true reformation may be the criterion and that prisoners assume such sentence reduction to be a "right." Most inmates are routinely awarded good time, but it may be reduced or eliminated by infractions of the disciplinary rules.

LENGTH OF SENTENCES

Ultimately, the legislature controls sentencing. In the past, most sentences were set for definite terms. Later, legislatures gave courts and parole boards greater authority (usually within some limitations) to achieve justice by permitting variable sentences. At present, some legislatures, as previously noted, have continued to set mandatory sentences for certain crimes, subject only to possible good-time reduction. In addition, for some crimes, judges can set specific sentences (within legislative limitations) with no possibility of early release. For some crimes, judges set a maximum and a minimum term, and the actual sentence is determined by a board. Judges resentful of the board's power may set the maximum close to the minimum in order to reduce board discretion. In response, legislatures sometimes have mandated that the minimum to be served must be a fraction (one third or one half) of the maximum. Another variant requires the court to sentence according to the law and leaves complete discretion with the administrative board. The Model Penal Code recommends that the legislature set the maximum, the court the minimum, and the board the actual release date. Finally, the by now discredited alternative adopted by some states was to have no maximum or minimum and to leave complete discretion to the board.

Indeterminate Sentences. Indeterminate sentences are really indefinite sentences, since they occur within a minimum-maximum range. An administrative board is authorized to specifically fix the sentence within the range. That board may be a parole board, but there is no necessary connection between parole and the indeterminate sentence. Parole may, of course, be achieved even with determinate sentences.

Minimum Sentences. The requirement of a minimum has been defended as necessary to ensure that courts do not become lax or corrupt. This reflects the general notion that all criminals should be punished, even severely so, since legislatively established penalties tend to be harsher than those imposed by judges. Removal of minimums in some states has not caused premature release of hardened criminals. On the other hand, where no minimum is prescribed, there is a danger of stiffer sentencing of blacks and the poor.

Maximum Sentences. The requirement of a maximum sentence is more controversial. Its existence (either as a true maximum or as a flat sentence) has led to the argument that many inmates have not been rehabilitated by the end of their term. This, in turn, engendered the indeterminate-sentence movement. Since rehabilitation is now conceded to be ineffective, the current trend is to a return to maximum or flat sentences. Maximum sentences were also once justified as limitations upon the power of the state to simply incarcerate those whom society did not like for long periods of time. Indeterminate sentences can and have been used as political weapons against unpopular or nonconforming prisoners.

Flat Sentences. Although there is a current trend toward either flat (fixed) or maximum sentencing, there is no proof that this system is better than the indeterminate (indefinite) system. Many reformers tend to trust legislatures more than judges or parole boards. Often these reformers are correct; judicially, the poor are frequently more severely punished than the rich. But legislatively mandated sentences are usually harsh and, of course, make no distinctions among different types of offenders. Despite acknowledged abuses of the "rehabilitative" function of indeterminate sentencing, the real question is whether someone or some agency will be able to exercise the power of mitigation now exercised by parole boards and courts. The flat-sentence argument assumes that legislatures will quickly mitigate any injustices caused by the system, but this does not always happen. Though the number of pardons may increase to mitigate legislative severity, the real sentencing decision will probably be made by the prosecutor. He decides what crimes to charge and, in effect, what sentence will be imposed, and his discretion is virtually unreviewable.

PAROLE

Parole is the system of release from incarceration prior to expiration of the maximum or flat sentence on certain conditions and under supervision, pending final release. It resembles probation in effect, though it is different in form and purpose. Probation suspends execution of sentence as a judicial substitute for punishment, while parole suspends completion of sentence as an administrative aid to rehabilitation.

Parole began indirectly as a system of indenturing (hiring out) prisoners to private employers. In time, juveniles so indentured were visited by state agents to prevent employer cruelty. Between 1776 and 1860, there was a growth of philanthropic organizations devoted to meeting postincarceration needs of prisoners. In 1845, Massachusetts became the first state to institutionalize concern for ex-convict aftercare. During this period, convicts were transported from England to Australia under a "ticket of leave." This, along with an Irish variant, became the basis of modern American parole. An English law allowing police surveillance of released convicts was another basis for the parole system. Parole was first formally adopted by New York in 1869 and quickly spread so that, by the end of the nineteenth century, twenty-five states had adopted it. Now all states provide for a parole system, although release on parole varies drastically from state to state.

Shock probation is a system whereby one sentenced to prison can secure early release by the sentencing judge. The rationale is that an offender serves only a short time in prison in order to (1) appreciate the seriousness of his offense; (2) be prevented from socialization into inmate culture; and (3) permit the judge to re-evaluate his initial decision. *Shock parole,* a variant *of shock probation,* was instituted in Ohio in 1974; it permits parole after six months to certain offenders. But this system may still expose relatively innocent offenders, if even for a short time, to the demoralizing effects of the inmate culture in jail or in prison. This system may also encourage judges to sentence to prison those who would ordinarily have received straight probation. Arguments favoring the system are that under it (1) public clamor for sentencing to prison is satisfied, but the offender is quickly returned to the community and (2) there are considerable tax savings.

The Parole-Board System.   Three types of boards determine whether inmates will be released on parole: (1) In some states, parole boards exist within institutions (the warden may or may not be a member). (2) In some states, the board is located within the Department of Corrections and has jurisdiction over all state institutions. (3) State boards with statewide jurisdiction may be located outside the Department of Corrections. In all but four states, the parole board has final jurisdiction to release, rather than merely advisory jurisdiction to make recommendations to the governor. In the vast majority of states, the board is an independent agency with statewide jurisdiction. Juvenile parole is handled, in part at least, by correctional authorities within the institution.

When parole boards were dominated by members of correctional institutions where the inmate is serving time, decisions in theory were made by those officials most closely involved in classification and rehabilitation programs. This, in effect, meant that parole was granted for compliance with institutional standards of good behavior rather than any overall assessment of rehabilitative potential. Also, the institution could use parole as a lever to, in essence, blackmail the inmate into compliance or to solve institutional problems of overcrowding. Most independent parole boards are composed of a diverse membership, although many states now require that at least one profession be represented. There is little consensus about which profession (law, penology, sociology, psychiatry) is most relevant, and different states mandate different forms of representation. Independent boards may tend to worry about public reactions to adverse decisions. Ohio has instituted a program to use ex-offenders as parole-officer aides; these positions are stepping-stones to the position of parole officer. The program appears to be highly successful.

The Parole Board in Practice.   Although most students of parole agree that close guidance, assistance, and supervision of parolees are desirable, these rarely occur. Many prisoners object to parole on the ground that it is little more than a police surveillance device. Some waive their rights to parole hearings, especially if they are to soon be released even without parole. Public belief that parole is a form of "coddling" is reflected in the current movement to eliminate parole or at least to limit its availability. In practice, most parole boards grant parole on the basis of the seriousness of the offense, thus reflecting the punitive philosophy of the general criminal-justice system and/or the belief that the prisoner may still be dangerous to society. There is also some relationship between prison conduct and early release. Only a minority of parole boards permit counsel to the applicant for parole; some permit witnesses; a few record parole decisions in writing; and some make and provide to the prisoner a transcript of the hearing. Many parole boards will not grant parole to an inmate who is wanted by authorities elsewhere or who has no guarantee of employment. The latter practice has been objected to because (1) many such guarantees are unreliable; (2) release comes to depend upon general economic conditions; and (3) employers may exploit parolees, since they know of their records. Also, there seems to be no correlation between lack of employment and recidivism. When an inmate has specific skills, a likelihood of employment, and a stable home life, some states will release him. Again, the recidivism rate is not related to release under these circumstances. Even "graduated release" programs—featuring gradual widening of freedom by work-release and halfway-house programs—may not be very effective. However, paroling inmates and providing money and assistance in securing employment may lower recidivism rates.

Parole boards will not release where (1) public outrage would follow and (2) influential people would protest. Such people include police, district attorneys, and those in the media. Another standard, that of prison conduct, is unreliable since (1) many well-behaved prisoners obtain early release to commit new crimes; (2) many prisoners who may not be rehabilitated desire close control and are well behaved under it; (3) some inmates are simply docile; and (4) some inmates actually benefit by prison. In contrast, some rebellious prisoners are not threats to the community at large.

Prisoner Attitudes Toward Parole. The combination of indeterminate sentences and parole (not an inevitable combination) creates anxiety and uncertainty among prisoners. Lack of knowledge about the date of release, and resentment over the injustice of the original sentence or of the amount of time actually served are some causes of anxiety and bitterness. This is especially true when inmates do not even know of the maximum fixed by the parole board in systems where the board is empowered to set the time period before parole eligibility occurs. The dangers inherent in parole (and sentencing generally) are magnified.

Indefinite sentencing means prolonged suffering, while definite sentencing creates the belief that the inmate (1) has only to serve his term to square accounts and (2) owes no other obligation to society.

Parole Supervision. Parole conditions, which may be fixed by parole boards or other agencies, generally require adherence to a law-abiding lifestyle; abstention from alcohol and gambling; support of dependents; changing of residence, employment, or marital status only with permission; and periodic reporting to parole officers. Many of these requirements, especially those related to morals, are often overlooked by parole officers. Since parole caseloads may run to more than two hundred per officer, close supervision is generally impossible; but as with probation, there seems to be no correlation between parole violation and caseload. Even low-caseload jurisdictions report that actual time spent with parolees is limited and inadequate.

Some parole officers view supervision as surveillance and threaten punishment for parole violation. Others "supervise" only to the extent of assuming that adherence to parole conditions should be maintained. In such cases, contacts are infrequent, though aid in obtaining jobs and money is stressed.

Some agencies believe that the task of reformation has just begun with parole and that a parolee needs help to truly and completely reform. This view is akin to the treatment view, which seeks to ascertain the "cause" of crime and then to eliminate it. Here, parole officers function as social workers and prescribe rehabilitation programs. Advocates of this system argue for "intensive supervision" and reduction of parole caseloads, though there is no proof that parolees will succeed more readily under this system than under its alternatives.

It may well be true that under any circumstances parole officers have little influence in parole success.

In reality, the role of parole officer is, in part, that of policeman and, in part, psychologist. Most parolees are concerned with reintegration into society, family, and employment, to counter the notion that they are criminal outcasts. Parolees are conscious of the fact that they are "different," and close supervision can only enhance this perception. In contrast, loose supervision will not diminish it. Probably, only establishment of close ties to law-abiding individuals will help to achieve parole success.

Violation of Parole. The law defines violation of parole conditions as violation of parole and hence requiring reimprisonment. However, some violations are overlooked by parole officers, and many never come to their attention. Thus, parole-revocation proceedings are often as much a reflection of the values of parole officers as of conduct by parolees.

A formal declaration of violation is followed by a warrant of arrest and a hearing before a parole supervisor, not a court. The U.S. Supreme Court has surrounded revocation hearings with some due-process safeguards, especially a right to counsel. A parolee who returns to prison may have to serve the remainder of his sentence or the maximum term of an indefinite sentence and may also lose good time earned prior to parole, or not be entitled to reimprisonment good time. Eligibility for later parole may be lost or delayed by law, by the parole board, or by other legal agencies. In some states, return to prison need not be triggered by parole violation. The parolee may voluntarily return because he is unemployed or needs medical attention, or parole officers may compel return because they believe that the parolee needs additional training or medical care.

Parole departments issue annual reports comparing the number of paroles granted and the number violated. Parole-violation rates tend to be somewhere between 10 and 40 percent of those granted (the most frequent percentage is about 25 percent). These rates, however, measure only (1) violations known to parole officers and (2) those considered serious violations requiring revocation of parole. Most criminal-justice scholars are suspicious of these figures, because they may reflect no more than manpower problems of parole officers. It seems true that the closer the parole supervision (surveillance), the lower the failure rate. Of course, since parolees frequently serve long periods on parole, many more will violate parole *at some time,* a statistic that cannot be computed within a given year. One major study showed that 55 percent of those paroled became know parole violators at some point, and perhaps another 5 percent violate parole secretly. Another study of parole failures in the federal prison system showed a 33 percent failure rate after two years. In 1972, California paroled sixty-seven hundred males, and within one year, 39 percent had failed; in another California study, 54 percent were shown to have failed within four years. Some studies have demonstrated that failure rates remain high even after the individual has been discharged from parole. Studies also show that the failure rate is higher for those discharged at the end of their term than for those discharged on parole. This may be attributable not to the "success" of parole, but to the fact that parolees are probably better risks from the beginning and that parole boards have "guessed" well.

Termination of Parole.   In all states, parole ends when the maximum sentence (time in prison plus time on parole) expires. Some states do not permit earlier termination while others do, by parole-board action. Civil rights lost by imprisonment may be regained in some states either by parole or by completion of parole; in a few, only a governor's pardon can restore such rights. Increasingly, at least some civil rights have been restored to parolees on the assumption that this will enable quicker reintegration into the community.

Factors in Parole Success.   Hundreds of studies of parole failure have attempted to correlate certain conditions with the likelihood of failure. These studies are flawed because they (1) do not account for the tendency of parole officers to overlook conduct that could lead to revocation and (2) depend on parolee information relating to certain factors such as "home life" and "work record." Despite these flaws, it appears that relevant factors are (1) age of first delinquency or crime (the younger the offender, the more likely he will fail); (2) number of arrests (the greater the number, the greater the likelihood of failure); (3) unsteady work record; (4) continuation of undesirable personal contacts; and (5) size of community (the larger it is, the more likely the failure). Young and black offenders have higher failure rates than do others. One parole study showed that paroled property-crimes offenders had higher failure rates than parolees who had committed crimes against the person. But paroled murderers, assaultists, and rapists were more often returned for technical violations of parole conditions than for new crimes. Thus, violations that did not result in return to prison of property offenders resulted in revocation of parole for those most feared by the general population. If this is true, then true parole success rates are even higher than the official statistics would suggest.

Parole Success Prediction.   Parole prediction studies have sought to isolate various factors and ascertain the relationship between those factors and parole failure. One major study demonstrated that the presence of fifteen or more negative factors characterized habitual parole violators, while those with fewer than five negative factors only occasionally violated parole. California, Massachusetts, Minnesota, Washington, Wisconsin, and Illinois (especially the latter) have produced significant statistical studies that (1) predict the probability of failure for future parolees, and (2) more important, guide parole agencies in techniques for dealing with parolees (close supervision for parole risks, virtually no supervision for good risks).

The U.S. Board of Parole has developed a matrix of various factors to use in parole decisions. More than three quarters of federal parole decisions conform to the guidelines, and the remainder must be justified in writing. Several states have adopted these or other guidelines.

The studies have not (1) provided a basis for *judging* just who should be paroled (Should an inmate with, let us say, a 50 percent risk, or only those running a lesser risk be released?); (2) taken into account the fact that prison behavior may modify preprison "bad risk" factors; (3) diminished the perceived injustice of telling inmates that they may be eligible for parole based upon prison conduct while actually conditioning parole on other factors that cannot be controlled by the inmates.

In addition, prediction tables may not adequately or meaningfully predict. Depending upon which table is used, they may somewhat reduce the margin of error (compared to pure chance) but not statistically by very much. Also, prediction tables generally are validated by follow-up studies. These studies often show that factors that may highly correlate with failure in the first five years after parole play little role after that, so that new and different factors must thereafter be substituted. Thus, knowledge of total violation rates may be a better predictive factor than the table itself.

Prediction also does not work when a new group of parolees becomes the selected sample. It is hard to attribute specific violations to specific factors. Particular parolee samples may have different characteristics, thus reducing the accuracy of a given predictive instrument. Also, information about parolee backgrounds may be unreliable, since the information comes from the convicts themselves or from records kept for an entirely different purpose. Finally, parole conditions, including the parolee's in-prison and postprison experiences, may change over time, as may parole-agency and public perceptions of "violations." Since criminal patterns develop because of interactions with others, parole violations will often be affected by future patterns of personal association; indeed, postprison social relations may tell more about proneness to recidivism than do personal characteristics.

CONCLUSIONS

Part VI

25. Contemporary Trends and Theories

Criminology has attempted to "scientifically" explain the causes of crime, but it has functioned in a context of ill-defined parameters (the subject matter, the criminal law, often changes) and social and political demands to arrive at "solutions." As with all behavioral sciences, many of criminology's postulates and procedures are difficult to test and verify. Criminology's claim to "value freedom" has been tested by both conservatives, who argue that the "science" embodies liberal optimism about the ability of society and government to change wicked or weak individuals, and radicals, who believe that criminality is merely a symptom of underlying social and economic class cleavages in American society.

While criminology's ability to describe may be great, its ability to explain has not yet been established, and its ability to predict is small. Yet, as crime inexorably rises, as ever newer (perhaps temporary) problems are added to criminology's agenda, it has become clear that it will continue to play a major role in any attempt to solve the frustrating problems that constitute its subject matter. How that role will be played will depend upon many factors, some intrinsic to the field itself, some quite extrinsic to it.

CURRENT CRIME TRENDS

In recent years, the data-collection procedures for the Uniform Crime Reports have improved; forty-five states now require all police agencies within the state to report UCR data to one central agency for transmission to the FBI. By 1978, such improvement meant that 94 percent of the rural population was included within UCR jurisdictions (along with 99 percent of the population in Standard Metropolitan Statistical Areas and 96 percent of the population in cities not included within those areas). Also, the reports are matched against national estimated population figures updated from the last census. Beginning January 1, 1980, the Reports included arson as a Part One offense.

According to the UCR, there was a mid-1970s' leveling of some serious offenses; the murder rate for 1978 was only 2.3 percent greater than for the previous year (the average is down to 9.0 per 100,000 population; see pp. 76–77). Again, the South accounted for almost half the total number of murders (42 percent), and had more than twice the rate for the north-central states (21 percent). The pattern of murder also paralleled previous findings: Large cities showed a 2 percent increase, while rural-area murders declined by 3 percent (the suburban rate increased the most, 4 percent). Overall, between 1974 and 1978, the murder rate declined by 6 percent. Also, consistent with previous years, three fourths of those murdered were male and 44 percent were black. The use of firearms in murders was high, from 52 percent in the Northeast to 70 percent in the South. The national average of 64 percent of murders by firearm was a minor decrease (though part of a continuous one) from a 68 percent rate in 1974. Of those murdered, 56 percent knew and 20 percent were related to their assailants. The clearance rate for murder also somewhat declined, from 80 percent in 1974 to 76 percent in 1978. Almost one half (49 percent) of those arrested for murder were black, and 43 percent were under 25 (9 percent were under 18); while the arrest rate of under-18-year-olds dropped 18 percent between 1974 and 1978 (arrests of those over 22 dropped 13 percent), arrests of 18-to-22-year-olds still accounted for 25 percent of all murder arrests in 1978.

The reported rape *rate* rose by 5.8 percent between 1977 and 1978 (the number of rapes increased by 6.5 percent), and by 18 percent between 1974 and 1978. The greatest increase was in the South, which also had the greatest number of reported rapes, and three fourths of all rapes were forcible. Again, rape was most often committed by young men; 54 percent of all arrests were of males under the age of 25 (most were between 18 and 22). Blacks and whites were equally represented among arrestees.

Robbery continued to be a frequently committed violent crime (39 percent), though still a small portion of the total UCR index crimes (4 percent). The number of robberies in 1978 was 6 percent less than in 1974. Seventy percent of robberies occurred in large cities, and almost half occurred in public places. Street robberies declined over the 1974-78 period, as did commercial ones, but bank robberies increased by 43 percent and gas-station holdups by 52 percent. The clearance rate, as usual, was low, only 26 percent; 75 percent of those robberies cleared were committed by those under 25 (56 percent by under-21-year-olds). Approximately one third were committed by those under 18. Fifty-nine percent of all arrested robbers were black.

Aggravated assault was more frequently committed than robbery in 1978 (53 percent of violent crime and 5 percent of index crime). More than one third of such assaults occurred in the South; the general rate increased by 6 percent over 1977 (and almost 20 percent over 1974). Weapons have been increasingly used; blunt objects and other dangerous-weapons use increased 48 percent between 1974 and 1978 (although the use of other weapons did not increase as rapidly as the general assault rate). Adults accounted for 69 percent of the 1978 arrests, and blacks for 39 percent. Seven times more men than women were arrested for this offense.

Larceny theft and burglary (except for auto theft), by far the most prevalent index offenses, both increased by slightly more than 1 percent in 1978 (the offense increase *rate* was less than 1 percent). Larceny theft accounted for 54 percent of all index offenses, and again, the South was the national leader (31 percent of the total). While both suburban and rural areas reported modest increases, the rate in large cities fell by 1 percent. Only 20 percent of these crimes were cleared. Despite the low clearance rate, arrests of thieves accounted for 50 percent of the total number of arrests for index offenses. Fifty-nine percent of the arrestees were under 21 (42 percent were under 18), and 32 percent were women. Twice as many whites as blacks were arrested for this crime. Between 1974 and 1978, reported larceny theft declined by 5 percent, but adult arrest rates increased by 16 percent, while arrest rates for persons under 18 declined by 6 percent, thus confirming that this phenomenon is likely to (1) occur and (2) be committed by adults, during times of economic difficulty. Burglary, which accounted for 28 percent of the total number of index offenses and 31 percent of the property crimes in 1978, was also mainly concentrated in the South (31 percent). The rate was rising in the South and declining elsewhere (the total number of burglaries nationally increased by 2 percent between 1974 and 1978). Daytime burglaries of both homes and stores increased substantially, while nighttime burglaries declined (substantially in businesses). Only 16 percent of burglaries were cleared. Whites accounted for 68 percent of total burglary arrests, while 84 percent of those arrests were of people under 25 (52 percent were under 18).

Almost 1 million cars were stolen in 1978, an increase of about 2.5 percent (the rate increased by 1.6 percent). Thirty percent of those cars were stolen in the Northeast (though large cities showed a 3 percent decrease between 1977 and 1978). The number of cars stolen has remained essentially static since 1974 (the rate has actually declined by 2 percent). Only 15 percent of the thefts were cleared (the New England states, which had the highest theft rate, had the lowest clearance rate). Seventy percent of those arrested were under 21 (51 percent were under 18). Blacks constituted only 27 percent of the arrestees.

In toto, violent crime constituted 10 percent of all index crime, though it rose more rapidly (5 percent) between 1977 and 1978 than did property crime (2 percent). Between 1974 and 1978, total index crime increased 9 percent, and both violent and property crime had the same percentage increase. The southern states, with almost one third of the nation's population in 1978, had slightly more violent crime and slightly less property crime than would be suggested by population figures alone. The big-city crime rate (as described by Standard Metropolitan Statistical Area data) was approximately 20 percent greater than for other urban areas and almost three times as great as in rural areas.

In general, more than 10 million arrests were made in 1978. Only about 20 percent of such arrests were for index crimes, while drunkenness, formerly the leader, accounted for only slightly more than 10 percent of total arrests (indeed, arrests for driving under the influence exceeded drunkenness arrests). Arrests for other public-order crimes, such as disorderly conduct, accounted for less than 10 percent of the total. Drug arrests remained high, about 6 percent of the total, while arrests for marijuana offenses totaled 445,800, a figure not very different from that of previous years. In 1978, 70.9 percent of all drug arrests involved marijuana, 61.3 percent for possession of the substance.

Between 1969 and 1978, the number of arrests for index crimes increased by 10 percent (the figure would be significantly higher if motor-vehicle arrest rates were excluded, since they declined by almost 16 percent). The arrest rates of those under 18 increased by 11.7 percent, and this figure would be even greater had it not been for a 23.7 percent decline in arrests for auto theft (for violent crime, the increase was 43.9 percent; for property crime, 23.3 percent). Among crimes for which, in general, arrest rate increases were greater than 50 percent were larceny theft, fraud (the only crime to show more than a 100 percent increase), vandalism, receiving stolen property, drug-abuse violations (almost 100 percent), and driving under the influence. Among crimes showing significant arrest decreases were embezzlement, gambling, drunkenness (46.5 percent), vagrancy (72.4 percent), and suspicion (86.3 percent, probably because of legal restrictions). While the male arrest rate rose only 5.5 percent in that decade, the female rate rose by 39.1 percent, most significantly for larceny theft (95.2 percent) and burglary (92.1 percent). The female arrest rate for all index crimes increased by almost 90 percent, while the male rate increased by less than 20 percent. By 1978, females were being arrested for more than one third of larceny thefts and for approximately 40 percent of all fraud, but these were the only offenses (apart from some sexual ones) where their rates even began to approximate male arrest rates. In 1978, 80 percent of females arrested for index crimes were arrested for larceny.

However, the crime rate climbed much more steeply in 1979 and into 1980. While inflation and the beginnings of a major recession may well account for some of that increase, it is too early to know whether the proportional decline of teen-agers in the population will prevent a repetition of the 1960s rates. Apparently, the increase in violent crime has come to parallel that in property crime (a historically unique factor), and the increase is as great, if not greater, in the outer suburbs and rural areas than in the large cities and adjacent suburbs. As more whites, more women, and more older people (older than 18, at least) are apparently committing more crimes, previous statistics on crime may be subject to drastic changes.

LESSONS FROM HISTORY

Throughout history, many crime-control methods have been attempted. They include (1) infliction of pain to deter the individual (specific deterrence) and others (general deterrence); (2) incapacitation of criminals to protect society; (3) reduction of opportunities to commit crime (for example, by physical means, such as improved lighting), which also serves a deterrent function; and (4) intervention to reduce the conditions that produce crime. The last method has been based upon the "medical" model of treatment or the social model of granting probation, parole, or otherwise diverting criminals from the "system" toward desirable social contacts and attitudes. The object—in part, at least—of all four methods is crime prevention, not merely punishment. In a democratic society, the primary means of crime prevention should of course be those that enhance the dignity of all individuals and that do not stress punishment for its own sake.

It is apparent that truly dangerous persons should be segregated and incapacitated to prevent further serious crime. It is difficult to change either these people or their environments—and if the latter could be changed, we do not know what the effect upon individual criminality would be. But it is too risky to use predictive data to apply this process of segregation, since such data are unreliable and capable of political and social abuse.

Public policy, for the majority of the population, both criminal and non-criminal, must stress incentives to "persuade" people to conform rather than to compel them by fear. Hence the necessity of giving all a greater stake in society should be stressed. Perception of crime now depends upon often tolerant social attitudes; many crimes are not reported or recorded, and many "criminals" maturate out of crime. That tolerance may become the basis for even greater willingness to accept errant but not truly dangerous individuals.

RECIDIVISM

Many of those arrested for serious crimes (55 to 85 percent) in a given year are recidivists—that is, criminal repeaters. Thus, recidivists commit a greatly disproportionate number of crimes, so that comparatively few people cause most of the work of criminal-justice agencies and constitute the most glaring failures of those agencies. Recidivism may be due to (1) personal characteristics of offenders, (2) failures of criminal-justice agencies, or (3) both. It is clear that the same factors, both personal and environmental, that conduce to crime also conduce to persistence in crime.

Despite the beliefs about recidivism, the data may not be accurate. General FBI recidivism data are biased in favor of overestimating the frequency. Many prisoners serving long sentences are of course repeaters and will be found in any survey. The prisons referred to in FBI data (which do not include all prisons) may contain a disproportionate number of recidivists. For instance, within a state the percentage of prisoners in particular prisons who are recidivists may range from 10 to 85 percent; thus the choice of the prison with the latter number will inflate the rate. One Minnesota study concluded that only 21 percent of all prisoners released were convicted of felonies, an additional 2 percent were parole violators and suspected felons, and another 15 percent returned only for parole violations, all within five years after release. Other studies of recidivism rates have produced wide discrepancies. One found that the rate was about one third in the 1960s, and less than a quarter in the 1970s (parole recidivism rates were lower than for those released without parole). Another analysis contended that the true rate was 61 percent for those paroled, 75 percent for those released without parole, and 56 percent for those released on probation. Such vast differences may be attributable to (1) different samples used (adult vs. juvenile-delinquent releases); (2) different definitions of recidivism; (3) different definitions of "success" (mere abstinence from crime versus the presence of certain factors such as steady employment); and (4) different time spans for the study conducted.

Of course, the recidivism rate ultimately depends upon certain institutional characteristics of sentencing practices in various states. It would be expected that where (1) probation is liberally granted so that only high-risk offenders go to prison at all and (2) where parole is liberally granted so that high-risk (as well as other) prisoners are released early, recidivism rates will be higher. Practices whereby noncriminal parole violators are readily returned to prison will also increase the "recidivism" rate.

Much recidivism has been attributed to persistence of criminal habits, but this theory tends to ignore social conditions. Theories of psychological or personality deficiencies, deficiencies that tend to persist over time, have also been formulated, but there is no proof that specific personality or psychological traits conduce toward either initial or repeated criminality. Sociological theory maintains that isolation of individuals from law-abiding behavior and status patterns and association with lawless behavior patterns (especially once the label of "criminal" has been affixed) are the critical factors underlying recidivism. It is difficult for many criminals to give up friendships and loyalty to other criminals, so that changes in communal attitudes toward ex-offenders to better reintegrate them may be more significant than individual therapy. The prevalence of crime in all of society, especially in its urban component, may also act to reinforce the potential for recidivism.

THEORIES ON CHANGING CRIMINALS

Failures of the criminal-justice system may be attributable to (1) inadequacy of the theories underlying the operations of those agencies and/or (2) failure, for various reasons, to implement otherwise sound theories. Since it is difficult to judge the quality of personnel and facilities (How good is good? How much is enough?), a brief recitation of the basic theories of "changing" criminals and their inadequacies should put the complex questions of change into perspective.

Early Theories. The traditional and most persistent theory is that change in criminals is accomplished by pain. Yet pain is often counterbalanced by resentment, isolation, and reinforcement of deviant-group allegiances. Infliction of pain deals only with symptoms. Compelling criminals to meditate about their fates was the second historic theory, and the assumption was that reflection upon their misery would produce change. Unfortunately, for every criminal who "reflected" his way to change, many others died or mentally deteriorated. Exhortation and moralizing to induce change were attempted, but this technique is effective only when used by members of a group upon other members who are already committed to or at least interested in the ideology of the group, not by outsiders attempting to change strangers. Another early method stressed the necessity of obtaining the offender's verbal commitment to change; this predictably resulted in failure. The culmination of these attitudes that involved tampering with some superficial element of the criminal's personality occurred in the regime of strict mechanical work and omnipresent surveillance of prisoners. Endless labor was thought to induce habits of obedience and industry, while endless surveillance was designed to reduce opportunities to "cheat." Jeremy Bentham, the great English nineteenth-century reformer, designed a prison called Panopticon to achieve this total effect, but it failed, in part because prisoners could observe guards as well as the reverse, and constant surveillance produced unbearable tensions.

Behaviorist Theory. In the twentieth century, a theory stressing form of psychological mechanical response replaced the physical and moral mechanisms of the past. Although in general a more sophisticated method of analysis, this newer theory shares the mechanistic orientation of any scientific or medical methodology. Thus crime, it was argued, much like physical illness, is caused by some individual disorder, and the cure can come after diagnosis and experimentation. Isolation of a specific mental disorder and its treatment will eventually cure the behavioral manifestation of that disorder. Believers in this theory came to recognize that certain social conditions may well "cause" the mental disorder, but then they sought to "cure" the disorder without changing the social conditions (many of these conditions, such as family background, could not be changed anyway). While psychoanalytically oriented theories stress clearing up of the particular disorder first, behaviorist theory deals with the delinquency itself and attempts to change behavior (through techniques such as reinforcement and aversion and other means of behavior modification) rather than "curing" the alleged cause.

Traditional "cure"-therapy treatment involves (1) encouraging the criminal to discuss his past; (2) requiring the therapist to identify a defect or set of defects, usually in broad categories such as "resentment of authority"; (3) feedback of this information to the criminal to enable him to "understand" why he does what he does; (4) probing of the past to ascertain the origins of the defect; and (5) a belief that enhanced awareness may "cure" the defect or awareness (further psychological treatment may, of course, be necessary).

Group Theory.   More recently, social psychologists have eschewed this highly individualistic mode of analysis and substituted for it "treatment" that emphasizes the social origins of human conduct. This stresses group affiliations; indeed, individual personality is perceived to be part of an overall group personality. Obviously, according to this theory individualized clinical treatment cannot solve any problems of crime. Changing criminals can be accomplished best in situations involving the following factors: (1) The criminal and the "change agent" are part of the same group and share certain attributes (apart from criminality). (2) The group meets ego and status needs of the criminal by providing legitimate outlets for his talents and by providing for his material and spiritual needs. (3) Ideally, the group should be organized for the purpose of changing criminals (much as Alcoholics Anonymous is organized to change chronic alcoholics) rather than for some other irrelevant or tangential purpose. (4) High-prestige group members strongly influence criminals admitted to the group. (5) The group is not dominated by unreformed criminals, so that the group norm will be anticriminal. (6) Pressures for change must come from the group and must be constant, especially from its anticriminal leadership. In accordance with the precepts of (1), it is obvious that merely appealing to a specific interest of a criminal is insufficient because it may result in fulfillment of that interest without fundamental change in other behavior. Officials who run such groups should reward anticriminal members of the group sufficiently so that they become the natural leaders of the new "subculture."

CRIME PREVENTION

Treatment of criminals, even sophisticated treatment and even if successful (more successful than is true at present), will have only a minor effect upon the incidence of crime. Few criminals are caught, few crimes are solved, and only a small percentage of even apprehended criminals are "treated" by the criminal-justice system. In order to prevent crime, the underlying social conditions that produce crime must be changed. In part, criminality has flourished because of the general atmosphere of criminality (especially white-collar criminality) within society. Historically, many reformers have argued for the fundamental change in social and economic conditions that would specifically reduce crime and generally make the society more responsive to the needs of its members. All crime-prevention theories, ranging from the psychological to the social-psychological to the sociological, cast their solutions in reference to certain beliefs about causes, though often these beliefs are not expressly stated. Thus what is needed is (1) greater understanding of crime causation and (2) social programs to deal with such causes. Professionals in the field, wedded to their own theories, may hamper objective research into causation and cure. Politicians who cater to public attitudes are not likely to advocate solutions unless they are presented with substantial evidence about these two factors.

Changing Social Groups. Since it has been established that local communities and close personal groups within those communities may influence criminality by providing an intimate and prestigious behavior pattern for individuals, it is clear that changing procriminal attitudes within these groups is necessary. There are many local groups (family, school, religious, neighborhood, work), and they may vary in their impact upon individuals. Whatever the impact, general crime prevention must concentrate upon some or all of these groups. General social, economic, and political arrangements may, of course, affect local communities, and, insofar as the effects are harmful, they must be changed. The most outstanding experiment in this realm is the Chicago Area Project undertaken by the University of Chicago to attempt to fundamentally change, by means of local community organizing, the criminogenic nature of many of these groups. Community committees, once active only in the field of preventing juvenile delinquency, now assist in the rehabilitation of those who have become enmeshed in the criminal-justice system. These groups often successfully modify the attitudes of their own members as well as those with whom they come into contact. Even ex-criminals who participate in these groups modify their attitudes and in turn influence those of youngsters. Since there is a great cultural similarity between the reformers and those they are attempting to influence, they have been more successful than a professionally led group would have been. While the Chicago Area Project results are controversial, what some believe to be its lack of success may be due to the fact that the project is now governmentally run and has become somewhat routinized and bureaucratized. Also, urban problems have significantly changed, along with the politics of dealing with those problems, and agencies may not have adapted quickly enough to such change. In other cities, local community organizing efforts to steer school dropouts back into education and assist parole and probation officers have shown little staying power as membership drifts away. Organized forms of recreation designed to keep youngsters off the streets are probably not successful unless they are part of a larger program for community organization.

Preventing Delinquency.   Many efforts have been made to identify and treat youngsters who have emotional problems that may lead to delinquency. Youth-Service Bureaus and other clinics have been established by schools, private welfare agencies, state mental-health agencies, or by independent agencies to deal with disturbed children. The record of these clinics has been mixed. Some studies have shown that there is greater delinquency among those so referred than among control groups that receive no psychiatric treatment. Again, this result tends to demonstrate that individual disorders do not cause crime and delinquency; rather, social conditions do. By being reactive agencies, clinics may not even be treating the worst disorders, which may not be brought to them. Professional social workers operating outside a clinical atmosphere, but providing educational and personal counseling, organized recreation, and medical treatment, had no significantly greater success than did normal maturational processes for a control group of similar children. Delinquency and probable delinquency were greatly overpredicted for members of both groups, and the number of actual delinquents produced was virtually identical. The only possible distinction between the groups lay in the fact that more control-group delinquents became persistent delinquents than did their "treated" counterparts.

Group work with delinquents and near delinquents has recently become increasingly popular. One type of group is the "activity" group, which (presumably) meets the needs and interests of a particular individual. Sometimes this group also provides some traditional psychological treatment. The agencies administering such programs are not usually organized by the community, and the agencies often do not deal with the most delinquent age groups. A second form of treatment involves redirecting the activities of an already existing group (usually a gang) into productive activities. Success in this often depends upon cooperation from the community, especially businessmen. Street workers have entered gangs and attempted to influence them into changing their activities, but the results have been disappointing. Failure may be attributable to simple time factors; it is difficult for street workers in a short time to undo many years of criminogenic influence. The difficulty may be compounded by the lack of identification between the middle-class agencies (funded by middle-class constituencies) and lower-class populations. This is true especially where some middle-class attitudes are repellent to local communities and where local leadership is not sought out or developed by the agency.

Changing Institutions. If it is true, as one prominent criminological theory argues, that the inability of lower-class people to achieve wealth, status, and success is due to their lack of opportunity in the general economic and social structure, then modification of that structure would seem to be indicated. A multifaceted attack on slum unemployment, featuring training and educational programs, along with numerous jobs within the agency itself, occurred in New York in the 1960s with a program called Mobilization for Youth. As the organization expanded into the field of protection of poor people's legal rights, the immediate goal of delinquency prevention receded. Aggressive defense of rights led to political conflicts with local and state governmental agencies and made it difficult to ascertain whether the project was successful, either as a delinquency-prevention experiment or as an antipoverty experiment. Other community programs, especially urban ones, seem to have had little effect on juvenile-delinquency rates. Educational changes designed to focus on delinquent and predelinquent youths in school and to provide smaller classes and trained teachers also have not had notable success. Some have argued that schools are themselves at fault, so that programs should be directed at reforming them rather then using them to change unruly children.

Some have criticized that vast array of programs aimed at specific and identifiable children and their parents as dealing only with the symptoms of a wider system of social deficiencies. Some sociologists have argued that crime is an inevitable concomitant of modern society and that crime reduction would require (1) economic stagnation, since competition and greed would have to be eliminated; (2) social stagnation, since cultural conflicts would have to be abated; (3) restriction of freedom, to permit closer monitoring of potential criminals; (4) restoration of religion as an agency of social control; and (5) a general slowing down of social change, since change produces both progress and maladjustment. The costs of such a radical change in society would, to say the least, be staggering.

Community organizers have argued that eradication of the basic correlates of crime—unemployment, poor housing, and general social disorganization—should be the focus of crime-control activities. Thus issues such as the economic system and private housing should be dealt with at the local community level. But these issues are usually beyond the range of activities (as well as the range of perceptions) of such local groups.

CHANGING LAWS AND PRACTICES

Since institutional change is unlikely, at least in the short run, many have agreed that modest changes in laws and practices may significantly reduce crime, or at least help victims. Perhaps these would attack only "symptoms" rather than "causes," but the effects of crime—surely a significant social issue—is what is truly at stake.

Gun Control.   Gun control, its nature and extent, is a controversial issue. Homicide and aggravated assault prevail in areas where guns are most readily available. The South has the most (1) guns, (2) killings, (3) aggravated assaults, and (4) percentage of serious offenses committed with a gun (as noted, 70 percent of murders in the South but only 52 percent of murders in the Northeast were committed with guns in 1978). The highest rate of both killings of policemen and accidental deaths by use of firearms are to be found in the South. Perhaps six times as many noncriminals (mostly children) as criminals are killed accidentally. Burglars account for most of the one hundred thousand weapons stolen each year; these weapons in turn arm criminals.

In 1871 New York State passed the first gun-control law, the Sullivan Act, which required police permits for gun owners. For a time, it was contended, this law lowered New York's murder rate. However, recent social developments and increased individual mobility have made the law less effective. More than three quarters of the states and the federal government have weak laws. It has been estimated that New Yorkers obtain guns originally purchased in the South at the rate of one hundred thousand per year. Since 1938, polls have shown the existence of substantial majorities for federal gun-control laws, although the National Rifle Association has effectively lobbied against licensing and other forms of control. In 1927, a federal law prohibited the shipment of handguns through the mail (this does not apply to rifles and long guns). Some laws ban shipment of particularly dangerous weapons and instruments, such as sawed-off shotguns, machine guns, and silencers, and require minimal registration on the part of dealers. The 1968 federal gun-control act forbids importation of handguns and some other weapons, though not of handgun parts. The law was passed at the behest both of citizens groups outraged at the assassinations of prominent political figures and of the American gun manufacturers. Efforts to ban or restrict parts for "Saturday-night specials" have failed.

Handgun registration would probably not decrease the availability of "street guns" acquired illegally by delinquents and criminals, though some apprehended criminals using registered stolen guns might be tried and convicted more readily. Restrictions on manufacturing of handguns would probably be more productive. Also, some reduction of crime might be achieved by increasing the penalties for illegal possession of handguns, whether used in crimes or not. Some states having such laws have experienced a reduction not in overall crime but in the fatalities accompanying crime.

Victim Compensation. The idea of victim compensation goes back to ancient law, where it was *the* penalty for crime. Tort law, which developed separately from criminal law, has always emphasized damages. Probation in modern times is frequently granted upon condition that restitution be made. In Europe, a criminal trial can involve the victim's claim for damages, unlike the situation in the United States, where civil and criminal trials are separate. (Probation conditions are one way of evading the rigidity of this distinction.) State payment to victims is relatively new and grew out of compassion. New Zealand commenced victim compensation in 1963. The scheme was rapidly adopted in England, and some American states soon thereafter. In some states, either the police or other agencies are required to notify victims of their rights. Numerous issues arise, including: (1) *What* is to be compensated, beyond medical expenses and loss of earnings? (2) *Who* is to administer the program—a specialized state board or, as in Massachusetts, local courts? (3) *What* is reasonable delay in a bureaucratic agency? (4) Is there discrimination against the poor because of a minimum-dollar-loss requirement? (5) Are maximum payment limitations just? (6) Is it fair to exempt (in all state programs, except California) victims of household assaults or homicides? (7) Is it fair to limit compensation to victims who have not participated in their own victimization (a subjective standard)?

RECENT TRENDS IN CRIMINOLOGY

This book has not studied the problem of deviancy, although some reference has been made to it. Since deviance labeling may be a factor in later criminality, the omission was practical rather than logical. Potentially, of course, so many fields relate to crime (history, political science, and sociology of law have been briefly mentioned) that the true and complete story of crime can be told only by an accurate analysis of society, in all of its manifestations—an impossibility. But criminology has tentatively expanded into at least one closely related field, victimology, and may, in the future, find—or create—newer, similar concerns. Victimology then is both important for itself and as an indicator of possible newer concerns.

Studies of Victimology.   Studies of victimology have widened the scope of criminology (although the direction is unclear). One wing of victimology stresses the responsibility of the state to compensate victims since it could not protect the victims. Another wing stresses the passive or active complicity of some victims with their offenders and argues that a true understanding of crime cannot be achieved unless this factor is studied. Both perspectives are essential to an understanding of crime: the former in terms of the relationship between the state and the individual, the latter in terms of the reality of criminal conduct. Just as it has been supposed that battered children ("victims") often become child and spouse beaters (thus, criminals), it has also been argued that victims may "learn" how to become offenders. Espousal of victims' rights would reintroduce into law the idea of compensation for victims, an early medieval notion that was ignored after the rise of the nation-state. These early concepts include compensation to the groups offended by criminal conduct, not merely the individual or his family or tribe or clan.

Criminal-Victim Relationships.   Although the field is new, some research indicates that (1) men not only commit more crimes than women, but also are the most frequent victims of crime, although the ratio is considerably reduced in homicide. (2) The age of victims tends to resemble the age of offenders for particular crimes. Marital status equates with victimization; married persons of both sexes are most often victimized. Most victims are strangers to the offender, although the second most frequent source of victims are friends or acquaintances. Close relatives are not frequently victimized in violent crimes against the person. Homicide is strongly intra-marital, and more women kill their husbands than vice versa.

Victim precipitation, whereby the victim was an active participant and perhaps even committed a crime, has also been increasingly studied. Even resistance by the victim—which may increase the gravity of the crime against him (as robbery may turn into homicide)—has been superficially studied; and the surprising though tentative finding is that resistance tends to be lower if the criminal is older. Spatial studies of the place of the crime and the relationship between that and the residence of victims and offenders have shown that both tended to live equally near (or distant) from the crime scene. When spatial factors are correlated with relational ones, strangers are victimized most frequently, but spouses are often victimized (by violent crime) in residential areas.

RADICAL THEORY

Many radical criminologists argue that fundamental or even important influential changes can be achieved only when and if capitalism as an exploitative system is eliminated. Marxists contend that the state's primary function is to protect private property, especially corporate property, and that state power is used against the working class to maintain domestic order by means of repression. Thus government has become the tool of the capitalist class and uses its power, especially its power to make and enforce criminal laws, to serve the interests of that class. Increasingly, capitalists feel insecure as the system gives way to its own failures ("contradictions" between private wealth and public good) and order that greater repression be used. Increasingly, the victims of that repression come to realize the reasons for that oppression and consciously begin to mobilize to fight it. Eventually the result will be revolution, which will overthrow both capitalist exploiters and the government that serves them. The questions are whether (1) this analysis is true and (2) even if it is true, whether the prediction will necessarily come about. Perhaps democratic processes that have spread political participation will continue to reduce economic inequality and control capitalist excesses; it is to be hoped that such democratic processes will be effective.

THE FUTURE OF CRIMINOLOGICAL THEORY

While crime certainly has a future, though perhaps only a moderately predictable one, and crime-control activities of society will certainly continue—probably without much enlightenment from the past—what generalizations are possible about future directions in criminology?

Positivism versus Interactionism. Criminology continues to veer between two fundamental approaches: that seeking scientific explanations of cause for all (or even some) crime and that seeking to make sense of the "meaning" of criminal behavior in terms of the life of the individual person. To believers in the latter approach, all human activity has a purpose and all theory must, eventually, make sense on the level of simple human experience. This approach calls for an almost intuitive testing of whether a "general law" or "principle" can actually be shown to exist in a concrete situation. While the first principle would eschew the relevance of "mental states" to validate any theory, the second insists upon that test. All positivist research stresses the search for "causes," and most American criminological research falls into this realm. Once supposed causes are discovered, then "cures" or treatment of the criminal become the logical consequence. Even functionalist theories are positivist in one of two senses: Either they stress deviant cultures that should be "treated," or they stress the "positive" function of deviance in upholding the social system (the notion of "latent" rather than patent function).

Thus for the positivist the criminal law is taken for granted (or, perhaps, made part of something called "natural crime"); there is a dichotomy between criminals and noncriminals; control-group studies can indicate the differences; and society is an organism infected by the alien virus of crime. Crime is an individual attribute or, at most, an attribute of a subculture that is alien.

Interactionist perspectives, on the other hand, concentrate upon the world of the individual criminal, his "social reality." Inevitably, such a concentration breeds some empathy and, most important, questions any need for treatment or change of the individual. The criminal law is studied to determine its origins and its processes. In this view crime is not pathological, but the result of an interrelationship between the individual or group and society, and is to be seen as the result of a combination of forces involving rule-making, rule enforcement, and rule violation. The battle between empirical "positivism" and the interactionists (ranging a broad span from labeling to conflict theorists) will probably continue, with perhaps the balance—of research, if not ideas—swinging to the latter.

"Scientific" versus "Historical" Models. The model used by at least positivist criminologists has been the "scientific" one. As has been noted, that model has failed to provide adequate explanations of "cause" and has only limited predictive value, thus failing to meet the most elementary tests of scientific validity. Some have suggested that the proper model should be the historical, a model that seeks to specifically define the "causes" of particular events, with only limited attempts to generalize those causes into universal "laws." Thus crimes and criminals would be looked at retrospectively by an investigator, who would solely seek to establish what (1) in the objective world and (2) in the offender's own "subjective" world combined to cause the event—the crime. To an extent, typological and interactionist models attempt to do this, and it is conceivable that further evaluation in these realms will suggest something like "tendencies." The strength of those "tendencies" would have to be evaluated by a comparison of offenders' conduct with nonoffenders' conduct, given the same histories and experiences. This is, of course, impossible, since criminology does not and cannot study nonoffenders, but the presence of many consistencies in certain crimes may, at least, shed light on the general social conditions that may produce those crimes and also on those conditions that have no relationship to such crimes. Any resulting theory would, however, have to be understood as involving "possible" causation, rather than one of "probable" or "inevitable" causation.

Correlates and Causes. Theories, especially multifactoral ones, should not continue to confuse correlates with causes. One major study of four hundred children whose lives were followed from the ages of eight to eighteen found that five factors—low family income, large family size, parental criminality, low intelligence, and poor parental conduct—could be equated with a vulnerability toward delinquency. But only half the sixty-three boys with three or more of these factors became delinquents, while most delinquents in the total sample did not come from this group. Another study of "causality" among fourteen hundred London schoolboys encountered severe methodological problems, despite its aim to find more than one cause (though a somewhat limited number of causes). Again, the issue of predictability, perhaps the more difficult one in current criminology, should be kept separate from both correlational and causal generalizations.

INDEX